AF600296

IBERIANISM AND CRISIS

Spain and Portugal at the Turn of the Twentieth Century

ROBERT PATRICK NEWCOMB

Iberianism and Crisis

Spain and Portugal at the Turn of the Twentieth Century

UNIVERSITY OF TORONTO PRESS
Toronto Buffalo London

Toronto Buffalo London
utorontopress.com

ISBN 978-1-4875-0296-6

Library and Archives Canada Cataloguing in Publication

Newcomb, Robert Patrick, author
Iberianism and crisis : Spain and Portugal at the turn of the twentieth century / Robert Patrick Newcomb.

(Toronto Iberic ; 33)
Includes bibliographical references and index.
ISBN 978-1-4875-0296-6 (cloth)

1. Comparative literature – Spanish and Portuguese. 2. Comparative literature – Portuguese and Spanish. 3. Spain – Relations – Portugal – History – 20th century. 4. Portugal – Relations – Spain – History – 20th century. 5. Spain – Intellectual life – 20th century. 6. Portugal – Intellectual life – 20th century. I. Title. II. Series: Toronto Iberic ; 33

PQ9019.N49 2018 460 C2017-906105-4

This book received support from the Davis Division of the Academic Senate of the University of California.

University of Toronto Press acknowledges the financial assistance to its publishing program of the Canada Council for the Arts and the Ontario Arts Council, an agency of the Government of Ontario.

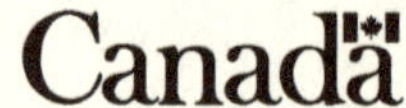

This book is dedicated to my wife, Kelley Weiss, and our sons, Simon Patrick and Ethan Francis Newcomb.

Contents

Acknowledgments

I would like to thank: my colleagues in the Department of Spanish and Portuguese at the University of California, Davis, and in the University of California Comparative Iberian Studies Working Group; the University of Toronto Press, particularly Siobhan McMenemy and Mark Thompson, for support of this project; Onésimo T. Almeida; Silvia Bermúdez; Leopoldo M. Bernucci; Sérgio Campos Matos; Thomas Harrington, Francisca González-Arias, Carmen Pereira-Muro, and Sharon Roseman, for helping me to formulate the ideas presented in chapter 3; and my external reviewers, for substantive and helpful feedback.

An earlier, abbreviated version of chapter 2 was published as "Antero de Quental, *Iberista:* Iberianism as Organizing Principle and Evolving Intellectual Commitment," (*Iberoamericana*, Nueva época, 8, no. 1 [September 2008]: 45–60). Chapter 4 builds from the articles "Portugal na visão unamuniana da Ibéria como unidade dialética" (*Estudos Avançados*, 24 [69] [2010]: 61–78), "Iberian Anguish: Unamuno's Influence on Miguel Torga" (*Luso-Brazilian Review* 49, no. 2 [2012]: 188–206), and "A Poetry of Flesh and Bone: Miguel de Unamuno and Miguel Torga" (*Portuguese Studies* 30, no. 1 (2014): 21–36), though its focus and argument are broader. All translations from the Portuguese, Spanish, Catalan, and Galician are mine except where otherwise noted. I take full responsibility for errors of fact, translation, or transcription.

IBERIANISM AND CRISIS

Spain and Portugal at the Turn of the Twentieth Century

Chapter One

Iberianism in a Time of Crisis

In a March 1855 article, the fourth in a series entitled "O Iberismo e os Seus Adversários" (Iberianism and Its Adversaries), the Portuguese writer and journalist José Felix Henriques Nogueira prophetically stated: "O iberismo é de ontem; mas invade tudo" (Iberianism is of the past, but it invades everything) (2: 67). A federalist, Nogueira was also a prominent defender of Iberianism, a minority intellectual current that sought to upend the Iberian Peninsula's political and intellectual status quo by advocating closer relations between Spain and Portugal, and a generally more equitable relationship between the Spanish state's constituent regions, which Iberianists sometimes expanded to include Portugal. Nogueira's 1851 volume, *Estudos sobre a Reforma em Portugal* (Studies on Reform in Portugal), was one of the first in a flurry of late nineteenth- and early twentieth-century Iberianist proposals published by prominent peninsular writers and public intellectuals. These proposals envisioned outcomes as diverse as a single, federal Iberian republic (Nogueira's objective), a centralized Iberian monarchy, and coordinated Spanish–Portuguese defence, trade, or infrastructure policies. Some Iberianists also proposed less tangibly political arrangements, such as increased and more substantive literary and intellectual exchange across peninsular state, regional, and linguistic borders, and the identification and literary flowering of a common Iberian "genius," "soul," or consciousness, whether in dialogue with or in contradistinction to Europe.

While, as Nogueira suggests, Iberianism is a long-standing feature of peninsular intellectual life, it cohered as a distinct mode of thought among the Spanish and Portuguese intelligentsia during the period we might broadly term the peninsular *fin de siècle*, which in the somewhat expansive periodization I adopt in this book ran from 1868 through 1910.[1] This period witnessed a succession of crises that shook the Spanish and Portuguese states to their foundations, and inspired some of the peninsula's most prominent writers to turn to the essay and other forms of literary non-fiction to examine the causes of a crisis many thought to be existential, and to propose potential remedies. This body of writing, which includes essays, speeches, pamphlets, newspaper articles, and longer academic studies, is commonly analysed in the context of the *fin-de-siècle* debate on peninsular "decadence" and possible "regeneration." What frequently goes unmentioned is that these texts were authored by literary intellectuals who were often explicitly Iberianist in their views. Indeed, this book will focus on some of late nineteenth- and early twentieth-century Iberia's most celebrated writers and thinkers, all of whom, in reflecting on the presumed crises facing Portuguese, Spanish, and perhaps even Iberian civilization, authored Iberianist proposals that were viewed by many as counterintuitive, if not downright anti-patriotic.[2] These include Antero de Quental and Oliveira Martins, both luminaries of Portugal's storied literary *Geração de 70* (Generation of 1870), Miguel de Unamuno, perhaps the best-known member of Spain's *Generación del 98* (Generation of 1898), and Joan Maragall, one of modern Catalan literature's most beloved poets. In addition to these names, which will be discussed at length in *Iberianism and Crisis*, several other prominent nineteenth- and early twentieth-century peninsular writers who engaged with Iberianism, either as sympathizers or opponents, will appear in this book. Among these are the novelists Emilia Pardo Bazán, Eça de Queirós, and Juan Valera, and political theorists and actors such as Francesc Pi i Margall, Joaquín Costa, Enric Prat de la Riba, and Joaquim Cases-Carbó, and the poet Manuel Curros Enríquez. Finally, in line with Henriques Nogueira's intuition that Iberianism was destined to periodically reappear on the peninsular scene, mid to late twentieth-century Iberianist writers and theorists will be mentioned in this book, particularly in its closing chapter. These later Iberianists include the Spanish federalist thinker Salvador de Madariaga, the Portuguese poet, fiction writer, and diarist Miguel Torga, author of a collection of *Poemas Ibéricos* (Iberian Poems, 1965), and the Portuguese novelist José Saramago, whose *A Jangada de Pedra* (The Stone Raft, 1986) imagines the Iberian Peninsula's cataclysmic physical separation from Europe as a prelude to a wholesale reconfiguration of intra-Iberian relations.

In order to appreciate the close conceptual relationship between Iberianism and crisis at the *fin de siècle*, this chapter will first analyse how nineteenth- and early twentieth-century Spanish and Portuguese writers understood the idea of crisis. Following this, I will offer a more detailed discussion of how peninsular writers used Iberianism to diagnose and propose remedies to crisis, both in the context of the specific challenges faced by Spain and Portugal and with reference to evolving ideas on the nation and natonalism in late nineteenth-century Europe. I will conclude with an argument for the importance of studying Iberianism, and a chapter-by-chapter summary of *Iberianism and Crisis.*

Discourses of Crisis in *Fin-de-Siècle* Spain and Portugal

The idea that Spain, Portugal, or perhaps Iberian civilization as a whole faced an existential crisis was commonplace among peninsular writers and essayists during the final decades of the nineteenth century and into the first years of the twentieth. This perception became particularly acute in the wake of traumatic, humiliating events such as Great Britain's 1890 "Ultimatum" to Portugal, which forced the Portuguese government to abandon territorial claims in southern Africa that would have connected Portugal's colonial holdings in Angola and Mozambique, and Spain's loss to the United States of Cuba, Puerto Rico, and the Philippines in the Spanish-American War (1898), a conflict remembered in Spain as *el desastre* (the disaster).[3] Beyond their political effects, among these the consolidation of Portuguese republicanism and an imperial rededication to colonies in sub-Saharan Africa (Portugal) and Morocco (Spain), these events prompted anguished reactions from Spain's and Portugal's leading literary intellectuals, in an emotional outpouring that at times threatened to drown out their programmatic calls for reform.[4] Reflecting on the Ultimatum, the Portuguese historian and polyglot intellectual Joaquim Pedro de Oliveira Martins – a man not afraid of hyperbole – described the events of 1890 in a letter to his friend, the novelist Eça de Queirós, as "uma catastrophe sem lyrismo" (a catastrophe without lyricism), and compared it to a collective death by drowning "n'um banho de lôdo" (in a pool of mud) (*Correspondencia* 137). As for the impact of 1898 in Spain, consider the mournful tone of Catalan writer Joan Maragall's poem "Cant del retorn" (Song of Return, 1899), one of the three "cants de la guerra" (songs of war) he penned in the wake of Spain's military defeat. Addressing the American continent, Maragall declares, "Som dèbils per tu" (we are too weak for you), and laments the "trista lluita sense fe ni glòria / d'un poble que es perd" (sad battle without faith or glory / of a lost people) (*Obres completes* [OC] 1: 173).

While *fin-de-siècle* peninsular writers seem to share what, following Gonzalo Navajas (278), we might term a "consciousness of crisis," they differed on the nature, scope, and causes of the crisis, and also on the possibilities for undertaking corrective measures. As Spanish philosopher José Ortega y Gasset, himself a theorist of crisis born during the agitated peninsular *fin de siècle,* reflected in *En torno a Galileo* (On Galileo, 1933; translated to English as *Man and Crisis*), genuine crises are rare, given that "la crisis es un peculiar cambio histórico" (crisis is a peculiar historical change) (*OC* 69; *Man* 85). Yet as R.J. Holton observes, the idea of crisis "resounds with all-embracing yet diffuse allusions to some multi-faceted yet unitary phenomenon" (503). This apparent contradiction, between Iberian intellectuals' consensus view that their country (whether Portugal or Spain), or perhaps the whole of peninsular civilization, faced a crisis, and their lack of agreement as to the nature of and possible solutions to the crisis, can certainly be seen in both the Portuguese *Geração de 70* and the Spanish *Generación del 98,* from which the principal writers discussed in this book – Quental, Oliveira Martins, Unamuno, and Maragall – hail. As German historian of ideas Reinhart Koselleck puts it, "[the idea of] 'crisis' remains ambivalent. The sense of experiencing a crisis becomes generalized but the diagnoses and prognoses vary with the user" ("Crisis" 370). Or as Holton explains, "Crisis has become such an all-pervasive rhetorical metaphor that its analytical utility for contemporary social thought has become devalued and confused" (502).

The simultaneous omnipresence and diffuseness of the concept of crisis – a juxtaposition that is particularly acute in the *fin-de-siècle* peninsular case – compels us first to define and historicize the idea of crisis, and then situate individual peninsular writers' pronouncements on crisis within the conceptual and historical framework that the idea of crisis describes. This will be our task in the following paragraphs.

Koselleck traces the idea of crisis to the Greek noun *krisis,* meaning discrimination, decision, or turning point, and the related verb *krinō,* meaning "to 'separate' (part, divorce), to 'choose,' to 'judge,' [or] to 'decide'" ("Crisis" 358). With the rise of Rome, "crisis" passed from Greek into Latin (as *crisis),* from which it entered the Romance languages, including Spanish (*crisis*), Portuguese and Galician (*crise*), and Catalan (*crisi*). Certain non-Romance languages, including Basque (*krisi*) and English (*crisis*), also adopted the term. As Portuguese cultural critic Carlos Leone observes, "O vocábulo, com a sua origem grega, presta-se admiravelmente a uma polissemia infelizmente esquecida. 'Crise,' momento de decisão, tanto pode referir o momento de perdição (destruição) como de salvação (resolução)" (The word [crisis], with its Greek origin, lends itself admirably to a polysemy that over time has unfortunately been forgotten. 'Crisis,' a moment of decision, can refer either to the moment of loss [destruction] or to that of salvation [resolution]) (10–11). Pointing to this same polysemy, Koselleck identifies two principal uses for the term among the ancient Greeks, which we might term the legalistic and medical discourses on crisis. As we shall see, these can be found, in varying degrees, in *fin-de-siècle* peninsular writing on crisis.

Koselleck identifies the legalistic discourse with Aristotle and other classical political theorists, who associated "crisis" with choice, judgment, or decision, particularly regarding public matters. They understood one's capacity to judge – that is, to criticize or critique (359) – as a precondition for participation in public life. With Greco-Roman civilization's encounter with early Christianity, the legalistic discourse of crisis gained, in Koselleck's words, both "a promise of salvation" and "apocalyptic expectations" (359). In other words, an idea that had previously referred to a worldly realm in which crises (of state, for instance) prompted political actors towards action, now gained a moralizing vocation and a transcendental importance. Indeed, the Greek *krisis* (judgment) and *krinō* (to judge) appear throughout the New Testament, as in Hebrews 9:27: "It is appointed unto men once to die, but after this the judgment [*krisis*]."[5] This juxtaposition of classical and biblical ideas shaped subsequent thinking on crisis, and helps explain the tendency of late nineteenth-century peninsular writers like Antero de Quental, who will be the focus of this book's next chapter, to adopt what Sérgio Campos Matos terms a "history-as-tribunal" approach in assessing the historical "causes" of so-called peninsular decline ("Nota" 9).

Koselleck also describes a classical "medical theory of crisis," which he traces to Galen among others (360). Here "crisis" refers to the moment at which an illness takes a decisive turn, either towards death or recovery. "Crisis" is widely used in this sense in nineteenth-century literature, particularly in realist-naturalist novels, whose authors were well known for their attempts to apply medical and scientific principles to the observation and analysis of life.[6] Koselleck notes that, "with its adoption into Latin," the medical idea of crisis "underwent a metaphorical expansion into the domain of social and political language" (360–1). In other words, medical "crises" came to describe not-strictly-bodily problems, such as emotional states, as in Eça's reference to his novelistic hero Carlos da Maia's romantic "crise de paixão e dor" (crisis of passion and pain) (653) in his realist masterpiece *Os Maias* (The Maias, 1888) (626).[7] Even the sorts of political crises that might intuitively have been addressed through the legalistic discourse became subject to this medically derived usage. Though unlike the legalistic discourse, here political crises were approached, rhetorically at least, from a "scientific" perspective, as states of transformative affliction affecting the body politic, and which required objective, dispassionate "diagnosis" and "treatment."

The medical idea of crisis led peninsular thinkers to describe, in the wake of the Ultimatum, the *desastre*, and other perceived humiliations, a gravely "ill" social body in need of life-saving "treatment" in the guise of modernizing reform or, alternately, collective recommitment to national tradition. As Lara Anderson comments for Spain: "The Regenerationists' use of the language of medicine to describe the symptoms and remedies for national decline was, at it were, endemic. Making explicit use of metaphors of sickness, their goal was to discover the nature of Spain's ailment" (quoted in Saler, 188). Maragall, for example, commented in an 1898 article on British Prime Minister Lord Salisbury's infamous speech on "Living and Dying Nations," which predicted the downfall of "Latin" empires at the hands of the more vigorous Anglo-Saxons, "España está enferma, no hay duda" (There is no doubt that Spain is ill) (*OC* 2: 555). And two years later, Joaquín Costa in his *Reconstitución y europeización de España* (Reconstitution and Europeanization of Spain, 1900) described post-*desastre* Spain as suffering a crisis, similar to an "enfermo que 'se siente' los brazos aún mucho tiempo después de haberle sido amputados" (sick man who "feels" his arms long after they have been amputated) (7–8). Further, he called for a policy approach that would treat the nation-state "como si España entera fuese un hospital" (as if all of Spain were a hospital) (19). The use of a medicalized rhetoric of "decadence" or "degeneration" was common among late nineteenth-century peninsular intellectuals. The Catalan federalist Valentí Almirall described conditions in Spain as follows in *Lo Catalanisme* (1886):

> Som un poble caduch, plé de vicis alimentats per la ignorancia, pero ab pocas forsas pera darlos tan sols apariencias brillants. Lo desenrotllo fatal

de la historia desde 'l comensament de la edat moderna nos ha conuhit á una caducitat prematura, sens haver passat per lo período de la virilitat. Som com aquells individuos infelissos, que corcats de cos y d' esprit, á vint anys repapeijan y á trenta moren de vells. (22)[8]

We are an aged people, full of vices that have been fed by ignorance, and with little strength to keep up appearances. The fatal progress of history from the beginning of the modern age has led us to a premature old age, without us having passed through a period of vigor. We are like those unhappy individuals who, their body and soul wrecked, at twenty years are in their dotage and at thirty die of old age.

In this respect peninsular intellectuals reflected the broader intellectual climate of *fin-de-siècle* Europe. In the opening pages of his highly influential study *Degeneration* (1892), Max Nordau, himself a physican, described "the *fin-de-siècle* mood" as "the impotent despair of a sick man, who feels himself dying by inches in the midst of an eternally living nature blooming insolently for ever" (3). Significantly, the volume's first book, dedicated to the *fin de siècle*, featured chapters entitled "The Symptoms," "Diagnosis," and "Etiology." Though as Sérgio Campos Matos notes, late nineteenth-century peninsular discourse on "decadence" partook of "una teoría de desviación histórica asociada a un sentimento de pérdida, de retraso a las otras naciones de la Europa occidental" (a theory of historical deviation associated with a feeling of loss, [and] of backwardness with regard to the other nations of Western Europe). Further, it was explicitly relational in civilizational and temporal terms, comparing Iberia to Europe "beyond the Pyrenees," and Iberia's "glorious" past to its beleaguered present ("Cómo convivir" 259).

Having briefly outlined the legalistic and medical discourses on crisis, I will now examine the work of Antero de Quental (1842–91) and Joaquim Pedro de Oliveira Martins (1845–94) – two "crisis-conscious" late nineteenth-century peninsular writers, who also happened to be Iberianists – with the aim of tracing these references back to the legalistic and medical discourses. Specifically, I will identify Quental's pamphlet *Portugal Perante a Revolução de Espanha* (Portugal Confronted by the Revolution in Spain, 1868) and his speech *Causas da Decadência dos Povos Peninsulares* (Causes of the Decline of the Peninsular Peoples, 1871) with the legalistic discourse on crisis, and Oliveira Martins's *História da Civilização Ibérica* (History of Iberian

Civilization) and *História de Portugal* (both 1879) with the medical discourse. While the "legalistic" or "medical" character of Quental's and Martins's thinking on crisis is not entirely an either/or proposition, their positions do gravitate, respectively, towards the legalistic and medical discourses.

Quental's essayistic writing addresses some of the most salient political events in nineteenth-century peninsular history, including Spain's Revolution of 1868. While Quental's thoughts are steeped in the late nineteenth-century debate on Iberian *decadência*, he makes few direct references to crisis in *Portugal Perante a Revolução*, and none in *Causas da Decadência* – texts in which he argues for Iberian federalism as a solution to Portugal's and Spain's precarious state. Nonetheless, the few references Quental makes to crisis in these texts are highly significant. In *Portugal Perante a Revolução*, written in response to the overthrow of Queen Isabel II at the opening of Spain's *Sexenio Democrático* (Democratic Sexennium, 1868–74),[9] Quental makes this semantic connection between the notions of *crisis*, *revolution*, and *revelation*:

> Uma das muitas traduções livres da palavra revolução é esta: *revelação*. No momento da crise apaixonada, as forças mais íntimas, os elementos mais profundos da sociedade revolvida nos seus abismos, agitando-se por chegar à claridade, sobem até à superfície e mostram-se à luz do dia com uma energia, uma verdade irresistíveis. É uma revelação: vê-se o que há, e vê-se com que tem de se contar, em bem e em mal, durante o longo período que se segue sempre àqueles momentos de impulso decisivo. Por vinte, por quarenta anos, por um século às vezes, a vida nacional não é mais do que o desenvolvimento, a combinação ou a luta daqueles elementos revelados na hora profética da revolução. (107; author's emphasis)

> Among the many indirect translations for the word revolution we find the following: *revelation*. At the moment of an impassioned crisis, the most intimate forces, the most profound elements of a society, which have previously circulated in the abyss and struggled to reach the light, rise to the surface and shine in the light with an irresistible energy and truth. This is revelation: consider what there is, what occurs, both the good and the bad, during the long periods that inevitably follow these moments of decisive action. For twenty, for forty years, at times for even a century, national life is nothing more than the development, the combination, or the struggle of those elements that were revealed in the prophetic moment of revolution.

Quental's lyrical description of a people's rise to power suggests Plato's cave allegory, in which a chosen few temporarily leave behind the darkness of ignorance and ascend into the light of truth, before descending again into the cave to liberate their unenlightened fellows. The mystically inclined Quental may also be alluding to Revelation 21:2, and its promise of a new society conceived as a "new Jerusalem." In underscoring Quental's indebtedness to both biblical and classical legal thinking, it bears recalling Revelation's descriptions of the dead rising from their graves (or from the abyss towards the light, as Quental had it) such that living and dead alike are "judged [*krinō*] every man according to their works" (20:13). This may be compared to Quental's historical judgment in *Causas da Decadência* that "o espírito peninsular descera de degrau em degrau até ao ultimo termo da depravação" (the peninsular spirit descended step by step to the utmost state of depravation), and his corresponding exhortation to his fellow Iberians: "Erguemo-nos hoje a custo, espanhóis e portugueses, desse túmulo onde os nossos grandes erros nos tiveram sepultados: erguemo-nos, mas os restos da mortalha ainda nos embaraçam os passos, e pela palidez dos nossos rostos pode bem ver o mundo de que regiões lúgubres e mortais chegamos ressuscitados!" (Today, we Spaniards and Portuguese must raise ourselves up, albeit with much effort, from this tomb in which our grave errors have buried us. Let us raise ourselves up, though we will stumble upon the scraps of our mortuary shroud, and the paleness of our faces will show from what dark and deathly realms we have escaped!) (28–9).

Through these biblical allusions, Quental presents *La Gloriosa* as a privileged moment of crisis for both Spain and Portugal, a singular opportunity in which, through revolution *qua* revelation, the peninsular peoples may be judged on a transcendental scale, either by God, or by "the spirit of truth," as he describes in *Causas da Decadência*. Quental retains the apocalyptic subtext of his argument in his 1871 speech, in which he calls for the "peninsular peoples" to repent of their historical "sins," which include monarchical tyranny, doctrinaire Catholicism, and a bloody overseas expansion:

> Se não reconhecermos e confessarmos francamente os nossos erros passados, como poderemos aspirar a uma emenda sincera e definitiva? O pecador humilha-se diante do seu Deus, num sentido acto de contrição, e só assim é perdoado. Façamos nós também, diante do espírito de verdade, o acto de contrição pelos nossos pecados históricos, porque só assim nos poderemos emendar e regenerar. (*Causas* 7–8)

> If we do not frankly confess our past errors, how can we aspire to a sincere and definitive correction? The sinner, only by humbling himself before his God, in a heartfelt act of contrition, is forgiven. Let us make the same act of contrition for our historical sins before the spirit of truth, because it is only in this way that we may correct and renew ourselves.

Despite occasional lapses into the organicist language in vogue throughout late nineteenth-century Europe, Quental's descriptions of 1868 in Spain and 1871 in Portugal as moments in which awareness and confession of a society's "sins" can set the stage for reform are solidly aligned with the legalistic discourse, and are particularly illustrative of its messianic, "apocalyptic expectations" (Koselleck, "Crisis" 359), along with its sense of moral culpability and its dependence on subjective judgment as opposed to objective, "scientific" analysis.[10]

Oliveira Martins, whose voluminous written output touched on history, historical fiction, literary criticism, anthropology, political science, and economics, presents something of a mirror image, or "pólo de contradição" (opposite pole), of his friend Quental (Saraiva 16).[11] While Quental's peers remembered him as almost monk-like in temperament, and as a highly disciplined writer and thinker, Martins was voluble, contradictory, and as a party activist, parliamentarian, and government official, was aggressively engaged in public life. Further, Martins possessed a swashbuckling personality and somewhat unhinged way with language that shines through in his colourful descriptions of the "crimes brutaes, paixões vis, abjecções e miserias [que] compõem, por via de regra, a existencia humana" (brutal crimes, vile passions, abjection and misery [that] as a rule characterize human existence) (*Portugal* x).[12] More germane to this discussion, Martins's views on crisis hewed much more closely to the medical discourse than did Quental. Though at the risk of muddying the waters, Martins's writing is at times marked by a near-apocalyptic negativity and a moralizing tone, both of which recall Quental. This said, Martins largely eschews subjective judgment and biblically derived pieties in his writing on the peninsula's historical and contemporary crises, emphasizing instead an organicist idea of society and the need for objective "scientific" analysis of the ailing social "body." The notion that societies, like individuals, follow a predictable trajectory of birth, expansion, decline, and death led Martins to a more fatalistic view of the prospects for reform than we find in Quental. Martins observes the following in his *História da Civilização Ibérica* (1879): "Caímos, passámos, porque é da natureza de todas as coisas vivas – e uma sociedade é um organismo – nascer, crescer e morrer" (We die, we pass on, because it is in the nature of living things – and society is an organism – to be born, to grow, and to die) (53). Later he declares: "As causas iniciais da vida e da morte são as mesmas: uma implica a outra; no princípio da primeira está a razão de ser da segunda … A decadência dos povos e a morte dos indivíduos são condições, necessárias ambas, da sua grandeza e da sua existência; e os fenómenos ou sintomas de corrupção colectiva ou de decomposição dos organismos animais, são também apenas a perversão do princípio da vida, no qual se contém a necessidade da morte" (The initial causes of life and death are identical; the one entails the other; the beginning of the former supplies the reason for the existence of the latter … The decadence of nations and the death of individuals are both necessary conditions of their greatness, nay, of their very existence; and the facts or symptoms of collective decay, like the decay of animal organisms, are merely the perversion of the principle of life – a principle which in itself entails death) (*Civilização Ibérica* 311; *Iberian Civilization* 264-5).

Martins's apparent determinism would seem to leave little room for corrective action, yet Martins was very much a reformer, was regarded as a competent administrator, and published several proposals for political and economic reforms in Portugal, some quite technical. As Martins reaches the end of the *História da Civilização Ibérica*, he confronts this difficulty, which was faced by numerous peninsular intellectuals of his generation, who for all of their reforming zeal had also imbibed enough scientific determinism to view their societies as "organisms" which they feared were close to senescence and death. Martins acknowledged as much in an 1891 letter to Oliveira Ramos, in which he characterizes the problem in the following, Nietzschean terms:

> Incontestavalmente, envelhecemos como especie. A semi-barbarie de que muitos desdenham, esse estado de relativa inconsciencia, mas de fecundidade, era, quanto a mim, preferivel ao poder incomparavel que hoje temos de esmerilhar e julgar todas as cousas. É possível extrair do criticismo contemporâneo uma synthese affirmativa que dê uma fé á humanidade? Eis a pergunta não respondida até hoje. Se não tiver resposta, a humanidade caducou, a civilisação demonstrou ser uma enfermidade propria e fatal da intelligencia humana. (*Correspondencia* 175)

> We have unquestionably aged as a species. The semi-barbarity, which many disdain, that state of relative unconsciousness, but of fecundity, for me was preferable to the incomparable ability we now have to polish and

judge any and all things. Is it possible to extract from contemporary criticism an affirmative synthesis that can give faith to humanity? This is the question that has yet to be answered. If there is no answer, then humanity has become senile, and civilization has been shown to be a fatal illness of the human intelligence.

If we apply to Quental and Martins the terminology of the more-or-less contemporaneous Spanish debate on *europeización* and *casticismo*,[13] we might describe Quental's position as largely free of biological determinism, and more open to "Europeanizing" reform.[14] Quental contended that through collective contrition for what we might term Iberia's "crimes against modernity," the peninsular peoples could create the conditions to transform their societies by accessing the most advanced ideas from Europe *além Pirenéus* (beyond the Pyrenees), among these Proudhonian federalism, which Quental enthusiastically advocated at the time.

Martins, in contrast, held to a moderate *casticista* position (recalling Miguel de Unamuno's argument in *En torno al casticismo*), and attempted to reconcile modernizing ideals with his views that societies possessed an essential and more-or-less immutable "genius" or underlying character (*intrahistoria*, for Unamuno), and were subject to a defined life cycle. As Unamuno notes in "Sobre el marasmo actual de España" (On Spain's Current Intellectual Morass, 1895; published as the final chapter of *En torno al casticismo*, 1902): "En nuestro estado mental llevamos … la herencia de nuestro pasado, con su haber y con su debe" (Our mental state carries with it … the legacy of our past, in both its positive and negative aspects) (*OC* 1: 858). It is in this context that Martins makes one of his only direct references to crisis in the *História da Civilização Ibérica*. Referring to what he viewed as Iberian propensities towards interpersonal equality and local autonomy,[15] he writes:

> A paixão da igualdade, impedindo toda a civilização progressiva, pôde nas tribos do Atlas impedir a constituição de um Estado; nas da Espanha resistiu, mas não pôde vencer os romanos que as arrastaram para o seio da vida europeia.
>
> Indicámos os sintomas dessa resistência, ainda hoje visíveis no federalismo semi-doutrinário, semi-histórico, tradicional e anacrónico, e no decurso do nosso trabalho vê-lo-emos surgir em todos os momentos de crise. (43)

> A passion for equality, which made progressive civilization impossible, prevented the constitution of a State in African tribes; in Spain there was resistance, but it was unable to withstand the Romans, and Spain was forcibly incorporated in the life of Europe.
>
> We have noted the signs of this resistance, which are still visible in a half-doctrinaire, half-historical, traditional, and anachronical theory of federalism; and in the course of our history we shall find them recur at all times of crisis. (*Iberian Civilization* 21)

For Martins, crises reveal latent, defining elements of national or civilizational character, such as the Iberians' stubborn spirit of independence and tendency towards localism. As he put it in his study *Portugal Contemporâneo* (Contemporary Portugal, 1881), "Quando a máquina social se desorganiza, aparecendo o que se chama revolução ou crise, vêem-se mais ao vivo çomo as coisas são na realidade" (when the social machine falls into disrepair, and what we would call "revolution" or "crisis" occurs, one sees more vividly how things really are) (2: 227). Similarly, Unamuno, who considered Martins one of Iberia's greatest historians, observed the following in "Sobre el marasmo actual de España":

> Atraviesa la sociedad española honda crisis; hay en su seno reajustes íntimos, vivaz trasiego de elementos, hervor de descomposiciones y recombinaciones, y por de fuera un desesperante marasmo. En esta crisis persisten y se revelan en la vieja casta los caracteres castizos, bien que en descomposición no pocos. (856)
>
> Spanish society is in deep crisis. Within it deep changes are occurring. There is a lively shifting about of elements, and stirrings of decomposition and recombination. Yet on the outside there is great stagnation. In this state of crisis the old caste of traditional types, many of who are in a state of decomposition, reveal themselves.

While crises may enlighten, they do not seem to provide writers like Martins and Unamuno with the conditions for the sort of decisive break with the past advocated by Quental – except to the extent that a cleareyed ability to see one's society "as it really is" is a necessary precondition for reform. Indeed, to the degree that Martins viewed peninsular society as an organism possessed of certain immutable qualities – and, I would argue, to the degree that he subscribed to the medical idea of crisis – he would have found Quental's position untenable. Martins and Unamuno both seem of the opinion that the Iberian peoples' deep-seeded characteristics or propensities will come to the fore during moments when the peninsular "organism" is severely tested – that is, in moments of crisis, as occurred in Spain in 1868 and 1898, and in Portugal in 1890. Given that these traits reflect a deeper peninsular or Iberian "genius," they, however unpleasant or counterproductive, cannot entirely be eliminated.

Yet for all of Martins's biological determinism, he did not close the door on reform, arguing at the conclusion of his *História da Civilização Ibérica* only against those reforms imitative of Europe, or otherwise out of step with the Iberian "genius":

> O que nos cumpre fazer, se queremos entrar no concurso das nações que ràpidamente caminham para a definição do sistema das ideais modernas, é reconstituir o nosso corpo social, mais que nenhum outro abalado e doente por uma enfermidade de três séculos … Cumpre-nos finalmente reconstituir o nosso organismo social; porque sem ter resolvido as suas questões internas, sem ter conseguido achar uma estabilidade na fortuna, jamais as nações puderam ter uma voz no concerto da humanidade … Por muitos lados a nossa história de hoje repete a antiga; e meditando-a bem, nós, peninsulares, acaso descubramos nela a prova da existência de uma força íntima e permanente que, libertando-nos da imitação das formas estrangeiras, poderá dar à obra da reconstituição orgânica da sociedade um cunho próprio, mais sólido por assentar na natureza da raça, mais eficaz porque melhor corresponde às exigências da obra. (337)

> What we must do if we wish to be numbered among the nations which are rapidly advancing towards a definition of the system of modern ideas is to reconstruct our social body, which more than any other has been undermined and weakened by an illness that has lasted three centuries … Finally we must reconstruct our social organism, since the nation which has not set its house in order and attained economic stability will never be in a position to make its voice felt in the councils of humanity … In many ways our history today repeats our ancient history, and if we consider that history carefully we may perhaps see in it the proof of the existence of an essential abiding energy which may free us from imitation of foreign models and give to the work of the organic reconstruction of society a native cast, the more solid because it will rest on the character of the race, and the more effective because it will better correspond to the essential requirements of the work of reconstruction. (*Iberian Civilization* 286–7)

Similarly Unamuno, at the conclusion of *En torno al casticismo* (On National Tradition; written 1895, published 1902), after hundreds of pages of argumentation aimed at asserting the continued hold on Spain of deeply rooted national tradition, addresses the possibility of change as follows: "¿Está todo moribundo? No, el porvenir de la sociedad española espera dentro de nuestra sociedad histórica, en la intra-historia, en el pueblo desconocido, y no surgirá potente hasta que le despierten vientos y ventarrones del ambiente europeo" (Is all lost? No, the future of Spanish society waits for us within our historical society, in its *intra-history*, in the unknown people, and it will not spring to vigorous life until it is awakened by winds and gales blowing from Europe) (*OC* 1: 866). For Unamuno as for Martins, under certain conditions crises may be resolved and "sick" social bodies cured, though in the Iberian case, the cure can come only through remedies that reconcile European modernity to Iberia's specific "physiology" – and this requires that the writer first accurately understand that physiology.

The question, then, is as follows: are the "remedies" proposed by Iberianism amenable to the peninsula's essential "genius" or to the conditions in which Spain and Portugal found themselves at the turn of the twentieth century? A substantial number of *fin-de-siècle* Iberia's most celebrated intellectuals, including Quental, Oliveira Martins, and in a certain respect Unamuno, thought so, as we shall see. But first, we must step back and look at the broader European intellectual context in which Iberianism emerged – one defined by shifting ideas concerning the nation, federalism, and decadence.

Iberianism as a Response to Peninsular Crisis

"Iberianism," rendered as *iberismo* in Spanish, Portuguese, and Galician, and *iberisme* in Catalan, refers to a body of peninsular thought that sought to disrupt conditions on the Iberian Peninsula by promoting various forms of approximation between Spain and Portugal, and by rebalancing relations among Spain's regions so as to be more equitable. At times, Spain's "regions" were made to include Portugal as home to the "peninsular" or "Iberian peoples," as in the title of Antero de Quental's 1871 speech on the *Causas da Decadência dos Povos Peninsulares,* and Oliveira Martins's chapter of the same name from his 1879 *História da Civilização Ibérica*. Iberianism's adherents and sympathizers held a range of political views, from the revolutionary

Proudhonian socialism of Quental, through the republican federalism of Francesc Pi i Margall, to the conservative monarchism of António Sardinha, author of *A Aliança Peninsular* (The Peninsular Alliance, 1924). Individual Iberianist proposals were similarly eclectic. Iberianism's political, philosophical, and programmatic diversity has led Luís Machado de Abreu to remark on late nineteenth-century Iberianism's "enunciações contraditórias" (contradictory enunciations) and to declare that "poucas palavras terão significado tão ambíguo como a palavra iberismo" (few words are as ambiguous in meaning as the word "Iberianism") (54–5). Late nineteenth-century Iberianist proposals included explicitly political calls for the Iberian Peninsula to be refashioned as a decentralized federal republic or joined as a centralized monarchy, as well as proposals for common Spanish–Portuguese defence, infrastructure, or economic policies, or for the creation of an Iberian customs union along the lines of the German *Zollverein*. But Iberianist proposals have also taken the form of appeals for greater intra-Iberian intellectual or cultural exchange, or literary expressions of a shared Iberian historical experience, culture, or soul, as in Miguel Torga's *Poemas Ibéricos* or José Saramago's novel *A Jangada de Pedra*.

Further, Iberianism's proponents, including those examined in this book, have drawn to varying degrees on the political, economic-strategic, and intellectual-cultural strands of Iberianism in fleshing out their programs, and have oscillated between more explicitly political stances and an Iberianism grounded in the perhaps more nebulous (but arguably less controversial) terrain of culture. This was the case of Oliveira Martins, who in his early article "Do Princípio Federativo e Sua Aplicação à Península Hispânica" (On the Federal Principle and Its Application to the Hispanic Peninsula, 1869) argued for the creation of a federal Iberian republic, as did his close friend Quental at the time. By the time his *História da Civilização Ibérica* was published in 1879 Martins had shifted towards a concern with identifying and defending a common Iberian civilization. Later still, in the 1889 article "Iberismo" (Iberianism), Martins argued for a Portuguese–Spanish political and strategic alliance, while explicitly opposing the political union of the two states. Martins's reversal on the question of peninsular federation has caused some scholars to exclude him from the Iberianist camp, as if to imply that explicitly political Iberianism is more legitimate or committed than an economic-strategic or intellectual-cultural approach.[16] Nonetheless, even as his specific views changed, Martins's overarching Iberianism remained intact between 1869 and 1890. What changed were the means Martins advocated for bringing about approximation between Portugal and Spain: where he once believed that the creation of an Iberian federal republic was best suited to achieving this goal, in his later years, and no doubt aware of the failure of the short-lived First Spanish Republic (1873–4), he found a strategic alliance more compelling. Regardless, Oliveira Martins did not stop being an Iberianist when he became disillusioned with the dream of an Iberian federation – and as I will argue in this book's next chapter, neither did Antero de Quental. In this sense, I concur with Víctor Martínez-Gil when he contends that "el rebuig de la unió ibèrica no implicava necessàriament el rebuig de qualsevol iberisme" (rejection of the Iberian Union did not necessarily imply rejection of all forms of Iberianism) (*El naixement* 41).

Iberianists have frequently grounded their arguments for political, economic-strategic, and intellectual-cultural Iberianism in the example of the united, Roman-era *Hispania*, which as many have noted is the linguistic ancestor of the modern *España*, *Espanha*, *Espanya*, and *Espainia*.[17] Looking back to a period in which most of the Iberian Peninsula was united under Roman rule, Iberianists have contended that the peninsula's political division, beginning in the early modern period, into two sovereign nation states (Portugal and Spain), is illogical and not in keeping with Iberia's deeper historical and cultural unity. Further, they have argued that Castile's traditional dominance within Spain is untenable and unjust, given the degree of regional linguistic and cultural diversity present within Spain's borders. These beliefs ground the view, common to all Iberianists, that some form of mutual re-approximation (perhaps political, perhaps not) between Spain and Portugal is desirable, and the opinion shared by many Iberianists that Castile's dominance within Spain must be challenged.

Of course, Iberian intellectuals have long been aware of the peninsula's internal diversity. Well before Iberianism emerged as a distinct body of thought during the mid-nineteenth century, peninsular writers commented, sometimes proscriptively, on how Iberian intra-relations were or should be configured. The great Portuguese Renaissance poet Luís de Camões offered the following description of the Iberian Peninsula, which he terms "a nobre Espanha, / Como cabeça ali de Europa tôda) (stately Spain, / As it were the head of Europe's commonweal)

(*Os Lusíadas* 81; *The Lusiads* 85), and its varied peoples in the third canto of his *Os Lusíadas* (The Lusiads, 1572), which despite its recognition of Iberia's internal diversity and multipolarity has functioned as Portugal's national literary epic:

Com nações diferentes se engrandece,
Cercadas com as ondas do oceano;
Tôdas de tal nobreza e tal valor
Que qualquer delas cuida que é melhor.

Tem o tarragonês, que se fêz claro
Sujeitando Parténope inquieta;
O navarro, as Astúrias, que reparo
Já foram contra a gente maometa;
Tem o galego cauto e o grande e raro
Castelhano, a quem fêz o seu planêta
Restituidor de Espanha e senhor dela;
Bétis, Leão, Granada, com Castela.

Eis aqui, quase cume da cabeça,
De Europa tôda, o reino lusitano,
Onde a terra se acaba e o mar começa. (*Os Lusíadas* 81–2)

Grown great from divers nations dwelling there,
Whom the wide waters of the sea contain,
And all so brave and noble, for the rest,
That every country thinks itself the best.

There is the Aragonese, whose fame grew bright
When the restless Neapolitans he quelled;
Navarre and the Asturias, who in fight
Against Mahomet's breed the bastion held;
There the Galician shrewd, and, great in might,
The high Castilian, whom his star impelled
Spain to restore and rule the commonweal,
Betis, León, Granada, with Castile.

And there, as crown of Europe it might be,
You may behold the Lusitanian reign,
Where the land ends and where begins the sea.
(*The Lusiads* 85–6)

Awareness among early modern peninsular intellectuals that "Spain" was a mutable term, and that an overarching peninsular identity could coexist with political diversity, was not limited to Portugal. Logically, it flourished in one of the peninsula's other non-Castilian "peripheries," the Crown of Aragon.[18] Vicent Josep Escartí lists a number of Catalan and Valencian writers from the fifteenth and sixteenth centuries for whom *Espanya* represented a "geographic reality" that did not require political uniformity (quoted in Sabaté and Fonseca, 328–9). And Antoni Simon, addressing the seventeenth and eighteenth centuries, contrasts a Catalan-Aragonese literary and historiographical tradition that "considered 'Spain' ... a designation of origin that encompassed all the inhabitants and kingdoms of the Iberian Peninsula," and that thereby allowed for Catalan-Aragonese political separation from Castile, with Castilian intellectuals' attempts to tie together the notions of Spanish-Iberian identity to political unity, and to assert their kingdom's pre-eminence as what Gregorio López Madera would in his *Excelencias de la Monarchía y Reino de España* (1597) refer to as the "'head of Spain'" (357, 363).

Projects aimed at achieving peninsular political unity – often under the aegis of Castile – were fixtures of Iberian history prior to the nineteenth century. In the prologue to his *Gramática de la lengua castellana* (Grammar of the Castilian Language, 1492), with its famous affirmation that "language [is] always the companion of empire," Antonio de Nebrija praised the unification of much of the peninsula under Queen Isabel of Castile, and reflected that "the members and pieces of Spain, which were scattered in many parts, were gathered and united into a single body and Kingdom, the form and joint of which, so ordered, the many centuries, injuries, and passage of time will not be able to break nor unravel" (203). Moving forward by a century or so, the 1580–1640 period of Iberian dynastic union under the Spanish Habsburgs, which was prompted by the death, without an heir, of the Portuguese king D. Sebastião in 1578, and which was retroactively cast in Portuguese historiography and Romantic nationalism as the "Spanish captivity," represented a brief window of time in which the whole of the peninsula was united under a common sovereign.[19]

As stated previously, Iberianism as such emerged during the peninsula's agitated "long nineteenth century," which if it was marked by any one theme, was marked by crisis, which we may define in terms of the many discrete challenges faced by the beleaguered Spanish and Portuguese states during this period, as well as a broader transformation of the idea of the nation state in the wake of the American and French revolutions. Crises faced by Spain and Portugal during the nineteenth century include Napoleon's invasion and occupation of the peninsula (1807), the independence of the greater part of Spanish America (1810–20s) and Brazil (1822), the Portuguese Civil War (1828–34), the First Carlist War in Spain (1833–9), the Maria da Fonte insurrection in Portugal (1846), *La Gloriosa* and the "Sexenio Democrático" in Spain (1868–74), the British Ultimatum to Portugal (1890), the Cuban War of Independence and the Spanish-American War (1895–8), and during the first years of the twentieth century, the Portuguese regicide (1908) and the *Setmana Tràgica* (Tragic Week) in Barcelona (1909). Given this litany of misfortune, one could argue that Iberianism is the intellectual product of peninsular crisis, or at minimum, one might contend that the profusion of Iberianist proposals during the second half of the nineteenth century was touched off by a widespread "consciousness" of crisis among peninsular intellectuals.[20] Iberianists and scholars alike have observed a strong correlation between peninsular crisis – or the perception of crisis on the part of peninsular intellectuals – and the popularity of Iberianism as a potential solution to Portugal and Spain's seemingly intractable problems. Oliveira Martins expressed precisely this view in an 1889 article, "Iberismo," in which he writes the following on the impact of crisis on the Portuguese psyche: "Nesta crise, como em tôdas as que sucessivamente teem açoitado Portugal desde o comêço do século, o pensamento de muitos portugueses tem-se voltado para a possibilidade de uma união com a vizinha Espanha" (During this crisis, just as in all those crises that have afflicted Portugal since the beginning of the century, the thoughts of many Portuguese have returned to the possibility of union with our neighbour, Spain) (*Dispersos* 2: 203).

Scholars of Iberianism – most of whom have been Portuguese – have borne out Martins's observation.[21] Manuela Mascarenhas, for instance, has observed the "aspecto cíclico" (cyclical aspect) of Iberianism in Portugal, and notes: "Após uma crise colonial surgem sempre projetos iberistas" (Iberianist projects always follow in the wake of colonial crises) (8). Similarly, Sérgio Campos Matos notes that, for Portugal, "os momentos de crise (1868–71; 1890–92) corresponderiam … a momentos de grande difusão do ideário iberista, como se da integração ou, pelo menos, da aproximação política e diplomática com a Espanha pudesse resultar a solução para essas graves crises" (The periods of crisis (1868–71; 1890–92) … are periods in which the Iberianist program gained ample projection, as if to imply that [Portuguese] integration within Spain, or at least political and diplomatic approximation to Spain, could resolve these grave crises) ("Iberismo" 355). And as José Antonio Rocamora observes: "La unidad [entre España y Portugal] fue vista por muchos como el único camino para reverdecer las viejas glorias, transformando dos países débiles en uno poderoso, capaz de actuar en la política mundial y restaurar el prestigio perdido" (Many saw unity [between Spain and Portugal] as the only way to revive past glories, and to transform two weak countries into a single strong country able to act in world affairs and recover its lost glory) (*El nacionalismo* 21).[22]

Rocamora, author of *El nacionalismo ibérico 1792–1936* (1994), characterizes Iberianism as an ultimately failed form of peninsular nationalism, one that maintained a complex relation with Portuguese and Spanish state nationalisms, and that, further, might be viewed alongside the "alternative nationalisms" that began to coalesce in Catalania, the Basque Country, and Galicia in the final decades of the nineteenth century (Angel Smith 1).[23] In casting Iberianism as a nationalist discourse and project, Rocamora highlights the broader political and intellectual context within which Iberianism emerged in a "peripheral" region of Western Europe during the European nineteenth century. By the close of the eighteenth century, the American and French revolutions, in challenging the dynastic principle, had offered as an alterative a pact-based, civic model for the nation state rooted in the social contract theory of John Locke and Jean-Jacques Rousseau. This model of national governance would memorably be described, decades later, by Ernest Renan in his 1882 address "What Is a Nation"? as "a great solidarity" and a "plesiscite of every day" (58). The European Romantics, active from the turn of the nineteenth century across the spectrum of literature, the arts, scholarship, and politics, offered as an alternative to the civic "plebiscite" an ethnic model of nationalism, which understood that "nations [are] gradually or discontinuously formed on the basis of pre-existing *ethnie* and ethnic ties" (Anthony Smith 137). The Romantic theorists of nationhood, many of whom were clustered in the as-yet-divided Germany and Italy, elevated over the state the notion of the organic nation, whether united in a single polity or separated by political borders "artificially" imposed by monarchies and petty fiefdoms. As Giuseppe Mazzini, who called for Italy to form a single republic, and then join a European federation, put it in 1849: "Without the nation there can be no humanity, even as without organization and division there can be no expeditious and fruitful labour. Nations are the citizens of humanity, as individuals are the citizens of the nation" (147). The Romantics viewed language as a privileged expression of the unity that substantiated a particular group's claims to national sovereignty. As J.G. Herder succinctly put it in his *Ideas for a Philosophy of History of Mankind* (1784–91): "Every distinct community is a *nation*, having its own national culture as it has its own language" (284; author's emphasis).[24]

Iberianism, which emerged as Spain and Portugal, two beleauguered, centuries-old, multicontinental dynastic monarchies, forced to contend with "the rapidly rising prestige ... of the national idea" (Anderson 85), took on alternately republican and monarchical, unitary and federalist guises. Further, Iberianism straddled the divide between civic and ethnic nationalisms – which as Angel Smith observes, "tended to intermingle" in nineteenth-century European nation-building projects (4).[25] While significant ideological differences separate, for example, the young Antero de Quental from the mature Oliveira Martins, or Miguel de Unamuno from Joan Maragall, we can say at a minimum that their turn to Iberianism reflected a pervasive sense of national malaise among their late nineteenth-century Iberian intellectual peers. This collective feeling of pessimism was the product both of localized political and economic crises, as well as Spain and Portugal's failure to successfully reconcile their state institutions with either the civic or ethnic model of nationalism, or the broader, unachieved demands of a modernity, felt with particular acuteness on an Iberian Peninsula by the *fin de siècle*. This feeling was given evocative expression by Cesário Verde in his 1880 masterpiece "O sentimento dum ocidental" (The Feeling of a Westerner), in which the poet-cum-*flâneur*, wandering around Lisbon, observes:

> Batem of carros de aluguer, ao fundo,
> Levando à via férrea os que se vão. Felizes!
> Ocorrem-me em revista exposições, países:
> Madrid, Paris, Berlim, S. Petersburgo, o mundo!
>
> (*O Livro* 94)

> Oh lucky travelers in hired coaches
> Now [heading] to the railway station! Countries
> And exhibitions file past me: Madrid,
> Paris, Berlin, St. Petersberg, the world! (*The Feeling* 25)

Certain Iberianist projects and efforts predated 1850, notably the founding by Spanish and Portuguese exiles in Paris of Iberianist groups and publications. However, the "Iberian question" truly emerged in

1851,[26] with the publication of two key Iberianist texts: the Catalan-born Spanish diplomat Sinibaldo de Mas's *La Iberia* (Iberia), and the Portuguese Iberian federalist José Félix Henriques Nogueira's *Estudos sobre a Reforma em Portugal*. Mas's and Nogueira's texts inspired the wave of Iberianist production that began in Portugal nearly twenty years later, with Antero de Quental's *Portugal Perante a Revolução de Espanha* (1868), and which arrived in Catalonia by the close of the century. Mas's *La Iberia* was quickly translated by Portuguese Iberianist Latino Coelho and published in Lisbon in 1852, where it went through three editions (in Spain it achieved five by 1868)[27] and deeply impacted the Portuguese intelligentsia.[28] Nogueira's *Estudos*, perhaps because it framed the problem of Iberianism in the context of a specifically Portuguese national reform agenda, one similar to that adopted by Joaquín Costa in *Reconstitución y europeización de España* (1900), was not, to my knowledge, translated to Spanish. This said, its federalism would be echoed by a number of younger Iberianist writers including Quental, Francesc Pi i Margall, and Joan Maragall.

Mas and Nogueira advocated distinct Iberianist programs, with Mas calling for a single Iberian monarchy and Nogueira advocating a decentralized Iberian republic. However, they agreed on the strategic benefits of union for both Portugal and Spain, and indeed, in August 1853 Nogueira reviewed the Portuguese edition of Mas's *La Iberia*.[29] Imagining a geographically imposing Iberian monarchy in possession of sizeable Caribbean, African, and Asian colonies – most of which, by the mid-nineteenth century, were in Portuguese as opposed to Spanish hands – Mas observed: "As vantagens de que gosa uma grande nação não consistem apenas em uma vaidade fôfa, senão nos beneficios positivos que a seus habitantes proporciona o seu governo por meio de tratados favoraveis ás vezes *impostos* a outras nações debeis na protecção que lhes dá nos paizes estrangeiros, nos mercados que lhes abre nas colonias que possue" (The advantages enjoyed by a great nation are not limited to superficial vanity, but rather consist of the positive benefits that its government can provide to the country's inhabitants through the favourable treaties that it can sometimes *impose* on weak nations through the promise of protection from other countries or through access to colonial markets) (50; author's emphasis). And in *Estudos*, Nogueira makes an argument on the advantages of Iberianism for both Portugal and Spain that recalls Mas. However, Nogueira arrives at his conclusion by following a federalist line of argumentation with which Mas would no doubt have disagreed: "Baluarte e última esperança dos povos oprimidos, que só na aliança com os seus iguais podem achar uma protecção benéfica e sincera, a forma federativa é destinada a libertar as nações fracas do predomínio das fortes" (The bulwark and last hope of oppressed peoples, who only by allying themselves with others on an equal basis can secure beneficial and true protection, federation is destined to free weak nations from domination by the strong). Nogueira then turns to the Iberian Peninsula specifically, contending that, by forming a federal republic, "Portugal e os outros povos peninsulares, irmãos em crenças, em costumes, em origem histórica, em grandes feitos, em grandeza e infortúnio, em interesses, em inspiração literária e artística, e quase em linguagem, não podem deixar de constituir, para o futuro, uma grande nação" (Portugal and the other peninsular peoples, who are brothers in their beliefs, customs, historical origin, great deeds, in both glory and misfortune, in their interests, their literary and artistic inspiration, and nearly so in language, cannot be, in the future, anything less than a great nation) (1: 162). Near the conclusion of the chapter, Nogueira goes further, declaring that through federation, "tu serás, ó ilustre Ibéria, o magnífico pórtico da Europa regenerada, a formosa princesa de suas nações!" (you will be, o illustrious Iberia, the magnificent gateway of a renewed Europe, a lovely princess among its nations!) (166).

Moving ahead by nearly twenty years, a young Antero de Quental, responding to the overthrow of Queen Isabel II in Spain in his 1868 pamphlet *Portugal Perante a Revolução de Espanha*, fused the pragmatic pro-Iberianist arguments of Mas and Nogueira with his belief that revolution, federation, and Proudhonian socialism were in the Iberian Peninsula's and Europe's immediate future:

> vemos o ideal revolucionário de Portugal tocar-se, confundir-se com o ideal da revolução espanhola. Para toda a Península não há hoje senão uma única política possível: a da federação republicana-democrática. E, em face desta formidável unidade de interesses, de ideias, de vontades, e de aspirações, que podem as *barreiras da nacionalidade* significar mais do que uma tradição, um símbolo poético, cujo sentido se perde de dia para dia, até se tornar de todo incompreensível, até desaparecer? (125; author's emphasis)

> We see that Portugal's revolutionary ideal approximates and fuses with the ideal of the Spanish revolution. Today there is only one political possibility open to the Peninsula: a republican and democratic federation. And

> in the face of this formidable unity of interests, of ideas, of wills, and of aspirations, what do *barriers of nationality* matter? What are they other than a tradition, a poetic symbol whose meaning diminishes day by day, until it becomes entirely meaningless and disappears?

This argument leads Quental to his perhaps deliberately scandalous statement that for the Portuguese people, "nas nossas actuais circunstâncias, o único acto possível e lógico de verdadeiro patriotismo consiste em *renegar a nacionalidade*" (given our present circumstances, the only possible, logical expression of true patriotism is that we *renounce our nationality*) (128; author's emphasis).

While Quental would refine his Iberianist views as he matured and conditions in Spain evolved, the bases of his Iberianist program – federalism, a moralizing call for the peninsular peoples to account for their historical errors, and an embrace of socialist-inspired interpersonal solidarity – are spelled out here. Similarly, we find typifying elements of Oliveira Martins's Iberianism in his early article "Do Princípio Federativo e Sua Aplicação à Península Hispânica" (On the Federal Principle and Its Application to the Hispanic Peninsula, 1869), which like his friend's 1868 pamphlet was at least partially inspired by *La Gloriosa*.[30] Like Quental, Martins argues for the practical benefits of a federal Iberian republic, which he describes as, "para nós, como para a Espanha actual, a solução de uma crise que a ela como a nós pode demorar a evolução progressiva por muito tempo" (for us, and for today's Spain, the solution to a crisis that might slow our progressive evolution for some time) (28). He further characterizes federation "como resolução da crise actual, e portanto como solução natural da questão peninsular" (as a way of resolving the current crisis, and therefore as a natural solution to the peninsular question) (37).

Quental's *Causas da Decadência dos Povos Peninsulares* and especially Oliveira Martins's *História da Civilização Ibérica* helped shape the late nineteenth-century Portuguese debate on national *decadência* and its potential solutions, and won Spanish admirers, including the novelist Juan Valera,[31] the scholar and historian Marcelino Menéndez y Pelayo, and, eventually, Miguel de Unamuno, whose reading of Quental and Martins will be discussed in chapter 4. By the turn of the twentieth century, however, the centre of Iberianist activity had passed from Lisbon to Barcelona, where Iberianism had taken root in the fertile soil of *fin-de-siècle* Catalonia. Here, in the midst of an ongoing Catalan cultural and linguistic revival, and increasingly loud Catalan demands for autonomy and even independence from Madrid, "tripartite Iberianists" like Joan Maragall and Ignasi Ribera i Rovira looked to Iberianism as a means to achieve more equitable relations between Catalonia, Castile, and Portugal, and to satisfy Catalan aspirations towards nationhood within an at least minimally united peninsula.[32]

The political situations of late nineteenth-century Portugal, an embattled though sovereign state, and Catalonia, a comparatively prosperous aspiring nation within the Spanish state, were distinct, despite the efforts of Catalan Iberianists and other commentators (Unamuno, Ribera i Rovira, Salvador de Madariaga) to present Catalonia and Portugal as opposing sides of the same Iberian coin. Nonetheless, the Catalan Iberianists echoed their Portuguese counterparts in arguing for the tangible benefits to Catalonia, and by implication, to the whole of Spain and Portugal, of a single federal Iberian state, to be led by the industrializing, dynamic, and European Catalonia. Maragall, the Barcelona-born poet, journalist, and translator, made the following observation on peninsular society in his article "El ideal ibérico" (The Iberian Ideal, 1906): "Ved que estamos muriendo … por falta de un sol que nos caliente el alma, por falta de un ideal, y he aquí el último ideal ibérico que se levanta de su Oriente" (You must see that we are dying … for lack of a sun, for lack of an ideal, and here we have Iberia's final ideal, which rises from its East) (*OC* 2: 726). While Maragall's pessimistic assessment was informed by the *desastre* of 1898, which impacted Catalonia just as it did the rest of the Spanish state, he identifies Catalan-led Iberianism (a sun rising in the Catalan East) as a potential solution to the crisis. In one of his final articles, "'Catalunya i avant'" (For Catalonia and the Future, 1911), Maragall argues that if the peninsular peoples succeed in identifying their common "alma peninsular" (peninsular soul), they may achieve "la gran civilización ibérica aún por hacer, y por la que seremos algo, mucho en el mundo" (the great Iberian civilization yet to be constructed, and through which we will be something, we will mean a great deal, in the world) (761).

Maragall's argument that a Catalan-led Iberian federation would allow the peninsular peoples to achieve greater international standing recalls statements made by more openly political Catalan Iberianists, namely Enric Prat de la Riba, a leader of conservative Catalanism and president of the Mancomunitat de Catalunya (1914–17), and Ignasi Ribera i Rovira, a Lusophile journalist and translator. Near the conclusion of his influential essay *La nacionalitat catalana* (The Catalan Nationality, 1906), Prat declares that through unification, "podrà la nova Iberia enlairarse al grau suprem d'imperialisme: podrà intervenir activament en el govern del món ab les altres potencies mondials, podrà altra vegada expansionarse sobre les terres barbres, y servir els alts interessos de l'humanitat guiant cap a la civilisació els pobles enderrerits y incultes" (the new Iberia will be able to achieve the highest degree of imperialism. It will be able to actively intervene in governing the world, along with the other world powers. It will once again be able to conquer barbarian lands, and serve the high interests of humanity by bringing civilization to backward and uncultured peoples) (128).[33] And in his volume *Iberisme* (Iberianism, 1907), which was prefaced by the Portuguese scholar and Republican politician Teófilo Braga (a contemporary of Antero de Quental and Oliveira Martins), Ribera i Rovira summarized the case for a tripartite Iberian federation as follows:

> La finalitat del nostre moviment politic, tant intens, tant triomfador, ha d'esser, catalans, definir momentaniament la personalitat de Catalunya, i després cercar-li l lloc que li pertoca en el concert de les nacionalitats iberiques. Destruint la falsa divisió de les províncies i de les regions, l'ideal suprem de l'iberisme reconeix la l'existencia de les tres nacionalitats hispaniques: la galaico-portuguesa a occident, la castellana al centre, i la catalana al llevant de la Peninsula. L'existencia d'aquestes hermoses i fortes nacionalitats, el reconeixement i el respecte mutuals entre elles, estableix l'equilibri hispanic i permet la realisació d'un desig latent en l'esperit de cada poble: la fraternitat, que ls lligui amorosament deixant-los lluires; l'igualtat, que ls torni senyors de lo propri sense temences; la llibertat, pera expandir-se profitosament, ajudant-se, no obstant, per les relacions internacionals, pels conflictes exteriors, obeint a una sola direcció, armonia de voluntats nacionals, a una veu collectiva que clamoregi a l'unissò, poderosa, ferma i temuda. (121)
>
> My fellow Catalans, the immediate goal of our political movement, which is so intense, and so triumphant, must be to define Catalonia's personality, and then fix Catalonia's place in the concert of the Iberian nationalities. Having destroyed the false divisions of provinces and regions, Iberianism's supreme ideal recognizes the existence of three Hispanic nationalities: the Galaico-Portuguese in the West, the Castilians in the Centre, and the Catalans in the East of the Peninsula. The existence of these admirable, vigorous nationalities, and the mutual recognition and respect they accord each other, establish an equilibrium between the Hispanic nationalities and allow for the achievement of the design that is latent in each of these

> peoples. This entails fraternity, which draws them together through love while preserving their freedom; equality, which allows them to govern themselves without fear; and the freedom to help each other profitably expand. But in international affairs and foreign conflicts, they will always follow a single course, in a harmony of national wills, a collective voice, powerful, firm, and feared, sounding as one.

In looking back on late nineteenth- and early twentieth-century Iberianism's succession of failed predictions (for instance, Quental's contention circa 1868 that Portugal would soon rise up to join Spain in republican revolution) and its ultimate failure to achieve a single peninsular state, it is tempting to dismiss Iberianism as a passing intellectual fashion, on a par with positivism, social Darwinism, and a variety of other *–isms* that while attractive to certain elite peninsular intellectuals, lacked popular support and failed to make the leap from theorization to political reality. Indeed, Portugal weathered the *fin-de-siècle* storm of the Ultimatum, the 1908 regicide, and the 1910 founding of the Republic and remained an independent, albeit beleaugured state that retained African colonies until 1974. Similarly, while Spain adopted a more decentralized form of government during the Second Spanish Republic (1931–9), which should have at least theoretically created a space for Iberianism, this gave way to the Franco dictatorship's centralization and suppression of the Catalan, Galician, and Basque languages, cultures, and national aspirations. And though Spain's 1978 constitution allows for a significant degree of administrative decentralization and regional autonomy, Spain's federal government, in the minds of many Catalan, Galician, and Basque autonomists and pro-independence activists, has not gone far enough, and continues to privilege Castilian language, culture, and political control.[34]

Even some of those closest to late nineteenth- and early twentieth-century Iberianism critiqued it as a quixotic dream or an intellectual fad. For instance, Portuguese novelist Eça de Queirós, a close associate of Antero de Quental and especially Oliveira Martins, poked fun at Iberianism in his 1888 novel *Os Maias*. In a famous dinner scene, the character João da Ega, a pseudo-intellectual dandy always ready to adopt the latest exotic intellectual fashion and an enthusiast of scandalous remarks, declares, to the horror of his more patriotic friends: "Portugal não necessita reformas, ... Portugal o que precisa é a invasão espanhola" (Portugal doesn't need reforms ... What Portugal needs is invasion by Spain) (213).[35] Were Iberianism's defenders all as comically superficial as Ega, it would hardly be surprising that Iberianism failed to significantly impact peninsular politics – except, perhaps, in a negative sense, as an impetus for Spanish "regenerationists" such as Joaquín Costa to call for colonial expansion in north Africa in the wake of 1898,[36] for the young Portuguese republic to reinvest in its African colonies as a bulwark against Spanish invasion,[37] and for conservative Catalanists to attempt to weed out Iberianism from their movement.[38] But as we have seen, Iberianism counted some of Portugal and Spain's most celebrated writers and thinkers, including Quental, Martins, and Maragall, among its defenders, and found a sympathetic ear in Miguel de Unamuno. This said, even those peninsular intellectuals who were most amenable to the Iberian union, and were best positioned to make this a reality, had reservations as to its feasibility. While Quental and Oliveira Martins's shifting Iberianist positions will be discussed in later chapters, let us now turn to Francesc Pi i Margall (Castilian spelling: Francisco Pi y Margall), a Catalan-born Spanish federalist and, briefly, president of the short-lived First Spanish Republic. After summarizing centuries of Spanish aggression and mistrust towards Portugal in his study *Las nacionalidades* (1877), Pi, who earlier in his career had confidently proposed federal democracy as a means for Portugal to rejoin Spain,[39] concludes:

> Comprenderá fácilmente el lector que esta conducta no era la más apropósito para atraernos ni la confianza ni las simpatías del vecino reino. Así hoy, no lo duden mis compatriotas, está Portugal tanto ó más enagenado de nosotros que en el siglo XVII. Importa poco que menosprecien allí la nacionalidad una pocas almas afligidas por la constante decadencia y la sin igual flaqueza de su patria: sus palabras de abatimiento y de amargura no llegan al corazon del pueblo, como las apasionados cantos de Tomás Ribeiro por la Independencia. Bajo el principio unitario, no vacilo en asegurarlo, no llegará a ser nuestro Portugal sino por las fuerza; aun bajo el de la federacion, tengo para mí que habia de hacerse difícil persuadirle á ser provincia de España. Tal ha sido la influencia de nuestra política, tal la obra del unitarismo. (258)[40]

> The reader will easily perceive that this behaviour was not conducive to gaining the confidence and sympathy of the neighbouring kingdom [i.e., Portugal]. You must see, my countrymen, that today Portugal is as alienated, if not more alienated, from us than was the case in the seventeenth century. It matters little that over there a few souls who are pained by the

unrelenting decadence and unparalleled weakness of their country, speak ill of their nationality. Their downhearted, bitter words do not penetrate into the hearts of the people, as do Tomás Ribeiro's passionate songs in favor of Independence. I can assure you that Portugal cannot become ours through force of arms, through a unitary policy. And even if a federal system were adopted, I believe that it would be difficult to persuade Portugal to become a Spanish province. Such has been the impact of our policy, and the result of unitarianism.

Notwithstanding Iberianism's historical failings, this book will make a strong case for the importance of studying Iberianism in the context of the intellectual culture of crisis-ridden late nineteenth- and early twentieth-century Spain and Portugal. I will make this case in this chapter's final section.

Iberianism as Critical History

The goal of achieving a united Iberian state, whether federalist or centralized, whether organized as a republic or monarchy, has remained elusive. Notwithstanding this apparent failure, if justification is needed for the study of Iberianism beyond the historical or literary interest of its writers and textual corpus, we might cite the following argument: Iberianism, in the mode of a Nietzschian critical history, serves the salutary function of contesting dominant peninsular narratives of national identity, by positing a single peninsular state and more equitable, dynamic relations between Iberian regions as desirable outcomes. As Friedrich Nietzsche observed in his essay "On the Utility and Liability of History for Life" (1874), "if the monumental view of the past" – which we would identity here with self-enclosed, unitary historical narratives for Spain, Portugal, and so on – "*prevails* over other modes of viewing it … then the past itself is *damaged*: entire large parts of it are forgotten, scorned, and washed away as if by a gray, unremitting tide, and only a few individual, embellished facts rise as islands above it" (100; author's emphasis). The German philosopher identifies three modes of historical discourse in his essay: the monumental, the antiquarian, and the critical. Iberianism, in Nietzsche's scheme, would likely serve as a critical history, one invested with "the strength to shatter and dissolve a past" – the same past monumental history seeks to elevate to the status of consecrated myth (106).[41]

Transposing Nietzsche's observations onto the topical terrain of *Iberianism and Crisis*, we might contend that the study of Iberianism serves to disrupt received notions of peninsular history, which traditionally have presented Iberia's political division into two sovereign nation states, Spain and Portugal, as self-evident, and, similarly, have normalized Castile's historical protagonism within Spain. All the while, these narratives ignore or marginalize potentially disruptive phenomena such as cross-border and cross-linguistic dialogues between peninsular writers and cultural actors, as well as alternate schemes for the peninsula's political organization, and pluralistic and historicized understandings of the categories used to configure the Iberian Peninsula, including "Iberia," "Spain," "Portugal," and the like. Viewed as critical history, Iberianism provides us with the source material to undertake disruptive actions in the present, whether political (for instance, advocacy of new forms for intra-Iberian dialogue) or academic (demonstrating through research and teaching the degree to which intra-Iberian relations are complex, contradictory, and historically contingent). Thomas Harrington has astutely observed that despite the tendency of peninsular historiography to construct "unitarily constituted discourses of national identity," in reality there exists "a rich history of attempts on the part of intellectuals to cultivate the idea of a Peninsula, and at times with it, a transatlantic Hispanic space that was unabashedly multinational, yet fundamentally conjoined in the pursuit of larger cultural, economic, and political goals" ("The Hidden" 139). The study of Iberianism provides us with a platform for accessing this sort of "unabashedly multinational" understanding of the Iberian Peninsula, and by extension, the peninsula's literary and cultural production.

Iberianism and Crisis is not a comprehensive history of Iberianism. Indeed, informative histories of Iberianism have been written by José Antonio Rocamora, Víctor Martínez-Gil, and Sérgio Campos Matos, among others. This book employs a critical or interpretive as opposed to strictly historiographical mode of writing, and has the following objectives. First, it aims to demonstrate the degree to which Iberianism informed the thought, writing, and public activity of some of the late nineteenth- and early twentieth-century peninsula's most celebrated writers and public intellectuals. Indeed, one would be hard-pressed to find writers more central to peninsular literary and intellectual life than were Antero de Quental and Oliveira Martins for late nineteenth-century Portugal, Miguel de Unamuno for turn-of-the-century Spain, or Joan Maragall for Catalan letters during the era of *modernisme*. Ironically, these men, despite their now canonical status within Portuguese, Spanish, and Catalan letters, respectively, were strongly informed by

Iberianism, a way of thinking that questioned the coherence of apparently self-enclosed national communities, and thereby subverted "Portugal" "Spain" and "Catalonia," as well as Portuguese, Spanish, and Catalan letters, as categories possessed of a self-evident, univocal meaning. Second, this book aims to underscore the relationship between the ideas of *Iberianism* and *crisis* by demonstrating how some of Iberia's most influential literary and public voices turned to Iberianism in order to address peninsular crisis at the *fin de siècle.* In making this connection, I will propose Iberianism as a line that connects a set of prominent peninsular intellectuals who are commonly and, to my mind, artificially separated by language, borders, regional identities, and canons, and by the distinct academic identities of Luso-Brazilian, Hispanic, and Catalan studies. And third and finally, this book takes up the challenge issued by Thomas Harrington and like-minded advocates of Iberian studies to work towards an "unabashedly multinational" understanding of peninsular literary histories and national and state identities, in their various entanglements. In so doing, in my conclusion I will propose a series of "lessons" provided by the Iberianist writers under analysis in this book to Iberian studies as an emerging academic field of inquiry.

Iberianism and Crisis is organized as follows: in chapter 2, "Antero de Quental, *Iberista*: A Portuguese Iberianist, the *Geração de 70*, and the *Sexenio Democrático* in Spain," I look to Iberianism to lend coherence to my analysis of Quental's socio-political prose as it developed over the course of his public life of nearly thirty years, from the 1860s through 1891. In casting Quental as a committed Iberianist, I break with the received critical tendency to limit his Iberianism to a brief phase of youthful enthusiasm sparked by the 1868 revolution in Spain. Rather, I argue for Iberianism as an enduring feature of Quental's thought, and propose that his Iberianism evolved rather than diminished over the course of his career. Concretely, I chart Quental's Iberianist engagement over three key periods: first, the early years of his intellectual career (1864–8), in which he wrote the poem "Ibéria" (1864) and, more substantively, the pro-Iberianist pamphlet *Portugal Perante a Revolução de Espanha* (1868); second, Quental's participation in the 1871 *Conferências do Casino* (Casino Conferences), a planned series of talks in Lisbon that included his address *Causas da Decadência dos Povos Peninsulares*, in which he engaged with the idea of a common "peninsular race," made a guarded defence of the Spanish republicans, and suggested a potential Iberianist future for Portugal; and third, Quental's final years, in which he published the philosophical survey *As Tendências Gerais da Filosofia na Segunda Metade do Séc. XIX* (General Tendencies of Philosophy during the Second Half of the Nineteenth Century, 1890). Here Quental returns to certain ideas he had applied previously to the Iberianist problem – namely, the notion of racial "genius" and the primacy of the value of freedom. This conceptual continuity illustrates the enduring impact on Quental of Iberianism (or at minimum, its underlying principles), if not his confidence that a workable Portuguese–Spanish political union could be achieved after the collapse of the First Spanish Republic in 1874.

In chapter 3, "'A Ribbon of Silver': Representations of the Portuguese–Galician Border at the *Fin de Siècle*," I move from Lisbon, the primary base of operation for Portugal's *Geração de 70*, to the Miño River (in Portuguese, *Minho*), which demarcates the Portuguese–Spanish (or Portuguese–Galician) frontier – one of the oldest stable political borders in Europe – for approximately seventy-five kilometres before emptying into the Atlantic. Daily life on the Portuguese–Galician border found ample literary expression during the late nineteenth century, a period that witnessed the *Rexurdimento*, a movement of Galician linguistic, literary, and cultural "rebirth" led by writers like Rosalía de Castro, Manuel Murguía, and Manuel Curros Enríquez. In this chapter I look beyond these more-or-less quotidian descriptions, and consider representations of the Miño and the Portuguese–Galician border that are invested with a greater degree of symbolism and which bear on Iberianism and on intra-Iberian relations. Specifically, I draw on reflections by Oliveira Martins, the Galician-born Spanish novelist Emilia Pardo Bazán, and Miguel de Unamuno. Their comments highlight cross-border cultural, geographic, and linguistic continuities between Galicia and Portugal in ways that disrupt received *fin-de-siècle* notions concerning the Iberian Peninsula's political division into two sovereign states, one of which (Portugal) was understood to be ethnically, linguistically, and culturally homogeneous, while the other (Spain) was viewed from Restoration-era Madrid as an essentially cohesive nationality whose linguistically and culturally distinct regions, such as Galicia, would over time be subsumed into a Castile-centred, monolingual, and monocultural whole. In challenging the Iberian status quo in this way, writers like Martins, Pardo Bazán, and Unamuno performed an important function that was complementary to the Iberianist project. By helping to illuminate the complexity of Galicia's position within the Spanish nation state, and within the broader Iberian Peninsula, Martins, Pardo

Bazán, and Unamuno each looked to the Portuguese–Galician border as a point from which to consider Iberia's other "possible nations" (Medeiros 9).

Chapter 4, "Miguel de Unamuno: A Peninsula of Flesh and Bone," is dedicated to perhaps the most storied member of Spain's *Generación del 98*. I focus here on how Unamuno used the notions of *carne* (flesh) and *hueso* (bone), biblically derived figures that repeatedly appear in his work, to articulate a theory of Iberian identity and intra-Iberian relations in which the constituent regions of the peninsula, and Castile and Portugal in particular, were strongly implicated. Unamuno's descriptions of an Iberian Peninsula built, metaphorically, of both "flesh" and "bone," provide a convenient means to explore his Iberianism in comparison to Quental and Oliveira Martins, who both deeply influenced Unamuno, and his friend and epistolary partner Joan Maragall. Writing against the backdrop of Spain's protracted imperial decline, which reached its culmination in 1898, Unamuno offered a vision of Spain (and by extension, Iberia) as a dialectical unity, that is, as an internally differentiated but ultimately unified whole. I argue that Unamuno's dialectical vision of the Iberian Peninsula can be understood as an effort to reconcile the competing if not opposed values of fealty to an "authentic" peninsular culture and openness to "modern" European ideas. In attempting through his dialectical vision of Iberia, or more bluntly, through Iberianism, to "square the circle" fashioned by the twin forces of Iberian particularity and European modernity, Unamuno followed in Quental and Oliveira Martins's footsteps. Further, he echoed – up to a certain point – the calls made by Maragall for an Iberianism that would affirm Catalan nationhood while maintaining the integrity of the Spanish state, and anticipated the Iberian federalist proposals of twentieth-century peninsular intellectuals including Miguel Torga and Salvador de Madariaga.

Portugal, a country both geographically near to Unamuno's adopted home of Salamanca, and dear to his heart, played a prominent role in his articulation of a dialectical theory of Iberian identity and intra-Iberian relations. For Unamuno, it occupied one side of the flesh/bone divide and stood in counterpoint to Castile. As such, in this chapter I first describe Unamuno's relationship with Portugal, which is notable for its depth and capacity to illuminate the broader contours of his Iberianist program. I then offer a more detailed analysis of Unamuno's dialectical understanding of the Iberian Peninsula, and discuss his call for Portugal and Spain to be brought into geographic, cultural, and linguistic confrontation as a means to achieve eventual synthesis. I conclude by tying Unamuno's dialectical vision of Iberia back to the vocabulary of "flesh" and "bone" introduced at the outset of the chapter.

Chapter 5, "Joan Maragall: Iberian Hymns from Catalonia," focuses on one of the most beloved figures in Catalan letters, a Barcelona-born poet, journalist, and translator whose popular, patriotic verses and public advocacy for Catalan language, culture, and nationhood transformed him into a symbol of Catalan identity and national aspiration. Like his friend and epistolary partner Unamuno, Maragall was aware of the complex interrelationships between the Catalan nation, the Spanish state, the Iberian Peninsula, and Europe. Maragall's multiple, shifting engagements – with Catalanism, Spanish regenerationism, and Iberianism – make him a difficult figure to pigeonhole, and make questions of Maragall's relationship to the Catalan, Spanish, and Iberian literary and intellectual traditions at the *fin de siècle* all the more complicated. Maragall's overlapping interests would suggest that he maintained a complex (or, less charitably, inconsistent or contradictory) sense of his Catalan, Spanish, and Iberian identities. Though as I demonstrate in previous chapters, in Antero de Quental's 1871 reference to his Lisbon audience as "nós Espanhóis" (we Spaniards) in *Causas da Decadência dos Povos Peninsulares*, and in Emilia Pardo Bazán's defence of her right to consider herself both Galician and Spanish in a passage from *La vida contemporánea (1896–1915)* (Contemporary Life, 1896–1915), disentangling Maragall's overlapping self-identifications may prove useful in illuminating the nuances of his Catalanist, Spanish regenerationist, and Iberianist programs. I attempt to do so in this chapter's first section. I then offer a detailed analysis of Maragall's Iberianism, and conclude by analysing Maragall and Unamuno's correspondence, assessing its possible impact on the deeper structures of Maragall's Iberianist thought and comparing Unamuno and Maragall's views.

Chapter 6, "The Iberianist Legacy: Salvador de Madariaga reads Oliveira Martins," brings closure to the analysis undertaken in the previous five chapters. After opening with a discussion of how prominent twentieth-century Portuguese and Spanish thinkers have interpreted the work of Oliveira Martins, I turn to an Iberian intellectual who was influenced by Martins, and whose thoughts on Iberian civilization, Iberianism, and intra-Iberian relations can be productively brought into dialogue with Martins: the Spanish writer, historian, diplomat, and political exile Salvador de Madariaga (1886–1978). While chronologically, Madariaga falls outside the *fin-de-siècle* period analysed in this book, I believe that he nonetheless merits inclusion as a figure who can help us bridge the gap between the turn-of-the-century heyday of Iberianism and current debates on Iberian culture and identity, which I address in this book's conclusion through an assessment of the burgeoning field of Iberian studies. Indeed, Madariaga's life spanned Spain's Restoration monarchy, Second Republic, Francoism, and the first years of post-Franco federal democracy. And the problems he addressed, including the tension between Castilian centralism and Catalan, Basque, and Galician aspirations towards autonomy or independence, and Spain's relationship to the dream of a federated Europe, are as timely today as they were during his lifetime – or indeed, as far back as the *fin de siècle*. Further, as an international diplomat who wrote in Spanish, French, and English, Madariaga enjoyed significant international prestige. This gave his writings a broad, extra-academic projection unavailable to mid-twentieth-century academic Hispanists. And finally, and perhaps most importantly for our purposes, Madariaga ties together and develops several of the strands of Iberianist thinking discussed throughout *Iberianism and Crisis*. Though Madariaga did not describe himself as an Iberianist – he preferred the term *federalist* – he nonetheless called for post-Franco Spain to reorganize itself as a federation, advocated European federalism more broadly, and affirmed the overarching unity of Iberian or "Spanish" civilization (a concept he viewed as inclusive of Portugal) even as he acknowledged internal peninsular differences.

While one can locate points of contact in Madariaga's work with the ideas and proposals of various *fin-de-siècle* Iberianists, including Quental, Unamuno, and Maragall, it was to Oliveira Martins's *História da Civilização Ibérica* that Madariaga turned in 1930, when he was tasked with choosing the inaugural title for a series of Hispanic classics to be published in English translation by Oxford University Press – hence my choice to focus on Madariaga as a reader of Martins. This chapter first offers a biographical sketch of Madariaga, then describes his role in the publication of *A History of Iberian Civilization*, summarizes his written references to Martins, and concludes by comparing Madariaga and Martins's ideas on Iberian history and culture.

Iberianism and Crisis concludes with "Iberianism's Lessons," which moves from the topical terrain of late nineteenth- and early twentieth-century Iberianism to contemporary academic debates. Concretely, I reflect on a series of proposals with the aim of radically reconceptualizing the discipline of peninsular literary and culture studies. Many of these proposals have been presented as interventions in an emerging field termed "Iberian studies," which asks how peninsular literary and cultural studies might be reimagined – and reinvigorated – by placing the Spanish and Portuguese canons into critical dialogue with each other, and with Galician, Catalan, Basque, and other peninsular texts, cultural expressions, and traditions. Meanwhile, Iberian studies have gained a certain institutional traction in the form of academic centres, departments, and publishing initiatives. In this conclusion I identify three key features of Iberian studies that differentiate it, at least in theory, from Hispanism, which proponents of Iberian studies present as the field's prevailing disciplinary paradigm. These are: (1) an embrace of multilingualism; (2) comparativism across borders and between peninsular states, nations, and regions; and (3) an inclusive, non-hierarchical approach to literary and cultural materials.

In "Iberianism's Lessons" I first summarize the debate on Iberian studies – a debate I view as highly relevant to the sort of multilingual, cross-border, and intra-Iberian analysis I attempt in *Iberianism and Crisis* – as it has developed over the last fifteen or so years. I then attempt to bridge the Iberianist past described in this book with the possible disciplinary futures projected by advocates of Iberian studies in the form of lessons provided by three writers discussed in previous chapters: Antero de Quental, Joan Maragall, and Miguel de Unamuno.

Let us now turn to the first of these three writers, Antero de Quental.

Chapter Two

Antero de Quental, *Iberista*: A Portuguese Iberianist, the *Geração de 70,* and the *Sexenio Democrático* in Spain

The *Geração de 70* stands as one of the most remarkable groupings in Portuguese letters, counting among its ranks celebrated writers, public intellectuals, and politicians such as José Maria Eça de Queirós, Joaquim Pedro de Oliveira Martins, Ramalho Ortigão, and Teófilo Braga.[1] The group's decisive rejection of received ideas, its receptiveness to European philosophical and scientific innovations, and its acute awareness of Portugal's degree of political, economic, and cultural marginality in the closing decades of the nineteenth century anticipated the similarly non-conformist Spanish *Generación del 98*.[2] At the centre of the *Geração de 70* stood Antero de Quental (1842–91), an Azorean-born writer, theorist, labour organizer, and political agitator who is often remembered as his generation's philosophical mentor or as an innovative, metaphysically minded poet rather than as an important contributor to Portuguese intellectual history in his own right. Like Eça and Braga, Quental attended the elite University of Coimbra, where he studied law between 1858 and 1864, though he was perhaps most notable during those years for his institutional and metaphysical rebellion: Quental organized an 1862 student walkout that led to the resignation of Coimbra's *reitor* (rector), and was remembered for his challenges to God to prove His existence by striking him down with lightening.

The young bohemians and aspiring radicals who clustered around Quental at Coimbra formed a campus counterculture characterized by adherence to progressive ideas from Great Britain, France, and Germany (Hegelianism, Darwinism, republicanism, and so on) and Romantic *causes célèbres* (Polish and Irish independence, Garibaldi's republican vision for Italy).[3] After graduation, the Coimbra cohort would reconvene in Lisbon, where they formed the *Cenáculo* (Cenacle), a reading circle and ongoing exercise in bohemia led by Quental at the home of his close friend Jaime Batalha Reis. The group also picked up new members, including Oliveira Martins, a polyglot and largely self-taught intellectual who had missed out on a university education because of his father's premature death and his consequent need to earn a living, and who in later years would emerge as one of Portugal's – and the Iberian Peninsula's – greatest historians.

Beyond the tales of inebriated conviviality it inspired, which Eça de Queirós dramatized so effectively in his novel *Os Maias* (1888), the *Cenáculo* was central in focusing the young members of the *Geração de 70* on a common set of influences and preoccupations – which were to a significant extent Quental's. Quental oriented the group towards his intellectual heroes, including Goethe, Jules Michelet, G.W.F. Hegel, Pierre-Joseph Proudhon, and Karl Marx. Moreover, his conviction that art and literature should be guided by a sense of social responsibility, or "bom senso" (good sense), rather than by rarified, abstracted aesthetic criteria, or "bom gosto" (good taste), became doctrine for the group. This assumed social mission would lead the members of the *Geração de 70* into a number of polemical ventures. These included the *questão coimbrã* (Coimbra question) of 1865–6, a fierce rhetorical battle on ethics and aesthetics fought in the press between Antero's circle and the aging don of Portuguese Romanticism, António Feliciano de Castilho, and the Iberianist agitation that followed Spain's revolution of 1868, in which Quental took a leading role.

In this chapter I will look to Iberianism to lend coherence to my analysis of Quental's socio-political prose as it developed over the course of his public life. In casting Quental as a committed Iberianist, I will break with the received critical tendency to limit his Iberianism to a brief phase of youthful enthusiasm sparked by Spain's 1868 revolution. Rather, I will argue for Iberianism as an enduring feature of Quental's thought, and will propose that his Iberianism evolved rather than diminished over the course of his career. Concretely, I will chart Quental's Iberianist engagement over three key periods: first, the early years of his intellectual career (1864–8), in which he wrote the poem "Ibéria" (1864) and more substantively, *Portugal Perante a Revolução de Espanha* (1868), an Iberianist pamphlet which he published in the wake of the overthrow of Spain's Queen Isabel II; second, Quental's participation in the 1871 *Conferências do Casino*, a planned series of talks in Lisbon that included his address *Causas da Decadência dos Povos Peninsulares*, in which he engaged with the idea of a common "peninsular race," made a guarded defence of the Spanish republicans, and suggested an Iberianist future for Portugal; and third, Quental's final years, in which he published the philosophical survey *As Tendências Gerais da Filosofia na Segunda Metade do Séc. XIX* (1890). Here Quental returns to certain ideas he had applied previously to the Iberianist problem – namely, the notion of racial "genius" and the primacy of the value of freedom. This conceptual continuity illustrates the enduring impact on Quental of Iberianism (or at a minimum, its underlying principles), if not his confidence that a workable Portuguese–Spanish political union could be achieved after the collapse of the First Spanish Republic in 1874.

Antero de Quental, Iberian Federalist: *Portugal Perante a Revolução de Espanha*

Spain's Revolution of 1868, which overthrew Isabel II and initiated the six-year "Sexenio Democrático" (Democratic Sexennium), brought Iberianism back to the forefront of Portuguese intellectual life nearly twenty years after the debate sparked by the publication in 1851 of Sinibaldo de Mas's *La Iberia* and José Félix Henriques Nogueira's *Estudos sobre a Reforma em Portugal.*[4] However briefly, 1868 opened up the possibility that radical political change might soon come to the Iberian Peninsula, and the young Quental was eager to seize on the opportunity. The revolution in Spain inspired Quental to write his pamphlet *Portugal Perante a Revolução de Espanha*, in which he argued that Portugal should join Spain in forming a decentralized Iberian federal republic.[5] Quental seems to have come to his federalist convictions by way of two principal sources: the French libertarian socialist and anarchist P.-J. Proudhon, author of *Du Principe fédératif* (The Principle of Federation, 1863) and a name repeatedly cited by Quental as one of his primary intellectual influences;[6] and Portuguese Iberian federalist Henriques Nogueira, author of the aforementioned *Estudos* and several articles in which he advocated the formation of an Iberian federation in which Portugal would participate.

Quental, as a reform-minded if not frankly revolutionary Portuguese intellectual of a generation known for its rebelliousness and almost instinctive rejection of the status quo, was doubtless attracted to Proudhon and Nogueira's argument that federation was the only means for weaker, smaller nations to achieve effective, as opposed to formal or nominal, independence. Proudhon and Nogueira contended that it was particularly important that second-tier or declining powers like

Portugal enter into federal arrangements with like-minded peoples, given the increasingly brutal tenor of European politics during the late nineteenth century. During this period, apologists for the established and rising European powers and for the United States cited Anglo-Saxon or Teutonic racial superiority and the ideal of civilizational progress to justify predation on the weak, whether in Europe or beyond – this logic was summarized in Lord Salisbury's infamous 1898 speech "Living and Dying Nations," which he gave while prime minister of the United Kingdom, and which received ample attention in the peninsular press.[7]

Proudhon argued that confederation with one's neighbours did not compromise national autonomy – quite the opposite. In *Du Principe fédératif* he contended that by aligning particular interests with the common good, "contracting parties, whether heads of family, towns, cantons, provinces, or states, not only undertake bilateral and commutative obligations [in the federal system], but in making the pact reserve for themselves more rights, more liberty, more authority, more property than they abandon" (39). Proudhon viewed federation, a "pact" based on "equal and reciprocal" agreement (38), as broadly applicable, though it held special benefits for states in real or perceived decline, like Portugal and Spain at the *fin de siècle*, by removing them from a deterministic, annexationist struggle in which established and emerging powers would expand at the expense of weaker rivals.

As for Nogueira, he characterized federation as follows in his *Estudos*: "Baluarte e última esperança dos povos oprimidos, que só na aliança com os seus iguais podem achar uma protecção benéfica e sincera, a forma federativa é destinada a libertar as nações fracas do predomínio das fortes" (The bulwark and final hope of oppressed peoples, who only by allying themselves with others on an equal basis can secure beneficial and true protection, federation is destined to free weak nations from domination by the strong) (1: 162). Quental summarized Nogueira's argument for Portugal to enter an Iberian federation as follows, in a laudatory article he wrote on Nogueira's *Estudos* in 1860, while a student at Coimbra: "Quizera ... que Portugal, como povo pequeno e opprimido, mas conscio e zeloso da sua dignidade, procurasse na – Federação – com os outros povos peninsulares a força, a importancia, e a verdadeira independencia que lhe faltam na sua tão escarnecida nacionalidade" (He proposed ... that the Portuguese, as a small and oppressed people, though a people conscious and zealous of their dignity, might find in Federation with the other peninsular peoples the strength, importance, and true independence now denied to this most ridiculed of nations) (*Prosas* 1: 21–2).

If we synthesize Proudhon and Nogueira's arguments, as the young Quental was likely to have done, we arrive at the conclusion that Spanish–Portuguese political union would, in theory at least, create a state too large and too powerful to conquer, and would prevent a repeat of Spain and Portugal's difficult resistance struggles against Napoleon during the first years of the nineteenth century. Simultaneously, the new state's federal structure would guarantee Portuguese autonomy by eliminating the Bourbon monarchy (and presumably the Braganças as well) and dissolving the former Spanish kingdom into its constituent parts, such as Castile, Aragon, Catalonia, Galicia, and the Basque Country. Each of these would, along with Portugal, constitute an autonomous, largely self-governing member of the federation. Portugal, in addition to representing a powerful presence in a devolved, federated peninsula, would as a component of a substantially larger and more populous state be better protected from external threats. It is in these terms that Nogueira and Quental understood that federation with Spain, despite the perhaps counterintuitive nature of the idea and the accumulated weight of centuries of anti-Castilian antipathy in Portugal, could be construed as being in the Portuguese national interest. As Nogueira wrote of his fellow Iberianists in *Estudos*: "Nós também nos prezamos de amar a terra em que nascemos, e de render culto às suas gloriosas memórias. Mas por profundo que seja em nós esse respeito, ele não chega a fazer-nos preferir a conservação de um nome falso" (We too are honoured to love the land of our birth, and to celebrate its glorious past. But as deep as this respect runs, it cannot permit us to preserve a false name). He identified the latter with a formally independent Portugal, and called on the Portuguese to pursue the "bem verdadeiro" (true good) he saw in peninsular federation (1: 165).

The distinction between effective as opposed to "false" or nominal independence featured prominently in Quental's defence of federalism in *Portugal Perante a Revolução*, which he concludes by declaring to his Portuguese readers that, "nas nossas actuais circunstâncias, o único acto possível e lógico de verdadeiro patriotismo consiste em *renegar a nacionalidade* (given our present circumstances, the only possible, logical expression of true patriotism is that we *renounce our nationality*) (128; author's emphasis). Despite the young Quental's penchant for rhetorical flair and categorical language, this declaration amounts to something more than a deliberately transgressive, anti-patriotic statement of the sort parodied by Quental's friend Eça de Queirós in his novel *Os Maias*, in which, as I discussed earlier, João da Ega scandalizes his fellow Lisbon intellectuals by declaring that "what Portugal needs is invasion by Spain." Rather, in calling on his fellow Portuguese to "renounce their nationality," Quental urges them to cast off a weak, nominally independent government in exchange for federation with their Spanish brothers and sisters.[8] If understood in federalist terms, "nationality" refers to one side of a binary that Quental, following Proudhon and Nogueira, describes between *nação* and *pátria*, with the former referring to the state apparatus and the latter referring to the ideas of "homeland" and "people."[9] Here Quental additionally draws on Romantic ideas of national spirit, in the mode of Herder's *Volksgeist* (folk soul or spirit) and Hegelian *Geist* (spirit). *Nação* and *pátria*, if understood in this way, are far from like terms, with patriotism residing in the people rather than the government, which is prone to ignore popular interests.

In his 1868 pamphlet, Quental links the people to the idea of the *pátria*, and argues that the Portuguese government has betrayed the people and *pátria*'s "mais formosas aspirações, os seus mais íntimos impulsos" (most beautiful aspirations, its deepest impulses) (127). For Nogueira and Quental, federalism offered true patriots a better way to defend the *pátria*: by casting off a debased, corrupted, and ineffective Portuguese state apparatus and entering into a natural and mutually beneficial alliance with like-minded, neighbouring Iberian peoples. Nogueira and Quental's arguments for the Portuguese to join an Iberian federation were largely pragmatic; indeed, Nogueira contended in his article "O Futuro da Península" (The Future of the Peninsula, 1853) that "a base da união federativa está na reciprocidade [de] interesses" (the basis for federal union lies in reciprocity of interests) (1: 208). At the same time, both men argued that beyond "reciprocity of interests," there were cultural, linguistic, and historical factors that favoured a specifically *Iberian* federation. Nogueira wrote: "Portugal e os outros povos peninsulares, irmãos em crenças, em costumes, em origem histórica, em grandes feitos, em grandeza e infortúnio, em interesses, em inspiração literária e artística, e quase em linguagem, não podem deixar de constituir, para o futuro, uma grande nação" (The Portuguese and the other peninsular peoples, who are brothers in their beliefs, customs, historical origin, great achievements, glory and misfortune, interests, literary and artistic inspiration, and are nearly so in their language, will in the future certainly form a great nation) (1: 162). For his part, Quental alludes to the artificiality of Portugal's historical separation from the "other Spanish peoples" in *Portugal Perante a Revolução*, asking rhetorically: "Mas Portugal, membro amputado desnecessariamente, ainda que sem violência, do grande corpo da Península Ibérica, vivendo desde então uma vida particular, estreita talvez mas sua e original, e tão apartado do movimento dos outros povos espanhóis como se fosse a fronteira, que deles o separa, um insondável oceano, que tem que ver Portugal com a revolução que acaba de trazer à superfície da sociedade espanhola, como em tumultuosa fermentação, os maiores problemas da política moderna, e com as resoluções que a filosofia e a necessidade, os princípios e os acontecimentos, impõem aos chefes em cujas mãos vão cair as rédeas agitadas dessa revolução?" (And Portugal, a limb amputated unnecessarily though without violence from the larger body of the Iberian Peninsula, which from that moment on has lived its own life, narrow perhaps though its own, original life, and which has stood at such a distance from the movement of the other Spanish peoples, as if the border which separates them were a limitless ocean, what does Portugal have to do with this revolution, which has caused the greatest problems of modern politics to bubble up to the surface of Spanish society, and what does it have to do with the decisions that philosophy and necessity, that principles and events, impose upon the leaders into whose hands the agitated reins of this revolution have fallen?) (118). For Quental:

> As duas sociedades, ainda que postas em face de problemas diferentes, acham-se hoje obrigadas a uma mesma solução, exactamente como dois doentes que, padecendo males diversos, encontrassem a salvação num mesmo e único remédio. O ideal da Espanha em revolução confunde-se com o ideal de Portugal que precisa ser revolucionado … Para Portugueses como para Espanhóis não há hoje senão um ideal político: democracia e federalismo. (118)

> The two societies, though they face different problems, are obliged to seek the same solution, just as two sick patients who suffer from different afflictions may find salvation in the same remedy. The ideal of a Spain in revolt becomes identical to that of a Portugal in need of revolution … For Portuguese and Spaniards today there is but one political ideal: democracy and federalism.

The events of 1868 gave young Portuguese Iberianists like Quental and Oliveira Martins reason to hope in the republican aspirations of the Spanish people as well as in the possibility that the Spanish monarchy might be replaced with a decentralized federal structure, thereby improving the prospects for Portugal to join a peninsular federation on equitable terms. As Quental explained: "A descentralização, quebrando nas mãos da *razão de Estado* a temível arma da unidade, restituindo à província e à iniciativa local todas as funções de que tinha sido cavilosamente despojada, ou de que cegamente abdicara … é quem só pode …, revestindo Portugal da luz serena e imaculada da república democrática, fazê-lo brilhar, gravitando, entre os astros da constelação ibérica" (Decentralization, which strips the fearful weapon of unity from the hands of *reason of state*, and restores to the provinces and to local initiative the functions that were either intentionally robbed from them, or blindly abdicated by them … is the only way that … Portugal, bathed in the serene, immaculate light of a democratic republic, will shine as one of the stars of the Iberian constellation) (124; author's emphasis).

In his 1869 article "Do Princípio Federativo e Sua Aplicação à Península Hispânica," Oliveira Martins echoed his close friend Quental (who as we have seen, himself echoed Proudhon and Henriques Nogueira) in arguing that true freedom for Portugal, and for Europe in general, could only be achieved through federation. He writes: "Existe um remédio só, a liberdade; a liberdade que é sòmente realizável pela federação" (There is but one remedy: freedom, a freedom that can only be achieved through federation) (27). Like Proudhon, Nogueira, and Quental, Martins viewed federation as particularly useful to Portugal and Spain as neighbours united by myriad linguistic, cultural, and historical ties, and which were both declining powers. Martins described federation as "para nós, como para a Espanha actual, a solução de uma crise que a ela como a nós pode demorar a evolução progressiva por muito tempo" (for us, and for today's Spain, the solution to a crisis that might slow our progressive evolution for some time), and moreover, "o único meio de salvação da nossa autonomia" (the only means to safeguard our autonomy) (28). Anticipating the traditional anti-Castilian sentiment that served as a potent argument against Iberianism in Portugal, Martins writes: "A recente revolução espanhola revelou a nação, revelou um povo diferente da horda de canibais que a monarquia bourbónica e o militarismo apresentavam à Europa" (The recent Spanish revolution has revealed the nation, it has revealed a people distinct from the horde of cannibals that the Bourbon monarchy and militarism inflicted upon Europe) (40). Freed from the stains of Bourbon centralism and militarism (and apparently, from the conquistador stereotype as well), Martins argued that the Spanish people posed no threat to the Portuguese. Given the deep ties binding the Portuguese and Spanish peoples, and the common problems faced by both, the formation of an Iberian union organized as a decentralized republic seemed a laudable and sensible goal to the young Martins, as it did to Quental.

Regardless of the explicit calls for union issued by Quental in *Portugal Perante a Revolução de Espanha*, scholars have tended to downplay the extent of his, and to a lesser extent, Martins's Iberianism. In truth, various members of the *Geração de 70* took up the Iberianist banner – a conspicuous fact given that this was the "cream" of the Portuguese intelligentsia openly engaging with ideas that were widely considered subversive, and even treasonous. While Martins is unquestionably the group's best-known Hispanophile, at various points Guerra Junqueiro, Teófilo Braga, and Manuel de Arriaga all expressed Iberianist sympathies, and developed friendships with Spanish writers. This openness to Iberianism is particularly striking in Braga and Arriaga's cases, as they would both later serve as president of the Portuguese republic, which was inaugurated in 1910. Indeed, Eça de Queirós and Ramalho Ortigão were virtually alone among the core members of the *Geração de 70* in consistently opposing stronger ties between Portugal and Spain, though they remained on generally friendly terms with their Iberianist colleagues.

Quental's Iberianist sympathies are not as well documented as those of Oliveira Martins, who dedicated a number of books and articles to the subject,[10] lived for a time in Andalusia as a young man, corresponded with Juan Valera, and addressed the Ateneo de Madrid in 1892. Nonetheless, they are significant and sustained. Four years prior to his 1868 pamphlet, Quental published the poem "Ibéria" (1864), in which he called on Spain and Portugal, in Hegelian fashion, to "como irmãos, reconhecer-se / Os amigos – há tanto tempo ausentes!" (like siblings, recognize each other / Friends – kept apart for so long!).[11] His republican and Iberianist sympathies clear, Quental accuses national leaders of "cava[ndo] oceanos" (carving out oceans) between the two nations, and declares: "Sejam-lhe ponte os corpos dos tiranos!" (Let the tyrants' bodies serve as a bridge!) (*Poesia* 76). The previous year, Quental wrote "Pepa." A Romantic-Orientalist fantasy ostensibly about an Andalusian girl, the poem can be read allegorically as describing Portugal's struggle to find in Spain its "outro peito, seu irmão" (other, twin breast) (76). After giving these inchoate Iberian-federalist feelings more comprehensive treatment in *Portugal Perante a Revolução*, Quental published his most significant statement on Iberian history and culture, *Causas da Decadência dos Povos Peninsulares*, in 1871. In this speech Quental reoriented his position towards the affirmation of a common "peninsular race" and made a more cautious defence of the Spanish republicans, who would briefly and unsuccessfully hold power in Madrid between 1873 and 1874 as the First Spanish Republic.

What Quental did not do as he matured was renounce Iberianism, as some contend. Scholars frequently cite a statement that Quental made to the German scholar Wilhelm Storck in a 14 May 1887 autobiographical letter, as evidence that his Iberianism was short-lived and was extinguished with the fall of the Spanish republic. Referring to *Portugal Perante a Revolução* in his letter to Storck, Quental writes: "Advogava aí a União Ibérica por meio da República Federal ... Era uma grande ilusão, da qual porém só desisti ... à força de golpes brutais e repetidos da experiência" (There I advocated an Iberian Union in the form of a Federal Republic ... It was a great illusion, of which I only freed myself ... after experience dealt me brutal, repeated blows) (*Obra Completa. Cartas* 2: 836). Indeed, scholars like Pilar Vázquez Cuesta and António Machado Pires have downplayed Quental's Iberianism, basing their analyses on the assumption that his Iberianism can be reduced to the goal of Iberian federation – which Quental did in fact seem to abandon by 1874. As was discussed in this book's opening chapter, however, Iberianism was an eclectic and flexible doctrine, taking in projects for Portuguese–Spanish political union, but also proposals for political, economic, and defensive alliances, as well as calls for greater cultural and intellectual exchange. These culturally Iberianist proposals did not necessitate a change in the peninsula's bipartite political structure. And certain Iberianists simply called on their peers to acknowledge the deep historical and cultural connections that bound together the peninsular peoples across borders, without necessarily advocating Spanish–Portuguese political union (though many nonetheless sympathized with this goal). As such, Quental's declaration to Storck need not be interpreted as a rejection of Iberianism *tout court*. While scholars like Cuesta and Pires would interpret the "grande ilusão" (great illusion) denounced by Quental as referring to the Iberian Union, we might also interpret Quental's self-criticism as applying exclusively to "a União Ibérica *por meio da República Federal*" (an Iberian Union *in the form of a Federal Republic*) (*Obra Completa. Cartas* 2: 836; my emphasis). According to this interpretation, the harsh lessons taught to Quental by the decline and fall of the republic in 1874 would have forced him to abandon an Iberian federal republic as a plausible political future for Portugal and Spain – though not necessarily the broader cause of Iberianism.

Not only is an exclusively political interpretation of Quental's Iberianism excessively narrow, but moreover, it prevents us from appreciating the seriousness with which peninsular intellectuals like Quental and Martins, and later, Miguel de Unamuno and Joan Maragall, viewed the project of defining, consolidating, and defending a common Iberian *pátria* above and beyond questions of governance. For instance, Cuesta characterizes Quental's Iberianism as a "pequena aventura juvenil" (brief youthful adventure) the product of a "patriotismo exigente e hipercrítico que, incapaz de aceitar a mediocridade presente, procurasse consolação na grandeza do que podia ter sido e não fora" (demanding and hypercritical patriotism that, being unable to accept the mediocrity of reality, sought consolation in the greatness of what might have been but which did not actually come to pass) ("Antero" 161, 182). For his part, Pires comments that the Iberianism of the *Geração de 70* was largely rhetorical and reactive, catering to an interest in Spain that was fashionable in Portugal around the time of *La Gloriosa*, or paradoxically, was concerned with inspiring the Portuguese to national renewal via the threat of Spanish aggression rather than with actually forming a single Iberian nation-state.[12] While Cuesta and Pires's characterizations may be appropriate for Eça, a noted anti-Iberianist who in his undated, posthumously published short story "A Catástrofe" (The Catastrophe), which he planned to expand into a novel, uses an imagined Spanish invasion as a catalyst for Portuguese national resurgence, they certainly do not apply to Quental, or to Martins.[13] Rather, in examining Quental's work we can trace a consistent preoccupation with Iberia and Iberianism that runs from his poem "Ibéria" (1864), through *Portugal Perante a Revolução de Espanha* (1868), the *Causas da Decadência dos Povos Peninsulares* (1871) and "A República e o Socialismo" (The Republic and Socialism, 1873), and up to the 1875 project undertaken by Quental and Jaime Batalha Reis to found the Iberianist publication *Revista Occidental*. Further, Iberianist traces may be found in Quental's later work, namely, his philosophical treatise *As Tendências Gerais da Filosofia na Segunda Metade do Séc. XIX* (1890) and his 25 November 1890 letter to Alberto Osório de Castro, written months before his suicide in 1891. Here Quental again speculates on the possibility of Iberian union, albeit with greater fatalism and less enthusiasm than he did in earlier years.[14]

In sum, I contend that we should think in terms of evolution rather than rejection in evaluating Quental's Iberianism. This approach aligns with statements made by Quental himself. In *O Que É a Internacional* (What the International Is, 1871), Quental, whose socialism was accompanied by a broader interest in Hegelianism and biological evolution, describes social change as achieved through gradual, "sucessivas transformações, por uma lenta preparação" (successive transformations, through slow preparation) (343). And in his 1887 autobiographical letter he characterizes his thinking during the 1870s as an "evolução de sentimento [que] correspondia a uma evolução de pensamento" (evolution in feeling [that] corresponded to an evolution in thought) (*Obra Completa, Cartas* 2: 837–8).[15] In the following section I will analyse *Causas da Decadência dos Povos Peninsulares* as an example of Quental's evolving Iberianism, and as a text that marks a transition between his early, explicit call for an Iberian federal republic, and his later affirmation of a shared Iberian history, race, and character, and interest in advancing common solutions to peninsular problems.

Causas da Decadência dos Povos Peninsulares as an Iberianist Text

Of the activities that occupied Quental's early career, the Casino Conferences stand out as the most significant in terms of their impact on Portuguese intellectual and cultural life. Quental and several associates, including Oliveira Martins, Eça de Queirós, and Teófilo Braga, organized a series of "conferências democráticas" (democratic conferences) that began in May 1871 at a casino located in the Largo da Abegoaria (now the Largo Rafael Bordalo Pinheiro) in Lisbon. The conferences' pilot program, released on 17 May 1871, reflects an overlapping of liberal concern for public dialogue with the conviction that Europe, rocked by that year's Paris Commune, faced the prospect of imminent, transformative crisis, and that revolution was in Portugal and the continent's immediate future. Since the organizers saw revolution as inevitable, they argued that the public should "estudar serenamente a significação dessas ideias [revolucionárias] e a legitimidade desses interesses; investigar como a sociedade é, e como ela deve ser; como as nações têm sido, e como as pode fazer hoje a liberdade; e, por serem elas as formadoras do homem, estudar todas as ideias e todas as correntes do século" (calmly study the meaning of these [revolutionary] ideas, and the legitimacy of these interests; calmly investigate how society is, and how it should be; how nations have been, and what liberty would mean for them today; and study all of this century's ideas and currents, as it is these that mould men) (quoted in Carreiro 1: 404). Or as Eça and Ramalho wrote in a May 1871 *farpa* on the Casino Conferences: "O Sr. Antero de Quental abriu no dia 19 as conferências democráticas no Casino … É a primeira vez que a revolução, sob a sua forma científica, tem em Portugal a palavra" (Mr. Antero de Quental opened the day of conferences on the 19th … This is the first time that revolution, in a scientific sense, has been given the floor in Portugal) (Ortigão and Queiroz 66). No doubt reacting to a pilot-program that featured "revolution" writ large, and that called for its attendees to help discover "como deve regenerar-se a organização social" (how the organization of society should be regenerated), and suspecting subversive and anticlerical intent, an alarmist government led by the Marquês de Ávila, president of D. Luís I's Council of Ministers, closed the conferences on 26 June after five sessions – the second of which featured Quental's speech on the *Causas da Decadência dos Povos Peninsulares,* which he delivered at the casino during the evening of 27 May 1871, and subsequently published.

In *Causas da Decadência,* Quental sets out to diagnose and propose remedies for the causes of Portugal's historical decline. In taking up the theme of *decadência,*[16] a term that suggests both "decadence" and "decline" in English, Quental joined a long tradition in Iberian letters of speculating on why Portugal and Spain's short-lived glory during the fifteenth and sixteenth centuries gave way to a protracted descent into political, economic, and cultural marginality, a process that was reaching its nadir by the late nineteenth century.[17] In addition, the text sees Quental fusing Romantic-era ideas of the nation as an organic social body, characterized by a common will, "genius," or nature, with more recent evolutionist and positivistic ideas that cast society as a collective organism operating according to supposedly scientific laws, and with notions of individual and collective "decline" and "degeneration," popularized by texts like Max Nordau's *Degeneration* (1892). If, as Quental believed, the social body was defined by gradual transformation, then Portugal and Spain's transition from expansion to decline might be traced back to historical causes. Here – though not in terms of their broader world views – Quental dovetails with the Spanish historian and conservative politician Antonio Cánovas del Castillo, who as a young man published a *Historia de la decadencia de España* (History of the Decline of Spain, 1854). Further, Quental anticipates the position articulated by Oliveira Martins in his *História da Civilização Ibérica*

(1879) – though Quental is less deterministic than Martins with regard to the prospects for correcting the peninsula's wayward evolution.[18] For Quental, peninsular decline resulted from the perversion of those qualities that gave rise to Iberian glory: genuine religious faith, local political liberties, and the drive to explore. Their debased versions – doctrinaire Catholicism, absolute monarchy, and a violent, ultimately unproductive overseas colonization – might be corrected, though only through an act of collective contrition and concerted, peninsula-wide effort.[19]

Quental's view that a people can intervene in its own history, even if this history is part of a broader Hegelian progression or pseudo-biological evolution, or more locally, if it is marked by a given racial or civilizational "genius," is made clear if we briefly return to *O Que É a Internacional*. Here Quental writes: "A sociedade é um organismo, e os organismos transformam-se, não se revolucionam. É pois necessário preparar essa transformação" (Society is an organism, and organisms transform themselves, rather than change through revolution. It is therefore necessary to lay the groundwork for this transformation) (347). For Quental as a socialist, economic relationships were determined by the conflict between capital and labour, which could only be overcome in the proletariat's final victory over the capitalist order. Likewise, Quental believed as an Iberianist that peninsular history was the partial (though not exclusive) product of an overarching peninsular character, which manifested itself in religious practice, governmental organization, and overseas expansion efforts. However, for Quental the historical determinism imposed by the "objective" facts of Hegelian-Marxian historical progress and Spencerian social Darwinism did not preclude judicious human intervention in the interest of effecting change. By contrast, for Oliveira Martins the road back to prosperity for the Iberian Peninsula was more complicated, as the causes of its past glory were also the causes of its present decline, merely evolved by some three centuries.[20] However, both men accepted historical diagnosis, public engagement, and the proposal of remedies as their operating method, with the Casino Conferences, charged with "investig[ando] como a sociedade é, e como ela deve ser" (investigat[ing] how society is, and how it should be), projected as a model for this sort of operation.

One curious problem raised by Quental's speech concerns the question of the social body he discusses – whether Quental understood it to be synonymous with Portugal, or if it comprehended the whole of the Iberian Peninsula and was therefore inclusive of Spain. The conferences' pilot program speaks in vague terms of "lig[ando] Portugal com o movimento moderno, fazendo-o assim nutrir-se dos elementos vitais de que vive a humanidade civilizada" (connect[ing] Portugal to the modern movement, allowing it in this way to be nourished by the vital elements upon which civilized humanity depends) (quoted in Carreiro 1: 404). However, Quental presents his argument as concerned with the decline of the "povos peninsulares" (peninsular peoples) in the plural, and his speech refers repeatedly to a common peninsular "raça" (race), "génio" (genius), and "pátria" (homeland). These references to peninsular unity and diversity underscore comments Quental made three years previously, in *Portugal Perante a Revolução de Espanha*, first, concerning Portugal as a "membro amputado desnecessariamente" (limb amputated unnecessarily) from the broader peninsular body, and second, regarding the common challenges facing Portugal and Spain, which he confidently declared could be resolved through a shared commitment to an Iberian republic.

Given Quental and his fellow organizers' concern with bringing about renewal in Portugal specifically, albeit with a certain degree of projection outward towards Spain and Europe, I would argue that two discursive registers can be detected in *Causas da Decadência*: a Portuguese national register and an Iberian register. Their simultaneous presence in Quental's speech reflects the changes Quental's Iberianist thinking underwent between 1868 and May 1871, no doubt in response to events in Spain. During this period, the Spanish provisional government's leadership coalition failed to secure a commitment from Fernando II, father of the future Portuguese King Luís I, to serve as king of Spain – a scheme that would in all likelihood have eventually united Spain and Portugal, though not as a republic, as Quental desired. The government then offered the crown to Amedeo, Duke of Savoy, who ruled as Spain's constitutional monarch between 1871 and 1873. Nonetheless, conditions in Spain remained agitated, and significant traditionalist and republican minorities opposed Amadeo I's rule. In his 1868 pamphlet, released during the heady first year of Spain's *Sexenio Democrático*, Quental had explicitly called for a peninsular federation, seemingly confident that left-leaning republicans would quickly rise to power in Spain, and perhaps inspire a similar revolt in Portugal. By May 1871 it would have been clear to Quental that these events, which would have created favourable conditions for an Iberian federal republic, were not in the immediate future – hence the relative moderation of his position in *Causas da Decadência*. As his correspondence from the

Sexenio Democrático period reveals, Quental was frustrated by the inability of the Spanish republicans to exert leadership and establish a stable government. Writing to Batalha Reis in July 1873, Quental declares his continued faith "no futuro republicano de França e de Espanha" (in the republican future of France and Spain). However, clearly frustrated by the weakness of the republic, he theorizes in a letter to Martins, written the same month, that Spain is not a united nation in the Portuguese sense, but a juxtaposition of peoples that, until recently, had been held together by monarchical tyranny: "Concluo, pois, para Espanha, para uma federação, semi-histórica, semi-revolucionária," but only "depois dum período de total desorganização" (I believe, in conclusion, that Spain will adopt a semi-historical, semi-revolutionary federal structure ... after a period of total disorganization) (*Obras Completas. Cartas* 1: 198, 208). While Quental remained committed to the Iberianist project, events across the border compelled him to change the focus of his Iberianism and to couch the argument he presented to his Lisbon audience in May 1871 in vaguer, more cultural or historical terms, thereby leaving interpretive room for Portugal to follow its own path should the situation in revolutionary Spain evolve in a direction unfavourable to his republican and Iberianist aspirations.

In the first pages of *Causas da Decadência* Quental presents us with a revealing case of ambiguous terminology, in referring to his Lisbon audience – which was predominantly if not entirely Portuguese – as *peninsulares* (peninsulars) and even *nós Espanhóis* (we Spaniards) (7–8, 12).[21] What does it mean for Quental to give the Portuguese the name of "Spaniards," who are frequently presented in the Portuguese historiographical tradition and national imagination as Portugal's rivals?[22] I suspect that despite his use of categorical, perhaps intentionally jarring language, Quental is actually describing the Portuguese as Iberians, and is thereby enlarging the idea of "nós" to include all of the "povos peninsulares." In doing so, Quental gestures towards, and attempts to recover, an understanding of the categories of "Spain" and "Spaniard" that prevailed in Portugal prior to the 1580–1640 period, during which the Spanish Habsburgs sat on the Portuguese throne. In this older sense, "Spain" referred to the whole of the Iberian Peninsula, irrespective of political boundaries, and to all Iberians, including the Portuguese, who according to this definition, could legitimately refer to themselves geographically and culturally as "Spaniards," though they did not live within the boundaries of the Spanish kingdom. In the centuries that followed the Iberian dynastic union, Portuguese intellectuals would selectively invoke this older, more inclusive definition of "Spain" to underscore Portugal's cultural and historical ties to the Spanish kingdom, or to advance Iberianist projects.[23]

In *Causas da Decadência dos Povos Peninsulares*, Quental attempts to accomplish both of these goals. More precisely, he describes an overarching peninsular history, culture, and "genius" in order to argue that Portugal and Spain must work in concert to correct shared historical mistakes and meet the demands of the future. Quental argues that the Portuguese, Castilians, Aragonese, Basques, Catalans, and Galicians are united as members of a common "raça peninsular" (peninsular race), and are possessed of an essential "génio" (genius), "espírito" (spirit), and "instinto" (instinct) that distinguish them from the rest of Europe. Invoking the Roman designation *Hispania*, which referred to the whole of the peninsula under imperial control, and which evolved into the modern *España* (in Portuguese, *Espanha*), Quental comments:

> Logo na época romana aparecem os caracteres essenciais da raça peninsular: espírito de independência local, e originalidade do génio inventivo … Na Idade Média, a Península, livre de estranhas influências, brilha na plenitude do seu génio, das suas qualidades naturais. O instinto político de descentralização e federalismo patenteia-se na multiplicidade de reinos e condados soberanos em que se divide a Península, como um protesto e uma vitória dos interesses e energias locais, contra a unidade uniforme, esmagadora e artificial. (10–11)

> As early as the Roman period the essential characteristics of the peninsular race made themselves known: a spirit of local independence, and an original, inventive genius … In the Middle Ages, the Peninsula, now free of foreign influences, shone in the fullness of its genius, of its natural qualities. Its political instincts in favour of decentralization and federalism manifested themselves in the many sovereign kingdoms and smaller domains into which the Peninsula was divided. This amounted to a victorious assertion of local interests and energies over a uniform, crushing, artificial unity.

Here Quental ignores the internecine violence that plagued the Iberian Peninsula during the Middle Ages in order to describe medieval Iberia, rather imaginatively, as an ideal federation, divided into several autonomous regions tasked with defending local liberties, but united by a shared Iberian character and loyalty to a common, overarching *pátria*.[24]

Quental comments that during this period, "fora da *Pátria*," here meaning beyond the Pyrenees, "guerreiros ilustres mostravam ao mundo que o valor dos povos peninsulares não era inferior à sua inteligência" (illustrious warriors showed the world that the valour of the peninsular peoples was equal to their intelligence) (19; my emphasis). For Quental, the trouble began when municipalities were subordinated to centralizing monarchies, one based in Lisbon and the other (eventually) in Madrid. The paradoxical result was that under these two monarchies, Iberians came to be divided into two opposing camps, one Portuguese and the other "Spanish," and both were subordinated to stifling central authority and the imperial ambitions of their respective political elites. Quental likens the proto-federalist, medieval Iberia he idealizes in this passage to the situation in 1871 by way of a proposal that Iberia recommit itself to federalism – now qualified as democratic and rooted in republican and socialist principles. Stepping back a bit from his argument in *Portugal Perante a Revolução de Espanha*, Quental does not explicitly advocate a federated Iberian republic in *Causas da Decadência*. Rather, he calls for a "federação republicana de todos os grupos autonómicos, de todas as vontades soberanas" (republican federation of all autonomous groups, of all sovereign wills) (76) – a statement that leaves ample room for Spanish–Portuguese political rapprochement, or even union, if Francesc Pi i Margall, Emilio Castelar, and other Iberian-minded Spanish republicans succeeded in taking the reins of government in Spain, and managed to successfully transform the country into a republic.

In qualifying the Iberianism that Quental defended in 1871, we should note that in *Causas da Decadência* he does not make exclusive reference to the Iberian register. He frequently refers to Portugal and Spain as separate entities, though the instances in which the ideas of "Portugal" and "Spain" are opposed are relatively few. In many cases, even when Quental mentions Portugal and Spain separately, he retains the idea of an overarching Iberian *pátria*, and describes the two as subject to common historical conditions, or plots for them a shared course of action. This strategy provides for the greatest possible conceptual unity for "Iberia" while acknowledging the historical reality of Spain and Portugal's separation into distinct, sometimes rival polities. Discussing peninsular decline generally, Quental poetically observes: "Portugueses e Espanhóis vamos de século para século minguando em extensão e importância, até não sermos mais que duas sombras, duas nações espectros, no meio dos povos que nos rodeiam!" (We Portuguese and Spaniards have diminished century by century in size and importance, so that now we are nothing but two spectral nations amidst the peoples who surround us!) (21). And speaking of the colonial and religious manifestations of peninsular decline, Quental poses the following questions: "E a nós, espanhóis e portugueses, como foi que o catolicismo nos anulou?" (And we Spaniards and Portuguese, how was it that Catholicism destroyed us?), and "nós, Portugueses e Espanhóis, que destinos demos às prodigiosas riquezas extorquidas aos povos estrangeiros?" (we Portuguese and Spaniards, to what end did we steal prodigious wealth from foreign peoples?). Finally, Quental calls for a concerted effort to combat decline, proclaiming: "Erguemo-nos hoje a custo, espanhóis e portugueses, desse túmulo onde os nossos grandes erros nos tiveram sepultados: erguemo-nos, mas os restos da mortalha ainda nos embaraçam os passos, e pela palidez dos nossos rostos pode bem ver o mundo de que regiões lúgubres e mortais chegamos ressuscitados!" (Today, we Spaniards and Portuguese must raise ourselves up, albeit with much effort, from this tomb in which our grave errors have buried us. Let us raise ourselves up, though we will stumble upon the scraps of our mortuary shroud, and the paleness of our faces will show from what dark and deathly realms we have escaped!) (28–9, 48, 61).[25] While in this rather gothic image the resurrected Spanish and Portuguese have separate "rostos" (faces), they share a "mortalha" (mortuary shroud), in the manner of conjoined twins.

Despite the conceptual unity that often accompanies his references to Portugal and Spain, Quental provides occasional evidence of a critical stance towards Portugal's peninsular neighbours. These criticisms are relatively infrequent, and, moreover, are tempered by Quental's support for the Spanish republicans. However, in the interest of full disclosure, Quental situates the moment at which the peninsula passed from expansion to decline during the first years of the "Spanish captivity," that is, the sixty-year period of Iberian dynastic union (1580–1640) set in motion by the young Portuguese king Dom Sebastião's disastrous 1578 military defeat and death, without an heir, at Alcácer Quibir in Morocco. Quental explains: "No princípio do século XVII, quando Portugal deixa de ser contado entre as nações, e se desmorona por todos os lados a monarquia anómala inconsistente e desnatural de Filipe II; quando a glória passada já não pode encobrir o ruinoso do edifício presente, e se afunda a Península sob o peso dos muitos erros acumulados, então aparece franca e patente por todos os lados a nossa improcrastinável decadência" (At the beginning of the seventeenth century, when Portugal was struck from the list of nations, and the anomalous, inconsistent, and unnatural monarchy of Philip II was crumbling on all sides, when past glory could no longer conceal our ruinous present state, and when the Peninsula was drowning under the weight of its accumulated errors, it was then that our undeniable decadence manifested itself fully and on all sides) (20).[26] It is also worth citing Quental's lamentation of Dom Sebastião's death, and specifically his reference to the *pátria*, which he understands here as exclusively Portuguese: "Se D. Sebastião não fosse absoluto, não teria ido enterrar em Alcácer Quibir a nação portuguesa, as últimas esperanças da pátria" (If D. Sebastião had not been [an] absolute [monarch], he would not have buried the Portuguese nation, the last hopes of the homeland, at Alcácer Quibir) (57).

Curiously, the tendency to situate the point at which Portugal began its long historical decline during the 1580–1640 dynastic union was popular in both the Portuguese Iberianist and anti-Iberianist camps. While the Iberianists sought to differentiate their projects for peaceful, equitable Iberian union from the lingering memory of alleged Castilian dominion and abuse under the Habsburgs,[27] anti-Iberianists marshalled these same memories as evidence of Spain's perennial ill will and desire to conquer Portugal. However, where an anti-Iberianist might have argued that the period of so-called occupation proved the Spaniards to be fundamentally untrustworthy, annexationist, and anti-Portuguese, Quental focuses his critique on the rulers, bemoaning Dom Sebastião's quixotic military campaign and the Spanish monarch's alleged inconsistency. Recall that for Quental, as the product of Romanticism and a socialist, the actions of rulers, so prone to forsake the popular interest, do not necessarily reflect the people's attitudes. Just as the Portuguese should not be held responsible for the misrule of their monarchs, nor should the Spanish be culpable for the crimes committed by their governing elite, whether concerning the "Spanish captivity" of Portugal or the "bestiality" of the conquistadors' activities in America (71).

In sum, Quental maintains the principal features of his 1868 argument in *Causas da Decadência* – he contrasts past glories to a troubled late nineteenth-century state of decline, he denounces political and religious elites, and he proposes a corrective course of action. However, in his 1871 address Quental does not explicitly advocate political union with revolutionary Spain, as he had earlier, but instead couches his argument in broad references to commonality of race, the demands of modernity, and a shared aspiration towards regeneration. Towards the end of his address, Quental states: "Somos uma raça decaída por ter rejeitado o espírito moderno: regenerar-nos-emos abraçando francamente esse espírito. O seu nome é Revolução" (We are a race that has decayed because we rejected the modern spirit: we will regenerate ourselves by openly embracing this spirit. Its name is Revolution) (77). Did this "modern spirit" as Quental understood it in 1871 imply the reorganization of the peninsula as a decentralized federal republic, possibly as a precursor to a wider European union, as it did in 1868? Did Quental's understanding of revolution, which he presented in *Causas da Decadência* as capable of reconciling the values of order and liberty, point towards Iberian federation, or do his continual references to a shared Iberian heritage imply another sort of relationship? I would argue that Quental's failure to answer these questions is reflective of his own evolving Iberianism during the early 1870s, as well as the unpredictable political climate of late nineteenth-century Portugal and especially Spain. Quental's retreat from his bold call in 1868 for political union to a more limited and nuanced defence in 1871 of the embattled Spanish republicans, coupled with more detailed analysis of Portugal and Spain's shared Iberian identity and history, most likely took these factors into account. Regardless, it is a mistake to interpret Quental's evolving position on Spanish–Portuguese relations between 1868 and 1871 as tantamount to a rejection of Iberianism. Indeed, doing so impoverishes Iberianism by reducing this eclectic body of thought to its most apparently radical and specifically political expressions.

The Afterlife of Iberianism in Antero de Quental

The first proof that Quental did not abandon his Iberianist convictions after the fall of the republic in 1874 lies in his involvement the following year with the *Revista Occidental*. This short-lived journal, which Quental was to co-edit with his close friend Jaime Batalha Reis, was envisioned as a forum for Portuguese- and Spanish-speaking intellectuals, both peninsular and Latin American. Further, it featured prominent Spanish republicans Francesc Pi i Margall and Ángel Fernández de los Ríos among its listed collaborators, and was premised on the typically Iberianist notion that Portugal and Spain (along with their former American colonies) were connected at the levels of race, history, and culture despite their political separation.[28] As the "Programa da 'Revista Occidental'" (Program for the "Revista Occidental") reads: "Se os hespanhoes e os portuguezes formam de ha muito duas nações distinctas, tiveram todavia sempre na organisação philosophica e sentimental de seus espiritos, na physionomia das suas litteraturas, no caracter dos seus actos, a afinidade que lhes deu a origem commum de raças e a acção, tambem egual para ambos os povos, do clima da peninsula hispanica" (While the Spanish and Portuguese have long formed two distinct nations, they have nonetheless, in the philosophical and sentimental organization of their spirits, the physiognomy of their literatures, and the character of their acts, shown an affinity derived from their common racial and historical origins, as well as the climate of the Hispanic Peninsula) (quoted in Quental, *Prosas* 2: 273–4).

Second, Quental again speculated on Iberianism in the wake of Great Britain's 1890 "Ultimatum" to Portugal, an event that, "dues dècades després de l'eclosió de l'iberisme durant el Sexenni Democràtic" (two decades after the first appearance of Iberianism during the *Sexenio Democrático*), caused Iberianism to experience "una breu però intensa revifalla" (a brief but intense revival) in Portugal (Martínez-Gil, *El naixement* 40). Quental's epistolary comments demonstrate that in a broad sense, Iberianism remained on his intellectual agenda long after the fall of the Spanish republic, and indeed, into his final years. As Batalha Reis revealed in a 2 March 1906 letter to Sampaio Bruno, despite his and Quental's opposition in 1875 to union between Portugal and Spain, "Ambos nos entendíamos haver muitos elementos essenciais comuns à História e criação das duas nações peninsulares" (Both of us understood that there were many essential elements that were common to the History and formation of the two peninsular nations) (quoted in Marinho 3). This appears to contradict the prevailing critical interpretation of Quental's 1887 epistolary declaration to Wilhelm Storck that Iberianism had been a "grande ilusão" (great illusion) apparently limited to his idealistic youth. While Quental may have stepped back from the explicitly political brand of Iberianism he forcefully advocated in 1868 – and this seems the substance of his comment to Storck – his argument in *Causas da Decadência* and subsequent intellectual engagements demonstrate that he remained sympathetic to Iberianism in principle, or at minimum was prompted by the Ultimatum to reconsider it, as were many other Portuguese intellectuals, including Oliveira Martins.

Finally, Quental returned to certain key concepts articulated in his earlier, explicitly Iberianist writings in his final major intellectual statement, 1890's *As Tendências Gerais da Filosofia na Segunda Metade do Séc. XIX*, published one year before his death. If Quental's rhetorical objectives had changed between his earlier, specifically Iberianist writings and *As Tendências Gerais*, from political exhortation and historical analysis to the presentation of a philosophical survey, certain ideas that underpinned his earlier writings can nonetheless be seen in his last major prose work. Granted, it would be an exaggeration to argue that Quental's discussion in his long 1890 essay of notions of racial "genius" and the value of individual freedom – ideas that had earlier appeared in *Portugal Perante a Revolução* and *Causas da Decadência* – demonstrates Quental's continued Iberianist commitment. However, I nonetheless consider it significant, in rounding out the case for Quental's evolving Iberianism, that certain guiding premises of his earlier Iberianist writings (namely, the ideas that peoples possess a unique collective personality and that freedom should be valued and cultivated) reappear in this late text.

Though not a central feature of his argument in *As Tendências Gerais*, Quental discusses the importance of racial "genius," along with the spirit of the age (in German, *Volksgeist* and *Zeitgeist*), in shaping philosophical systems. He explains: "O espírito da época penetra-os a todos [os sistemas filosóficos]: o génio da raça e da civilização, que os viu nascer, imprimiu em todos igualmente o seu cunho indelével" (The spirit of the age penetrates all [philosophical systems]: the racial or civilizational genius, which saw them born, indelibly mark[s] all of them) (44). While for Quental the truths enunciated by distinct thinkers or philosophical schools may be universal in application, they are nonetheless conditioned by the cultural and historical context in which they are developed and articulated.[29] Nonetheless, Quental relativizes the importance of *Volksgeist* and *Zeitgeist*, arguing in a broadly Hegelian fashion that over time, philosophical ideas and systems tend towards convergence, exchange, and mutual influence. Similarly, Quental had affirmed the existence of a peninsular "raça" (race) or "espírito" (spirit) in *Causas da Decadência dos Povos Peninsulares* as a force that conditioned the historical behaviour of the peninsular peoples, though as we saw, he did not subscribe to racial determinism to nearly the same degree as did Oliveira Martins, or Teófilo Braga, for that matter. Indeed, near the conclusion of his 1871 speech Quental exhorts his audience towards "um esforço viril, um esforço supremo: quebrar resolutamente com o passado" (a virile effort, a supreme effort, to resolutely break with the past) (75), as if to say that ultimately, individual or collective will to action may trump ingrained racial or civilizational tendencies. Whereas in *As Tendências Gerais*, Quental looks to the forward movement of history to temper the influence of racial "genius," in *Causas da Decadência* he cites the possibility that individual and collective choice can accomplish the same.[30]

Indeed, the valorization of individual freedom constitutes an important thematic holdover from Quental's earlier Iberianist writings, and was one of the major themes of his intellectual life. While a student at Coimbra, Quental published a series of three articles on "A Indiferença em Política" (Indifference in Politics, 1862), in which he characterized freedom as "o meio principal, o essencial para que chegue um povo ao termo do seu destino" (the principal, essential means by which a people fulfils its destiny) and "a primeira condição para que alcancem as sociedades o fim para que as destina a Providencia" (the first condition that must be met for a society to achieve the end to which it has been destined by Providence) (*Prosas* 1: 150, 152). Five years later, in *Portugal Perante a Revolução de Espanha*, Quental characterized the 1868 Spanish revolution as motivated by a collective desire for freedom, asking in the first section of his pamphlet, "O que vai a Espanha fazer da sua liberdade?!" (What will Spain do with her freedom?!) (105). Further, he argued that in order for the Spanish people to maintain their freedom, they needed to adopt a democratic, republican government. And in *Causas da Decadência dos Povos Peninsulares*, Quental argued that the peninsular peoples, in adhering to a doctrinaire form of Catholicism, had missed out on one of modernity's greatest conquests, namely, "liberdade moral" (moral freedom). Quental explains the incompatibility of "moral freedom" with Catholic orthodoxy as follows: "Ora, a *liberdade moral*, apelando para o exame e a consciência individual, é rigorosamente o oposto do catolicismo do Concílio de Trento, para quem a razão humana e o pensamento livre são um crime contra Deus" (Now then, *moral freedom*, which compels the individual to examine his conscience, is in point of fact the opposite of the Catholicism of the Council of Trent, for which human reason and free thought were crimes against God) (31; author's emphasis). In sum, in his earlier writings Quental presents political and moral freedom as preconditions for progressive reforms, such as the formation of an Iberian democratic republic in *Portugal Perante a Revolução*, or the more nebulous, modernizing "federação republicana de todos os grupos autonómicos, de todas as vontades soberanas" (republican federation of all autonomous groups, of all sovereign wills) that he advocates in *Causas da Decadência* (76).

In *As Tendências Gerais da Filosofia na Segunda Metade do Séc. XIX*, Quental generalizes the principle of freedom that he had described in piecemeal fashion earlier in his career, such that the political and moral reforms he advocated in his Iberianist writings become particular manifestations of a broader principle – namely, that freedom is the driver of human consciousness, history, and indeed the universe itself. Quental explains: "É uma razão imanente que preside a esse universal movimento, que se exprime nele, que nele palpita. Uma ideia instintiva lateja surdamente, como uma pulsação de vida, nesse universo que a ciência mede e pesa, mas não explica: é a aspiração profunda de liberdade" (There is an immanent cause presiding over this universal movement, which expresses itself in it and pulses through it. An instinctive idea throbs silently, like the pulse of life itself, in this universe that science measures and weighs, but does not explain: this is the deep desire for freedom) (89). This in turn leads to "a espiritualização gradual e sistemática do universo" (the gradual and systematic spiritualization of the universe), such that "a história é especialmente o teatro da liberdade" (history is in particular the theatre of freedom) (90–1).

In a 1904 article, Miguel de Unamuno described Antero de Quental as "un poeta filósofo, cuyos cantos resuenan lúgubres en la dulce lengua portuguesa" (a philosopher-poet, whose songs resound with sadness in the sweet Portuguese language) and a writer "cuya fama fué tablado de la tragedia humana" (whose fame was marked by human tragedy) ("¡Plenitud de plenitudes y todo plenitud!" [1904]; *OC* 1: 1181). Unamuno, who was a great reader of Quental, of the *Geração de 70*, and of Portuguese literature generally, characterized Quental, along with Oliveira Martins, as one of the keys to understanding "el sentido del pesimismo ibérico" (the meaning of Iberian pessimism) ("Sobre la Tumba de Costa [a la más clara memoria de un espíritu sincero]" [1911]; *OC* 3: 946). Nearly fifty years later, in a 26 August 1951 diary entry, another Iberianist writer, Miguel Torga, would offer what I consider a more exact description of Quental, describing him as falling within "a recta linha ibérica da angústia" (the straight line of Iberian anguish) (6: 45). Unamuno, who shared Quental's preoccupations with Iberianism and with human anguish, might also be placed within this tradition of "Iberian anguish." We will address the case of Unamuno's Iberianism in chapter 4 after taking a brief detour to the Portuguese–Galician border at the *fin de siècle*, to examine how prominent Portuguese and Spanish writers, including Oliveira Martins, Emilia Pardo Bazán, and Unamuno, used the border to explore the complexities of Portuguese–Galician relations, which have been marked simultaneously by political separation and by deep linguistic, cultural, and historical affinities.

Chapter Three

"A Ribbon of Silver": Representations of the Portuguese–Galician Border at the *Fin de Siècle*

nessa água, que não pára, de longas beiras: e, eu, rio abaixo, rio a fora, rio a dentro – o rio.

this water, which doesn't stop running, along long banks: and I, river below me, river outside me, river within me – the river.

João Guimarães Rosa, "A Terceira Margem do Rio"
(The Third Bank of the River, 1962)

Borders and border regions are paradoxical spaces, particularly when considered from the perspective of the nation state. Political borders embody a series of contradictions: they are lines of separation and spaces of encounter. They are sites at which the nation state's authority is affirmed, but also challenged. And while borders often rely on "natural" topographical features, they are man-made, and as such, at least minimally artificial.[1] Given these contradictions, commentators have looked to borders and border regions to challenge the nation state and its claims to coherence. The geographer Gabriel Popescu argues that the incongruence between territorial borders and group identities reveals that the nation state is a "theoretical impossibility" (13). And critical theorists such as Homi Bhabha and Walter Mignolo have looked to borders as sites at which power attempts to impose ultimately false binaries – such as the notion that nation states like Portugal and Spain are self-evident and mutually exclusive – onto spaces that are "irredeemably plural" (Bhabha 149). And Mignolo, seizing on the image of the border, has coined the term "border thinking" as a disruptive critical practice.

The paradoxical quality of borders and border regions is underscored when rivers serve as borders. This is the case of the Miño River (in Portuguese, *Minho*), which marks the Portuguese–Spanish (or Portuguese–Galician) frontier – one of the oldest stable state borders in Europe – for approximately seventy-five kilometres before emptying into the Atlantic. As Enric Bou notes, rivers often function as "symbol[s] of renovation, a statement against fixation and stillness, contrary to what is identical and cannot be modified" (6). Though rivers "set landmarks and borders … their significance is transferable" (7). Rivers suggest transit, motion, and resistance to political, cultural, and personal strictures. As such they demonstrate to Bou an approach to peninsular or Iberian literary studies that is "more akin to issues of center and periphery, otherness and non hierarchical assumptions" – that is, a "non-centripetal" alternative to traditional Hispanism (4). These connotations of rivers are evocatively expressed in Brazilian writer João Guimarães Rosa's story "A Terceira Margem do Rio" (The Third Bank of the River, 1962), in which a father abandons his family to paddle along a river in search of an ineffable other space, a liminal territory or "third bank" located neither here nor there, somewhere beyond the sensible world – a sort of Couto Mixto of the mind.[2]

The fluidity and mobility suggested by rivers contrasts with the fixity nation states attempt to impose through cartographic mechanisms such as borders. As Joan Ramon Resina observes, "nationalism tends to be seen geographically, even cartographically" ("Scale" 61). This cartographic nationalism "map[s] states onto previously existing nations." In other words, by attempting to "reduc[e] historical complexity," states impose allegedly "national" borders which may disrupt the familial, economic, and cultural ties that bind communities now separated by boundary lines, generally drawn in far-off capital cities.[3] Rivers, in contrast, suggest the circularity, continuity, and sense of interpersonal and natural connection associated with traditional village life. This is the case in Galician writer Manuel Curros Enríquez's poem "A emigración" (Emigration), included in the volume *Aires d'a miña terra* (Airs from My Land, 1880), which describes the Miño emptying into the Atlantic as a fulfilment of a desire, which the river shares with Galician emigrants, to return in death to the place of its birth: "Dicen que como o Miño, o noso pobo / na terra donde nace quer morrer" (They say that like the Miño, our people / wish to die in the land where they were born) (*Obra poética* 234).

What, then, do we do with the Portuguese–Galician frontier, with its contradictory symbolic values as political *border*, suggestive of the rigid division of *além* and *aquém Minho,* and *river,* which suggests underlying continuities and connections between the land and inhabitants of the Miño's northern and southern banks? How did late nineteenth- and early twentieth-century peninsular writers understand this river-as-border, the Miño, which in the words of Pilar Vázquez Cuesta, "ó mesmo tempo, nos separa e nos une" (at the same time, separates and unites us)? ("Portugal-Galicia" 5). What do representations of the Miño tell us about the state of Portuguese–Galician relations and the imagined configuration of Iberia at the *fin de siècle*?

Daily life on the Portuguese–Galician border found ample literary expression in Galicia during the late nineteenth century, a period that witnessed the *Rexurdimento,* a movement of Galician linguistic, literary, and cultural "rebirth" led by writers like Rosalía de Castro, Manuel Murguía, and Manuel Curros Enríquez. This period also largely coincided with the literary career of Emilia Pardo Bazán, a Galician-born, Spanish-language novelist who figures with Benito Pérez Galdós and Clarín among the giants of realism-naturalism in Spain, and as the author of *La cuestión palpitante* (The Burning Question, 1883–4), which addresses Émile Zola, is arguably its most important early theoretician. Of particular interest to peninsular writers, in terms of the Portuguese–Galician border, was a tradition of illicit but more or less routine cross-border smuggling, and the migration of labourers from Galicia to Portugal. Pardo Bazán's novel *Los pazos de Ulloa* (The House of Ulloa, 1886) – published, incidentally, in the inaugural year of the first international bridge over the Miño[4] – touches on conspiracies hatched by Galician *caciques* (local political bosses) just over the border in Portugal, and describes a Galician border village whose women cuckold their absent husbands while they are off working in Portugal. And in her short fiction, Pardo Bazán refers to the Miño as the "natural frontera" (natural border) between Galicia and Portugal, and describes Galician runaways who slip across the border to Portugal before striking out for the New World (*OC* 3: 219).[5] And Curros Enríquez refers to a smuggler in his poem "As cartas" (The Cards), also from *Aires d'a miña terra*: "Polos gardas fronteiros atrapado, / vindo de Portugal, / entróu, sobre unha besta esmiolado, / o traficante en sal" (Caught by the border guards, / on his way from Portugal, / the salt smuggler, / entered on a ragged horse) (*Obra poética* 196). Decades later, fellow Galician writer Camilo José Cela would insert Portugal and smuggling into his novel *La familia de Pascual Duarte* (The Family of Pascual Duarte, 1942); the father of the eponymous narrator-protagonist is described as Portuguese, and a former smuggler.

In this chapter I will look beyond these quotidian descriptions, and consider representations of the Miño and the Portuguese–Galician border that are invested with a greater degree of symbolism and which bear on Iberianism and on intra-Iberian relations. Specifically, I will draw on reflections by Portuguese historian Joaquim Pedro de Oliveira Martins, along with the aforementioned Emilia Pardo Bazán, and Miguel de Unamuno. Their comments highlight cross-border cultural, geographic, and linguistic continuities between Galicia and Portugal in ways that disrupt received *fin-de-siècle* notions concerning the Iberian Peninsula's political binarism – that is, its division into two sovereign states, one of which (Portugal) was understood to be ethnically, linguistically, and culturally homogeneous, while the other (Spain) was viewed from Restoration-era Madrid as an essentially cohesive nationality whose linguistically and culturally distinct regions, such as Galicia, would over time be subsumed into a Castile-centred, monolingual and mono-cultural whole.

In challenging the Iberian status quo in this way, Martins, Pardo Bazán, and Unamuno perform an important function that is complementary to the Iberianist project. First, they help illuminate the complexity of Galicia's position within the Spanish nation state, and within Iberia as a whole. As Kirsty Hooper and numerous others have noted, Galician identity is located somewhere between Spain, in which Galicia is situated politically, Portugal, to which Galicia is tied by linguistic and cultural affinities, the Americas, to which generations of Galicians have immigrated, and the Celtic world, whose mythology Galician nationalists have drawn on in affirming Galicia's cultural specificity within Iberia (1–2). With its plurality of cross-border and transnational ties, Galicia provides a privileged space from which to question the Iberian status quo, and to propose new paradigms for intra-Iberian relations that would, in Thomas Harrington's words, be "hybrid, overlapping, or multi-polar" ("The Hidden" 139). To varying degrees and from distinct places of enunciation, Martins, Pardo Bazán, and Unamuno each looked to the Portuguese–Galician border as a point from which to consider Iberia's other "possible nations" (Medeiros 9). It is to my mind not coincidental that of these three imaginers of "possible nations," one (Martins) was a declared Iberianist and another (Unamuno) was sympathetic to Iberianism.

Curiously, all three writers fell victim to the identitarian strictures imposed by the Iberian status quo, which in one way of another they all challenged. As public intellectuals, they regularly crossed Iberian regional and state borders, physically and metaphorically, in terms of their literary world views. They participated in what might be described as a common effort on the part of late nineteenth-century peninsular intellectuals who, prompted by the rise of regionalism within Spain and Iberianism across the peninsula, attempted to disentangle potentially overlapping or competing categories such as fatherland (*pátria/patria*), land (*terra/tierra*), country (*país*), nation (*nação/nación*), and region (*região/rexión/región*). Though I contend that in the specific cases of Martins, Pardo Bazán, and Unamuno, their disentangling efforts might additionally be understood in light of their conflicted relationships with their nations and regions of birth.[6]

As described in the previous chapter, Joaquim Pedro de Oliveira Martins (1845–94) was a Portuguese historian of Iberianist sympathies, and author of a *História da Civilização Ibérica* (1879) that was well received in Spain, and which he dedicated to Spanish writer Juan Valera.[7] Martins's controversial historical interpretations, included in his *História de Portugal* (History of Portugal, 1879), among other texts, made him a polemical figure in his home country. Further, Martins was unique in the Portuguese intellectual climate of his time, even within the Iberianism-minded *Geração de 70*, for his degree of contact with Spain at the levels of ideas, travel, and personal and institutional connections. While not particularly engaged with Galician issues, Martins was familiar with Rosalía de Castro and Manuel Curros Enríquez.[8] And as we shall see, he addressed Portuguese–Galician relations in his historiography. Further, Martins substantially influenced younger Spanish writers, in particular Unamuno, who in his article "La literatura portuguesa contemporánea" (Contemporary Portuguese Literature, 1907) attributed to Marcelino Ménendez y Pelayo the declaration that Martins was "el historiador más artista que ha tenido la Península en el pasado siglo, y yo creo que el único historiador artista de ella. El más artista y el más penetrante" (the most artistic peninsular historian of the last century, and in my opinion, the only artistic peninsular historian, the most artistic and the most penetrating) (*OC* 1: 191).

Emilia Pardo Bazán (1851–1921) is one of Spain's best-known novelists and arguably its best-known woman prose writer. Born in La Coruña (or A Coruña) to an aristocratic Galician family, the eventual *condesa* identified as Galician and set her novels in Galicia. One of these bore the eminently Galician title *Morriña* (1895), a reference to a feeling of melancholy said to be essential to the Galician collective spirit, and comparable to Portuguese *saudade*. Indeed, Pardo Bazán's contemporary, the conservative Galician regionalist Alfredo Brañas, vouched for her Galician credentials in his study *El regionalismo* (Regionalism, 1889). Brañas noted that in Pardo Bazán's novels "solo se respira el ambiente de la tierra [gallega]" (one breathes only the air of the [Galician] land) (341). Despite her distance from the *Rexurdimento*, Pardo Bazán was active in the Galician literary and intellectual milieu. She edited the *Revista de Galicia* (1880) and served as president of the Sociedad del Folklore Gallego (Galician Folklore Society, founded 1883). Pardo Bazán considered herself Galician as well as Spanish, and confessed frustration at finding these two identities incompatible, at least in the eyes of more militant regionalists such as Rosalía de Castro, her husband Manuel Murguía, and Manuel Curros Enríquez. In her non-fiction volume *La vida contemporánea* (1899), Pardo Bazán wrote:

> Por conocer mi españolismo, no faltaron regionalistas gallegos que me acusasen de desafecto a Galicia, no obstante haberme pasado buena parte de mi vida literaria pintando costumbres, estudiando caracteres y pintando paisajes gallegos, con filial interés. Así es que se produce un caso curioso: mientras los que me traducen allá por lueñes tierras creen que yo profeso el más apasionado regionalismo artístico y que del perfume de mi tierra está enteramente impregnada mi producción, los que acá me conceptúan *castellana* y no me reconocen. La explicación, pardiez, que es sencilla; yo seré regionalista por amor e instinto ; separatista, jamás." (quoted in Pereira-Muro 74; author's emphasis)

> Given my well-known loyalty to Spain, there were not a few Galician regionalists who accused me of hostility toward Galicia, despite the fact that I have spent a good part of my literary life painting a picture of its customs, studying its people and depicting Galician landscapes with the interest proper to a native-born daughter. This leads to a curious phenomenon: while those who translate my work in faraway lands see me as a passionate artistic regionalist and believe that my work is doused in the perfume of my land, here people call me *Castilian* and do not recognize me [as Galician]. The explanation is simple, by God! I am a regionalist through love and instinct, but I will never be a separatist.

Pardo Bazán's choice to write in Castilian – albeit a Castilian influenced by Galician vocabulary, syntax, and phonology[9] – no doubt contributed to her detention by later generations of Galician critics, along with Ramón del Valle-Inclán, Cela, and other Spanish-language writers from Galicia, at Galician "passport control."[10] And her monarchism, Catholicism, and anti-separatism ruffled the feathers of the republican *galeguista* camp to which *Rexurdimento* notables like Rosalía, Murguía, and Curros belonged, and confirmed her later exclusion from the Galician canon. The title of Galician writer Antón Villar Ponte's 20 September 1917 open letter to Pardo Bazán, "Ilustre enemiga" (Illustrious Enemy), captures the paradox of the *condesa*'s relationship to Galician letters:[11] though unquestionably Galicia's best-known prose writer, Pardo Bazán has been cast by *galeguista* intellectual and political actors as the "enemy" of the values the *Rexurdimento* and its heirs claimed to defend. This made, and makes, her a potentially disruptive presence in Galician literature.

While no political revolutionary, Pardo Bazán nonetheless offers substantive reflections on the complex relationship between Galicia and Spain, and on the prospects for Galician regionalism to exist in the context of the Spanish state. These reflections are principally found in her articles and speeches. As a corollary, in her literary non-fiction she evinces a notably deep engagement with Portuguese literature and culture, and acknowledges persistent cultural and linguistic ties between Galicia and Portugal, notwithstanding centuries of political separation. These observations on intra-Iberian relations and on the peninsula's internal diversity make her, to my mind, a necessary reference in discussions on Iberianism at the *fin de siècle*, even though she would have likely rejected the Iberianist label, and adhered to a fairly conservative political centralism that would have been anathema to Iberianism's more radical proponents.

For his part, Unamuno (1864–1936) earned the enmity of fellow Basques for his (in retrospect, incorrect) predication that the Basque language, being unfit for the modern world, would die out, and for his aggressive criticism of Basque separatism, which he derisively termed *bizkaitarrismo*.[12] At the same time, as with Pardo Bazán in relation to Galicia, Unamuno identified himself as both Basque and Spanish.[13] And like his friend the *condesa*, Unamuno was a noted Lusophile who corresponded with, met, and befriended Portuguese intellectual luminaries such as Guerra Junqueiro, Eugénio de Castro, a young Vitorino Nemésio, and Teixeira de Pascoaes, whose own connections to the

Galician *Grupo Nós*, as well as Catalan *noucentisme*, are well known.[14] Unamuno acknowledged the influence on his writing and thought of Portuguese writers, particularly the *Geração de 70* (Martins, Quental, Junqueiro, et al.), and had nearly three hundred Portuguese-language and Portuguese-themed texts in his personal library.[15]

Unamuno also travelled to Galicia, and developed a deep friendship with Emilia Pardo Bazán. And as I will argue in greater depth in this book's next chapter, Unamuno was a strong cultural Iberianist whose dialectical vision of Spanish and Iberian identity, articulated across his voluminous essayistic production, engaged with a plethora of issues germane to the debate on intra-Iberian relations during the late nineteenth and early twentieth centuries. An epistolary partner of Joan Maragall, one of the architects of Catalan tripartite Iberianism (a scheme the Basque thinker partially endorsed), Unamuno called on peninsular writers to familiarize themselves with a variety of Iberian linguistic and literary traditions by reading texts in Castilian, Catalan, and Galician.[16] Let us begin our examination of the representation of the Portuguese–Galician frontier with Oliveira Martins.

Oliveira Martins: Dismembering Galicia

In his *História de Portugal*, Oliveira Martins anticipated the observations cited at the opening of this chapter on the artificiality of borders. Martins argued against the providential narrative of Portuguese history, and evinced what historian Sérgio Campos Matos terms "a sensible scepticism toward [Portuguese] ethnic uniqueness" ("Portugal" 87). Martins contended that Portugal's independence amounted to the "desmembração da Galliza" (dismembering of Galicia) (57) – a term also employed by Martins's contemporary Teófilo Braga to describe the separation of Galicia and Portugal, as in the prologue to his *Parnaso Português Moderno* (1877), where Braga declares: "Efectivamente, a Galiza deve ser considerada como um fragmento de Portugal, que ficou fora do progresso de nacionalidade. Apesar de todos os esforços de desmembração política, a Galiza não deixou de influir nas formas da sociedade e da literatura portuguesa" (In effect, Galicia should be considered a piece of Portugal that has been excluded from our nation as it has progressed. Despite all the efforts to dismember us politically, Galicia has influenced Portuguese literature and society) (quoted in Cuesta "Portugal-Galicia" 13). In Martins's account, Portugal's early rulers affirmed the county-turned-kingdom's independence in a

Nietzschean expression of personal will, and in defiance of "natural" borders and affinities. Indeed, if a "natural" political, linguistic, and cultural unit existed in western Iberia during the Middle Ages, for Martins this was Galicia (in the expansive sense of the term, referring to territory both *além* and *aquém Minho*), and not the incipient Portugal, which Martins viewed, initially at least, as the unnatural product of the first Portuguese kings' egotism and political talent. As Pilar Vázquez Cuesta notes for Martins's *História de Portugal*, "Nin a xeografía nin a raza – di – xustifican a independencia portuguesa como pretenden algúns historiadores. Dun lado e outro da raia fronteiriza atopamos tipos humanos semellantes e, en troques, existen nos dous reinos diferencias ben visibles entre as poboacións do Norte e do Sur do país" (neither geography nor race – he says – justify Portuguese independence, despite what some historians say. Similar human types are found on both sides of the border and in contrast, in the two kingdoms there are substantial differences between northern and southern populations) ("O amor" 41).[17] As we shall see, for Martins the Miño, *despite* its role as a dividing line between Galicia and Portugal, served during the Middle Ages to connect the two countries and peoples. Matos notes for Martins: "In his view the border resulted from an arbitary convention, the rivers as much as the mountain ranges extending far beyond it" ("Portugal" 83–4).

In his *História de Portugal*, Martins writes:

> Qualquer que fosse o valor dado no XI seculo á expressão geographica de *Portucale*, é facto provado por todas as memorias e documentos d'esses tempos, que para ninguem deixava de considerar-se o territorio de entre Minho e Mondego como parte da Galliza. O facto da constituição do condado de nada vale contra esta opinião; porque demasiado se sabe que a formação dos Estados medeivaes, na Peninsula e fóra d'ella, jámais obedecia ás prescripções geographicas ou ethnologicas. Não se atribua pois a causas d'esta ordem, nem á consciencia de uma solidariedade nacional, o facto da desmembração da Galliza dos fins do XI seculo. A scisão que o Minho demarcou obedeceu apenas a motivos de ordem politica. (1: 54; author's emphasis)

> Whatever meaning was granted to *Portucale* as a geographic expression during the eleventh century, all of the accounts and documents from this period are in agreement that the territory located between the Miño and Mondego rivers was part of Galicia. The fact that the county [of Portucale]

> had been constituted as such in no way negates this fact, for we know all too well that the formation of medieval states, both within and outside the Peninsula, in no way respects geographic or ethnic criteria. We must not attribute the dismembering of Galicia at the end of the eleventh century to these sorts of causes, nor to any consciousness of [Portuguese] national solidarity. The division marked by the Miño was the product of purely political causes.

Martins declares more succinctly: "Nos primeiros tres seculos, isto é, na primeira epocha da historia portugueza, a independencia é um facto originado no merecimento pessoal dos chefes militares dos barões de áquem Minho. Nacionalidade [portugueza] propriamente dita, não a ha" (During the first three centuries, that is, during the first period of Portuguese history, independence was achieved and maintained due to the personal merits of the military chiefs in the employ of the noblemen of the lower Miño. There was no [Portuguese] nationality, in the strict sense of the term) (1: 55). Hence Martins's perhaps surprising reference in this same section of his *História de Portugal* to the lower Miño – Portugal's historical heart – as "a metade portugueza da Galliza" (the Portuguese half of Galicia), and his mention of the "barões gallegos das duas zonas divididas pelo Minho" (Galician noblemen from the two parts separated by the Miño) and "a facilidade com que os reis portuguezes transpõem armados as aguas d'esse rio" (the ease with which the Portuguese kings crossed that river armed) in their attempts to form a "homogeneous" Galician state under Portuguese rule (1: 54–5). Martins went further in a 2 June 1891 letter to Galician intellectual Salvador Cabeza de León. Citing Galicia and Portugal's shared history, Martins declared: "Portugueses e galegos somos um e o mesmo povo na língua e no sangue" (We Portuguese and Galicians are one and the same people in terms of language and blood) and more succinctly, "Galegos somos" (We are Galicians) (quoted in Araújo 78–9). According to Martins, the Portuguese nobility's failure to reunite Galicia helped shift Portugal's expansion southward, away from the lands north of the Miño. This relegated "a Galliza portugueza" (Portuguese Galicia), the site of the former *Condado Portucalense*, to the status of northern province of Portugal as opposed to the vital centre of Portuguese national life (57). With the conquest of Lisbon in 1147 and Portugal's later maritime voyages, the kingdom's "caracter maritimo e colonial" (maritime and colonial character), which would further distance it from peninsular and European affairs, would be secured (24).

Concurrently, Galicia and Portugal's disparate historical destinies conspired to distance the Galician and Portuguese tongues. Martins describes Galician and Portuguese in his *História da Civilização Ibérica* as two dialects of the same language, which significantly he terms Galician as opposed to Portuguese. He writes that Galician is a national language, "embora ... nos apareça hoje, de um lado como dialecto da parte da província que ficou incorporada na monarquia espanhola, do outro como língua fixada e culta da monarquia portuguesa, cujo núcleo foi a Galiza, de entre Minho e Douro" (though ... today it appears to us, on one side [of the border] as the dialect spoken in the part of the province that was incorporated into the Spanish monarchy, and on the other as the standardized and refined language of the Portuguese monarchy, whose birthplace was the portion of Galicia located between the Minho and Douro rivers) (164). Martins builds on this view in his letter to Cabeza de León: "Desde o Finisterra pelo menos até ao Mondego, o povo é absolutamente o mesmo, e se não tivesse sido o facto da cisão política pelo Minho, a língua seria absolutamente idêntica. O português não é outra coisa senão o galeciano que tomou caracteres próprios com a cultura principalmente quinhentista" (From Finisterre to at least the Mondego, the people are absolutely the same, and if not for the fact of the political division marked by the Miño, their language would be absolutely identical. Portuguese is nothing but a Galician that gained its own characteristics through cultural influences, principally during the sixteenth century) (quoted in Araújo 78). With Galicia unnaturally "dismembered" and a Portuguese kingdom formed in defiance of nature, the question becomes how to characterize what Martins viewed as residual connections between Portugal and Galicia, connections that have been felt with particular force along the border, and in spite of the peninsula's binary political division. As Martins wrote to Cabeza de León: "Ainda hoje, no entrelaçamento das famílias e propriedades dos dois lados do Minho vemos os restos de uma história antiga" (Even today, we see the remains of an earlier history in the interconnections between families and property on both sides of the Miño) (78). Emilia Pardo Bazán offers us one possible model for characterizing these lingering connections.

Emilia Pardo Bazán: Invincible Affinity

On 2 September 1885, Emilia Pardo Bazán delivered a speech at the Liceo de Artesanos in La Coruña, entitled "La poesía regional gallega"

(Galician Regional Poetry). The speech, Pardo Bazán's first public address, was purportedly delivered in honour of Rosalía de Castro, who had died some months earlier – though as Catherine Davies and Justo Beramendi describe, Pardo Bazán had a strained relationship with Rosalía and her husband Manuel Murguía due to ideological and personal differences.[18] After dispensing with platitudes to the recently deceased poet ("Quién no ha leído sus versos? ¿Quién no se ha… suspirado con sus melancólicas *saudades*?"),[19] Pardo Bazán elucidates a vision of Galician literature that places it squarely within a broader, identifiably *Spanish* whole (*OC* 3: 672; author's emphasis). This vision contrasts starkly with the determined autonomism of the *Rexurdimento*, which sought to defend Galician language and culture against what, in the prologue to her highly influential *Cantares gallegos*, Rosalía termed the "risa de mofa" (mocking laughter) of Spain's "máis ilustrísimas provincias" (more illustrious provinces) (9).

Pardo Bazán identifies the revival of an "espíritu de raza" (spirit of the race), what Herder would have termed *Volksgeist*, as the propelling force behind regionalist literary movements during the latter part of the nineteenth century, such as the Galician *Rexurdimento* and the Catalan *Renaixença*. In her study *La cuestión palpitante* (1882–3), Pardo Bazán identified as a feature of contemporary intellectual life "cierto renacimiento de las nacionalidades, que mueve a cada pueblo a convertir la mirada a lo pasado, a estudiar sus propios excelsos escritores, y a buscar en ellos aquel perfume peculiar o inexplicable que es a las letras de un país lo que a ese mismo país su cielo, su clima, su territorio" (a certain rebirth of national feeling, which inspires each people to look to the past, to study its celebrated writers, and to find in them the unique, inexplicable perfume that is to a country's literary life what the sky, climate, and land are to the country itself) (3: 590). In her 1885 speech she notes a "renacimiento" (rebirth) of regional literatures in "Cataluña, Valencia, las Baleares, las Vascongadas, Asturias y Galicia, o sea cuantas provincias tienen dialecto propio" (Catalonia, Valencia, the Balearic Islands, the Basque Country, Asturias and Galicia, that is, the provinces that have their own dialect) (674).

Pardo Bazán described Galician interchangeably as a language and dialect, arguing in her 1888 article "¿Idioma o dialecto?" (Language or Dialect?) that the distinction is ultimately meaningless.[20] However, she could not resist in her 1885 speech noting the *Castilian* cultural formation of the Galician regionalists, and the artificial character of a movement whose principal architects, perhaps more so than their Catalan contemporaries, had been educated in Castilian and were more comfortable speaking Castilian than Galician. Pardo Bazán writes: "Hoy el gallego posee, como el catalán y el provenzal, una nueva literatura propia; pero a diferencia de estos dos romances meridionales, el gallego no lo hablan los que lo escriben" (Today Galician has a new literature of its own, like Catalan and Provençal. But unlike these two eastern Romances, those who write in Galician do not speak it) (*OC* 3: 926). This said, Pardo Bazán admitted the Galician language's autonomous identity, and appeared to view Galician as distinct from Castilian in terms of its individual "genius" or character, writing in her article "Vidas y rosas: Benito Losada" (Life and Roses: Benito Losada, 1888): "A pesar de las innumerables semejanzas del gallego y del castellano, su *genio* es muy distinto (por lo cual siempre he considerado algo pueril empeñarse en establecer que estas dos formas del romance en la Península Ibérica proceden la una de la otra, y no admitir la explicación racional de su desarrollo paralelo) (Despite the innumerable similarities between Galician and Castilian, their *geniuses* are quite distinct [this is why I have always considered it somewhat puerile to attempt to determine which of the two forms of Iberian Romance gave rise to the other, as opposed to accepting the rational explanation that they developed in parallel to one another]) (*OC* 3: 900–1; author's emphasis). Here Pardo Bazán rejects the claim, made by Murguía and Brañas, for Galician's historical precedence over Castilian.[21] Rather, Pardo Bazán concurs, in all likelihood unconsciously, with Martins, who held in his *História da Civilização Ibérica* that "o castelhano e o galeciano desde o princípio parecem como idiomas diversos" (from the beginning, Castilian and Galician were distinct languages) (163).

For Pardo Bazán, Galician, whether a language or dialect, was distinct from Castilian, and Galicia's aspirations to possess a regional literature were legitimate, provided this literature retain its place within a broader Spanish canon and retain a "universal" character, as she argues for Basque in her article "El fuerismo en la novela" (*Fuerismo* in the Novel, 1890). However, as she argued in another 1882 article, given the disparate conditions faced by Spanish- and Galician-language poets, the notion that "el mejor poeta gallego debe parecerse a un buen poeta castellano" (the best Galician poet should appear equal to a good Castilian poet) amounted to a "pretensión imposible y absurda" (impossible and absurd pretension) (3: 882). Pardo Bazán's insistence on Galician literature's distinctiveness and the allowances she makes for its apparent lack of quality fail to mask her implication that Galician-language writing is in some essential sense inferior to work written in Castilian. What, then, was the basis of her critique of the Galician regionalists? We find the answer in "La poesía regional gallega," in which Pardo Bazán characterizes the regionalists' "complaints" against Castile as a case of confusion between the categories of *patria* and *tierra*:

> [Las] quejas [poéticas, contra Castilla] no son mero juego retórico; si, como es de creer, expresan una aspiración sincera, contenida en el movimiento intelectual de Galicia, tenemos que reconocer que el renacimiento lleva en sí un germen de separatismo, germen poco desarrollado todavía, pero cuya presencia es imposible negar, y que acaso sea el único fruto político y social de este florecimiento poético. ¡Qué otra cosa significa la frecuente confusión del concepto de *patria* con el de *tierra* o región nativa, confusión que aquí se repite tan a menudo en el lenguaje hablado y escrito!
>
> Galicia no es sino la *tierra*, algo íntimo y dulce, algo quizás más caro al corazón, más necesario para la vida que la misma patria; pero la patria representa una idea más alta aún, y la patria, para los españoles todos, dondequiera que hayan nacido, desde la zona tropical hasta el apartado cabo de Finisterre, es España, inviolable en su unidad, santa en sus derechos. (*OC* 3: 686; author's emphasis)

> The poetic objections against Castile are not merely a rhetorical game. If, as is likely the case, they express a sincere desire on the part of the Galician intellectual movement, then we must recognize that this rebirth carries within it the seed of separatism. This seed is still small, but its presence is impossible to deny, and it might be the only political and social fruit of this poetic flowering. What else can we infer from the frequent confusion, so often repeated in speech and in writing, of the concepts of *homeland* and *land* or native region?
>
> Galicia is a *land*, something that is close to the heart and is sweet, and perhaps is more closely felt and more necessary for one's life than even one's country. But the *homeland* represents an even greater idea. And the country of all Spaniards, wherever they are born, from the tropics to the lonely cape of Finisterre, is Spain, inviolable in its unity and sainted in its rights.

For Pardo Bazán, Galicia could legitimately be described as a *tierra* (land), *región* (region), or even *país* (country) – terms that fall on a sliding scale of geographic specificity and which, for Pardo Bazán, invoke feelings of belonging and personal affection.[22] Indeed, Pardo Bazán used these terms more or less interchangeably when referring to Galicia in her own writing, as in an 1888 article on Eduardo Pondal, in which she refers to Galicia as both a "país" and "mi tierra" (my land) (3: 888). For Pardo Bazán, Galicia was *not*, however, a *patria*, a designation she reserved solely for Spain as a broader political, geographic, and cultural entity. Pardo Bazán's vision of the Galician *tierra*, falling somewhere short of nationhood and located within an identifiably Spanish *patria*, contrasts with the *galeguistas'* views.[23] This difference becomes apparent in examining Rosalía's poem "A Gaita Gallega" (Galician Pipes), published in her *Cantares gallegos* (Galician Songs, 1850) in which she declares: "Probe Galicia, non debes / chamarte nunca española, / que España de ti se olvida / cando eres, ¡ai!, tan hermosa … Galicia, ti non tes patria, / ti vives no mundo soia, / i a prole fecunda túa / se espalla en errantes hordas" (Poor Galicia, you should never / call yourself Spanish, / for Spain has forgotten you / when, oh!, you are so fair … Galicia, you have no homeland, / you live alone in the world, / and your hordes of children, / go forth across the earth) (110–11). As Beramendi and Seixas argue, "en defensa de Galicia [Rosalía] acada unha intensidade suficiente como para traducirse en práctica negación de súa españolidade" ([Rosalía's] defence of Galicia reaches sufficient intensity to practically amount to a negation of her Spanish-ness) (33). And in 1899, Manuel Murguía argued for Galicia's right to call itself a *nación*, chastizing Spaniards unable to understand "cómo un territorio, una raza, una vida común consciente y continuada durante siglos, pueda hacer de una región – haya sido o no independiente – una nación cuya vida nadie puede ya anular por entero" (that a territory, a race, a way of life consciously shared by all, can make a region – regardless of whether it has been independent – into a nation, whose life no one can entirely annul) (quoted in Beramendi and Seixas 56).

Pardo Bazán evidently did not share these positions. This said, it would be incorrect to class her views as beyond the pale of "acceptable" Galician regionalist opinion during the late nineteenth century. Pardo Bazán's position may, for instance, be productively compared with that of conservative regionalist Alfredo Brañas, who in *El regionalismo* (1889) attempted to resolve the question of competing loyalties to Spain and Galicia (or Catalonia, the Basque Country, etc.), by establishing a hierarchy in which the region *(Región)*, a term he sometimes substitutes for *país*, is subordinated to the state (*Estado*), which he uses interchangeably with *patria*. Echoing and building on Pardo Bazán's idea that loyalty to the *patria* supersedes loyalty to the region, Brañas forecloses the possibility of competing loyalties to Galicia and Spain by making the former subordinate to, and productive of, the latter.[24] He explains: "El amor á la región engendra el amor al Estado ó á la patria: el ciudadano no aspira en último término más que á defender hasta con su propia sangre la unidad y la independencia nacionales: sabe que de esa unidad depende la vida de la región, del municipio y de la familia, y por consiguiente también la libertad y seguridad del indivíduo; luego al defender á su patria defiende al pais, á la región que adora ... He ahí el *patriotismo*, ó sea el amor de la patria" (Love of one's region engenders love for the State or homeland: the citizen merely aspires to defend national unity and independence even with his own blood: he knows that regional, municipal, and family life, and therefore individual liberty and security, depend on this unity; thus in defending his homeland he defends his country; he defends the region he adores ... This is *patriotism*, that is, love of one's homeland) (38–9; author's emphasis). This allows Brañas to claim that *regionalism*, as distinct from *federalism*, is free of the "seed of separatism" that Pardo Bazán attributes to the underlying ideology of *Rexurdimento* literary culture. Indeed, both Pardo Bazán and Brañas rejected the federalist argument, which was most famously articulated in Spain by Francesc Pi i Margall in *Las nacionalidades* (The Nationalities, 1877), and in Portugal by José Félix Henriques Nogueira, in *Estudos sobre a Reforma em Portugal* (1851) and a young Antero de Quental in *Portugal Perante a Revolução de Espanha* (1868). For Pardo Bazán and Brañas, there could exist only one, *Spanish* nationality within the boundaries of the Spanish kingdom. As Pardo Bazán wrote in an 1888 declaration to which we shall return, and which might be interpreted as an implicit rejoinder to Pi i Margall, "no hay *nacionalidades peninsulares*" (there are no *peninsular nationalities*) (*OC* 3: 902; author's emphasis). It is unclear, however, whether Pardo Bazán shared Brañas's confidence that Galician regionalism could be cleansed of its separatist connotations. There is a note of fatalism in "La poesía regional gallega" that leads me to believe that she did not.

According to Pardo Bazán, militant regionalists, driven by an unfortunate combination of "apego al rincón natal" (connection to the land of one's birth) and "un germen de rencor ... contra las provincias dominadoras y puestas a la cabeza del Estado" (an element of resentment ... against the dominant provinces that have been placed at the head of the State), "subvert" the idea of the Spanish *patria* by circumscribing their national feeling to the borders of their particular *tierra*. She explains: "La noción de *patria* llega a subvertirse, y los regionalistas de buena fe la reducen a las fronteras de su región, y aun hay quién la circunscribe a una localidad determinada" (They subvert the notion of the homeland. Regionalists of good faith reduce it in size so as to correspond to the borders of their region, and there are even those who circumscribe it to a particular locality) (685; author's emphasis). Pardo Bazán implies in "El fuerismo en la novela" that there is a misguided nostalgia in this combination of affection for one's homeland and anti-Castilian resentment. The "nostalgia del tiempo pasado que sienten todos los defensores de las causas maltratadas por el tiempo presente" (nostalgia for the past felt by all those who encounter difficulties in defending causes that are today beleaguered) places the militant regionalist on the wrong side of history, for there are "dos corrientes en que se divide nuestra patria" – note again Pardo's exclusive use of *patria* to describe Spain – "la España estática y la España dinámica, el ayer y el hoy irreconciliables" (two camps into which our homeland is divided, the static Spain and the dynamic Spain, the irreconcilable past and the present) (*OC* 3: 929).

Given Pardo Bazán's opposition in "La poesía regional gallega" to militant Galician regionalism and her description of Spanish national unity as "inviolable" and "sainted," it is curious that in the same address she offers an extended reflection on the ties that bind Galicia and Portugal, and reveals a *lusofilia* the depths of which were not entirely typical of the intellectual culture of *fin-de-siècle* Galicia. This compels us to view Pardo Bazán's position on intra-Iberian relations as something more than a categorical affirmation of Spanish centralism. While *lusofilia* would become an important component of later Galician literary culture, beginning in the 1920s with the *Grupo Nós*, the notion that a writer so apparently out of step with *galeguismo* could have flown the flag of *lusofilia* decades before it became fashionable in Galician intellectual circles does not accord with Galician literary historiography, which has tended to downplay the *lusofilia* of *Rexurdimento*-associated writers like Rosalía, Murgía, and Curros – not to mention Pardo Bazán.[25] Yet as Ana María Freire López documents, Pardo Bazán made various trips to Portugal, befriending and exchanging letters with Portuguese intellectual luminaries of the *Geração de 70* such as Teófilo Braga, Eça de Queirós,[26] and Ramalho Ortigão. Further, in language that anticipated José Martí's call for Latin American solidarity in "Nuestra América" (Our America, 1891), she lamented in the title of a 21 November 1883 article published in the Portuguese *Almanach das Senhoras* (Ladies' Almanac) how Spain and Portugal resembled "vecinos que no se tratan" (neighbours who do not speak to each other) (quoted in López).

As I alluded to earlier, Pardo Bazán wrote the Portuguese–Galician border into her fiction. Moreover, she addressed medieval Portuguese history in the short story "La rosa" (The Rose, 1903), and told of a Galician returnee from Brazil in "El brasileño" (The Brazilian, 1911). And in a poem published in the 11 April 1880 edition of the *Revista de Galicia*, "Lectura de 'Os Lusíadas.' A orillas del Tajo" (Reading "Os Lusíadas" on the Banks of the Tagus), Pardo Bazán recounts reading Luís de Camões's epic poem while in Portugal ("Doraba el sol al declinar la tarde / las torres de Lisboa, / y esplendían del Tajo, como fuego, / las aguas tembladoras"), and celebrates the achievements of Camões and the Portuguese navigators ("Pensé ver en galeras lusitanas / hervir las sacras ondas, / y brillar, del poniente en los reflejos, / el numen de la gloria") (*Poesías* 141).[27]

Pardo Bazán explains how her Spanish patriotism and *lusofilia* might be reconciled in an 1888 article on José Pérez Ballesteros's *Cancionero popular gallego* (Galician Popular Songbook), for which Braga wrote a prologue. Here Pardo Bazán recounts an exchange with Braga during an 1883 trip to Lisbon: "Repito aquí lo que entonces dije: que no hay *nacionalidades peninsulares* ... Ahora añado que la opinión anterior no me impide estimar cumplidamente la genialidad propia y las buenas letras de cada país, ni deleitarme muchísimo con las poesías regionales, si son bonitas, ni reconocer gustosa el parentesco de consanguinidad que existe entre Galicia y Portugal" (I will repeat here what I said then: that there are no *peninsular nationalities* ... I would add that this opinion does not prevent me from properly esteeming the unique charm and fine literature of each country, nor does it prevent me from getting a good deal of enjoyment from examples of regional poetry, if they are pretty, nor from happily recognizing the degree of resemblance and consanguinity between Galicia and Portugal) (*OC* 3: 902; author's emphasis).

In short, Pardo Bazán shared with Iberian federalists like Quental, the younger Braga, and Joan Maragall, as well as the conservative regionalist Brañas, the view that peninsular regional differences existed at the levels of language, culture, temperament, and environment. Further, Pardo Bazán, in acknowledging the underlying "resemblance and consanguinity between Galicia and Portugal," effectively accepted the notion that Spain's regional identities could not entirely be contained within the boundaries of the Spanish state, but rather might in certain ways "transcend" them (Hooper 6). Just as Catalans may feel tied to the "Països Catalans" (Catalan countries) beyond Spain's borders (southeastern France, Andorra, northern Sardinia), and Spanish Basques may feel connected to Basque territory in southwestern France, so might Galicians look to Portugal as a land that, while politically separate, is not exactly foreign. Iberian federalists believed that the peninsula's plural nationalities – in Maragall's words, "una armonía de varias libertades" (a harmony formed of various liberties) – could act as a dynamic force.[28] Pardo Bazán and Brañas agreed with federalists like Maragall (as well as Unamuno) that regional and local identities were essentially affective, though as we have seen, they maintained a hierarchy of feeling that cast these sentiments as local, as opposed to properly national, and of a lower order than one's loyalty to the *patria*.[29]

In addition to describing the Galician language in "La poesía regional gallega" as "el habla gallega o su derivada la portuguesa" (the Galician tongue or its derived form, Portuguese) (*OC* 3: 677) – a characterization with which Martins would have concurred – Pardo Bazán declares:

> A semejanza de esos ríos que se hunden en un punto para reaparecer algunas lenguas más lejos, los anales literarios interrumpidos en Galicia se reanudan en Portugal.
>
> Mejores que regiones análogas podemos considerar a Portugal y Galicia un país mismo. El Miño que entre ellas corre no es término que las divide, sino cinta de plata que las estrecha; sus orillas, labios húmedos con que se dan un beso fraternal. En la benignidad del clima, en el ameno verdor que viste el suelo, en la orientación cara al mar de Atlante, en las costumbres y carácter de sus hijos, no es dudoso que esa larga zona de tierra ibérica que comprende los territorios galaico y lusitano ha sido destinada por Dios, a completarse moralmente, con tan invencible afinidad como la que une a las regiones levantinas Valencia, Cataluña y las Baleares. Después de la amputación de Portugal, quédase Galicia como miembro destroncado, sin vida propia. Cuando Portugal se alza y señorea el Océano ... Galicia se anula: mientras la hermana de allende el Miño se viste de brocado y oro, la de aquende suelta entristecida su viejo laúd, retírase a la montaña, calza zuecos de pastora, y sólo al morir la tarde y recoger sus ganados entona alguna copla rústica.
>
> No es posible dudar que la literatura gallega, a no ahogarla en su adolescencia acontecimientos y vicisitudes políticas, hubiera sido lo que fue la de Portugal, en la cual hay que ver el cumplido desarrollo de un germen

galaico, y esta gloria que Galicia reclama, no la funda en que el mayor y más excelso poeta lusitano – el tuerto ilustre colocado por los portugueses a la cabeza de su literatura, allí donde los españoles ponemos al manco inmortal – haya sido de origen y solar gallego; sino que la basa en razones más serias y científicas; en la evidente prioridad demostrada, aparte de otros documentos más añejos, por la existencia de las *Cantigas* alfonsinas, libro de versos gallegos escrito antes que Portugal poseyese monumento alguno de su literatura arcaica.

Fueron el idioma portugués y el gallego, según todas las probabilidades, una misma cosa hasta el siglo XV, y, por lo tanto, el desarrollo actual de aquél revela lo que pudo éste dar de sí. Fuerza es reconocer que al portugués le falta la amplitud, nobleza, entereza, valiente musculatura y sana complexión del castellano, ofreciendo solamente en recompensa una mimosa molicie, una modulación variada y expresiva, y cierto humorismo irónico que distingue también al gallego. Es el portugués menos opaco, más resonante y metálico que nuestro dialéctico; diríase que el oxígeno de la vibradora atmósfera indiana, el salitre de las olas, las emanaciones de la flora brasileña, han prestado a la lengua de Portugal color y sonido. Salva esta diferencia, fruto de elementos históricos, en el idioma de Almeida Garrett puede Galicia ver reflejada la evolución probable del suyo. (*OC* 3: 679–80)

Like those rivers that disappear in one spot only to reappear a few leagues away, the segments of Galician literary history that were once separated are reconnected in Portugal.

Rather than considering Portugal and Galicia as analogous regions, they are really a single country. The Miño that runs between them is not a dividing line, but rather a ribbon of silver that binds them together; its banks are the moist lips with which they give each other a loving kiss. There is no doubt that the large swath of Iberian soil that includes both the Galician and Lusitanian lands, with its gentle climate, its land that faces the Atlantic, and the customs and character of its children, has been destined by God for moral unity, with as invincible an affinity as that which binds together the easterly regions of Valencia, Catalonia, and the Balearic Islands. After Portugal was amputated, Galicia was left as a severed, lifeless limb. While Portugal took to the sea and mastered it, Galicia annulled itself. While the man from the other side of the Miño dressed in brocade and gold, his brother on this side mournfully played his lute, retreated to the mountains, and donned shepherd's shoes, only to intone a rustic couplet at the end of the day, after bringing in his flock.

> There can be no doubt that Galician literature, had it not been drowned in political circumstances and ill fortune during its adolescence, would have achieved what Portuguese literature did. In Portuguese literature we see the flowering of a Galician seed. Galicia claims glory for this literature not because the greatest and most celebrated Portuguese poet – the illustrious one-eyed bard placed by the Portuguese at the head of their literature [Camões], where we Spaniards place the immortal cripple [Cervantes] – was Galician in ancestry. Rather, our claim is based in more serious and scientific arguments, namely because the *Cantigas* of Alfonso X was a book of Galician verses written before old Portuguese literature had any monuments to its name.
>
> It is quite likely that Portuguese and Galician were the same language until the fifteenth century, and as such, the subsequent development of the former reveals what the latter might have achieved. We must admit that Portuguese lacks the breadth, nobility, strength, heroic musculature, and healthy complexion of Castilian. In compensation it offers a lovely softness, a varied and expressive modulation, and a certain ironic humour that is also typical of Galician literature. Portuguese is less opaque, and more resonant and metallic than our dialect. One might say that the air of lively India, the salt of the ocean waves, and the scents of Brazilian flowers have imparted certain colours and sounds to the Portuguese language. Save these differences, which are the fruit of history, one can perceive in the language of Almeida Garrett the probable evolution of Galician.

Pardo Bazán's narrative of Portugal's early history mirrors Martins in its use of surgical metaphor. Where Martins speaks in his *História da Portugal* of the "dismembering of Galicia" at the hands of Portugal's early rulers, Pardo Bazán writes of Portugal's "amputation," which left Galicia a "severed, lifeless limb."[30] Indeed, in a 17 October 1898 column published in *La Ilustración artística* Pardo Bazán describes the problem in binational terms, writing: "Me llevo la impresión de que nada efectivo y real nos separa a españoles y portugueses ... Por qué razones se separó Portugal de España y quiso ser independiente, mientras Aragón o Galicia se adherían más y más a la nacionalidad española, es cuestión que a primera vista no se resuelve de un modo satisfactorio" (I have the impression that nothing effectively or really separates the Spanish and Portuguese from each other ... The question of why Portugal separated from Spain in order to be independent, while Aragon and Galicia, for example, came to adhere more and more closely to the Spanish nationality, cannot at first glance be satisfactorily explained). Further, citing Martins's *História de*

Civilização Ibérica and recalling his formula of Iberian civilizational unity combined with Spanish–Portuguese political dualism,[31] Pardo Bazán explains: "España y Portugal, separados, han corrido igual suerte, como si continuasen juntos, porque, si es fácil realizar la división política y geográfica, es inasequible infundir alma distinta en pueblos que la tienen idéntica, y cuyos elementos tradicionales nada difieren" (Spain and Portugal, though separately from one another, have encountered the same fate, as if they had remained as one. For while political and geographic divisions are easily established, it is impossible to infuse distinct souls into two peoples who share a common soul, and whose traditional elements are in no way distinct" (quoted in López).

This argument would have satisfied Martins, as well as Antero de Quental, who in his *Causas da Decadência dos Povos Peninsulares* (1871) described a common civilizational trajectory for all the "peninsular peoples," organized into two independent states: Portugal and Spain. Quental, lamenting the state of peninsular decline, declares: "Portugueses e Espanhóis vamos de século para século minguando em extensão e importância, até não sermos mais que duas sombras, duas nações espectros, no meio dos povos que nos rodeiam! (We Portuguese and Spaniards have diminished century by century in size and importance, so that now we are nothing but two spectral nations amidst the peoples who surround us!) (21). Curiously, Pardo Bazán's argument also recalls comments made by three *Rexurdimento*-identified writers to whom she is frequently opposed: Manuel Curros Enríquez, Rosalía de Castro, and Manuel Murguía. In the prologue to his anthology of Portuguese poetry in Spanish translation, *La lira lusitana* (The Lusitanian Lyre, 1883), Curros refers to Portugal as "la nación hermana" ([our] sister nation) and writes: "Apenas se comprende cómo siendo España y Portugal de un mismo origen; siendo tal la identidad de sus razas; teniendo ambas casi una mismo lengua y una misma historia; uniéndolas unos mismos recuerdos del pasado y unas mismas esperanzas para la porvenir; ligadas en lo moral por los mismos lazos y en lo físico por los mismos continentes, no han logrado todavía fundir en una sus literaturas, viviendo, por el contrario, los dos pueblos gemelos identificados en todo menos en la santa comunión del pensamiento" (It is difficult to understand how Spain and Portugal – given their common origin, their degree of racial resemblance, their shared language and history, their common memories of the past and hopes for the future – have not yet managed to unify their literatures. Rather, these two twin peoples are linked in every way except through the Holy Communion of thought) (17).

For her part, Rosalía presents Galician and Portuguese literary culture as symbolically connected through the waters of the Miño and Mondego rivers, and through Luís de Camões's account of Galician noblewoman Inês de Castro in his *Lusíadas*. In an 1884 poem, Rosalía writes:

> Dende as fartas orelas do Mondego,
> e dente a *Fonte das lágrimas,*
> que na hermosa Coimbra
> as rosas de cen follas embalsaman,
> do Miño atravesando as auguas dondas
> en misteriosas alas,
> de Inés de Castro, a dona mais garrida
> i a mais doce i a mais triste namorada;
> do gran Camoens que inmortal a fixo
> contando as súas desgracias,
> de cando en cando a acariñarnos veñen
> non sei que saudades e lembranzas. (297–8)
>
> From the lush banks of the Mondego,
> and from the *Fonte das Lágrimas,*
> which in lovely Coimbra
> the hundred-petaled roses bathe in scent,
> from the Miño, in whose waters
> on the mysterious wings,
> of Inês de Castro, the most beautiful woman
> and the sweetest and the saddest lover;
> immortalized by Camões,
> who told of her misfortune,
> from time to time affection comes
> and I know not what longing and memories.

Referring to Camões's death in 1580, the same year Portugal's "Spanish captivity" under the Habsburgs began, she declares:

> Pesan dos xenios na eisistencia dura
> tanto a fama i a groria canto as bágoas.
> A que cantache en pelegrinos versos
> morréu baixo o poder de mans tiranas;
> ti acabache olividado e na miseria

i hoxé es groria da altiva Lusitania.
¡Ou poeta inmortal !, en cuias venas
nobre sangre gallega fermentaba!
Esta lembranza doce,
envolta nunha bágoa,
che manda dende a terra onde os teus foron
un alma dos teus versos namorada. (298)

In the difficult lives of geniuses,
fame and glory but also tears weigh heavily.
You sang in lively verses
of what died under the power of tyrants;
you died forgotten and penniless
and now you are the glory of prideful Lusitania.
Oh immortal poet, in whose veins
noble Galician blood flowed!
This sweet memory,
wrapped in a tear,
from the land of your ancestors
I send to you, a soul in love with your verses.

Manuel Murguía provides the most expansive of the three *Rexurdimento*-connected reflections in his volume *Galicia* (1888), published in Barcelona as part of the multivolume series *España: sus monumentos y artes – su naturaleza é historia* (Spain: Its Monuments and Arts, Its Nature and History). In the introduction, Murguía writes:

> Cuando se penetra en nuestro país, por Portugal, la hermosura de los paisajes no permite pensar en cosa alguna. Pero antes de vadear el Miño, por los encantados lugares en que sus aguas pertenecen á dos reinos distintos, es imposible escapar á las diversas reflexiones que surgen en nuestra alma. Cielo y tierra dicen á una voz que los que allí viven son nuestros hermanos; que la bandera blanca y azul de los Braganza, cubre á pueblos que son de sangre gallega. Su lengua es tan nuestra como sus mares. Nuestras montañas salvan todo límite, y con sus brazos de granito unen, como en otros tiempos, á los que tienen un mismo origen y una misma historia. Á veces arraiga el árbol en tierra de ambas naciones y da sombra á gentes que siendo unas, se tienen por diversas ... ¿Por qué están separados? Sólo el cielo lo sabe; aunque es lo cierto que aquellas gentes, hijas de un mismo padre, alimentan entre sí rencores como los de Caín y Abel. (viii–ix)

When one enters our country from Portugal, the beauty of the surrounding lands does not allow one to think of anything else. But before crossing the Miño, at those enchanting spots whose waters belong to two kingdoms, one cannot ignore the various reflections that surge forth from the soul. The sky and land declare with one voice that those who live on that side are our brothers; that the white and blue flag of the Braganzas shields people whose blood is Galician. Their language is as much ours as is their ocean. Our mountains are not detained at the border, and their granite arms embrace, as in times past, those who share a common origin and a common history. There are trees whose roots extend into both nations and provide shade to peoples that, though they are one, are thought of as distinct ... Why are they separated? Only God knows; though it is true that these peoples, children of the same father, nurse resentments against each other like those of Cain and Abel.

And regarding Afonso Henriques's failed attempt to incorporate the city of Tui, on the Miño's northern bank, into the nascent Portuguese state, Murguía reflects:

Tuy volvió á su libertad, y Galicia quedó desde entonces y parece que para siempre, limitada por el Miño ... Porque desde que del lado de allá del Miño, se entendió que eran distintos de los de acá, se echaron ciegamente los infranqueables límites. Aquel gran escritor lusitano nuestro contemporáneo casi [Alexandre Herculano, en su *História de Portugal*] ... lo ha visto así y dicho con toda claridad. 'Una idea de nacionalidad distinta radicada en el ánimo de los pueblos de aquende del Miño, al mismo tiempo que les daba fuerza y unidad política, tornábase en una barrera moral que iba levantándose paulatinamente entre ellos y los habitantes del noroeste de la península, con los cuales no hacía un siglo, tenían comunidad de patria, de principios, de intereses y de lengua.' Error gravísimo en que también nosotros caímos, y que separando los que eran hermanos los hizo enemigos, privando al nuevo reino de una gran fuerza, dando á los que no eran nuestros, poderosos aliados y territorio que no estaba bien que poseyeran otros que no fuesen los suyos! Que no sin gran misterio contribuyeron los nobles gallegos á la formación de aquel reino; que no en vano Galicia y Portugal tienen una misma historia, una misma sangre, y una misma lengua y literatura inicial! (782–3)

Tuy was returned to freedom, and from that day forward, Galicia would be limited by the Miño, as will seemingly always be the case ... Because

> the moment those living on the other side of the Miño began to believe that they were different from those who lived on this side, barriers that could not be crossed were blindly erected. The great Lusitanian writer, our near contemporary [Alexandre Herculano, in his *History of Portugal*], puts the problem as follows, with utter clarity: "The idea of a distinct nationality which took hold in the souls of the people from this side of the Miño gave them power and political unity, but also created a moral barrier that slowly arose between them and the inhabitants of the northwest of the peninsula, with whom one hundred years before they had shared a common homeland, and common principles, interests, and a common language." This is a grave error to which we also fall victim. By separating those who were brothers, the new kingdom [Portugal] was deprived of a great source of strength, and those who were not like us [the Castilians] were given powerful [Galician] allies and territory that they should not have possessed! It is no mystery that Galician noblemen contributed to the formation of that kingdom [Portugal], and it is not coincidental that Galicia and Portugal have the same history, blood, and language and early literature!

In sum, by examining Pardo Bazán's *lusofilia* within the context of her attempts to reconcile her loyalty to Spain and her affinity for Galicia – that is, her *españolidad* and *galeguidade* – we may better appreciate the complexity of Iberian identities during the late nineteenth century, as well as Pardo Bazán's centrality to the debate over Galician regionalism at the *fin de siècle.* While Pardo Bazán, along with Brañas and against the grain of the *Rexurdimento,* forcefully argued for Galicia's place within Spain, she acknowledged that Galicians might legitimately look to their cousins living south of the Miño, and to the Portuguese tradition broadly, in articulating a historically grounded and culturally, though not politically distinct, Galician identity. This position is not far removed from the mature Oliveira Martins's calls for Portuguese and Spaniards to take a lively interest in each other's affairs, and if desired, to identify with fellow Iberians across the border, while at the same time respecting the fact of Portugal and Spain's political separation. More radically, in granting that Galicia might look southward to Portugal in affirming a distinctive identity, Pardo Bazán effectively countered the Restoration-era government's attempts to present the boundaries of the Spanish state as corresponding to those of a cohesive, unified Spanish nationality. This crack in the edifice of nineteenth-century official Spanish nationalism provides a convenient point of entry for Iberianist proposals of the sort authored by Quental, Maragall, and to a lesser extent, Unamuno. While Pardo Bazán provided the basis for Galicia to affirm its uniqueness within Spain (albeit at some cost to the myth of Spanish national cohesiveness), she failed to comment on the future of Galicia and of Spain's regions. We will now turn to Unamuno to address this gap.

Miguel de Unamuno: Galician Nature and the Iberian Dialectic

An inveterate traveller and very public intellectual, Miguel de Unamuno made various trips to Galicia during his life, and commented on numerous occasions on Galician literature, identity, language, and regionalism. In an article written in 1912, "Junto a las rías bajas de Galicia" (Along the *Rías Baixas* of Galicia), later published in the volume *Andanzas y visiones españolas* (Spanish Journeys and Visions, 1922), Unamuno describes one such journey to Galicia:

> Desde que hace ochos años visité una parte de Galicia – Orense y Coruña –, ansiaba conocer el resto, y sobre todo la encantadora comarca de las rías bajas, de que se hacen lenguas cuantos la visitan. Y allá he tenido ocasión de ir en romería este verano.
>
> Fué atravesando mi bien conocido Portugal, por las orillas del Duero asceta que corre en lecho de rocas y yendo a buscar luego las del Miño manso, que como una caricia lenta baja al mar, restregándose en la verdura de sus vegas.
>
> La tierra toda del Miño, de un lado y otro de la ría, por España y por Portugal, se abre a los ojos como una visión del ensueño que nos ata a la tierra. La he visto entre llovizna, recibiendo resignada el jugo fecundante de las nubes, y es como mejor sentimos su significación íntima toda. Es un paisaje carnal y crepuscular a la vez, y, si me es permitido, más musical que pictórico. Los montes del horizonte languidecen entre neblinas. Por dondequiera el verdor vela al esqueleto rocoso de la tierra, que acá, en esta ósea Castilla, asoma por dondequiera sus juanetes. (1: 383)[32]

> Ever since I visited one part of Galicia – Orense and La Coruña – eight years ago, I have been eager to visit the rest of it, and especially the enchanting region of the *Rías Baixas*, which inspire the praise of all who visit. And this is where I've gone on a pilgrimage this summer.
>
> I approached it from my well-traveled Portugal, along the banks of the ascetic Duero, which runs along a bed of rocks. I was seeking the banks of

> the gentle Miño, which like a slow caress descends to the sea, watering the greenery of its meadows.
>
> This whole region of the Miño, on both sides of the *ría*, in Spain and in Portugal, presents the eyes with a vision of earthly fantasy. I have seen it in the drizzle, resignedly receiving the clouds' precious liquid, and it is in these conditions that we best appreciate its deep, underlying meaning. This is a landscape that is both fleshy and crepuscular, and if I may, more musical than visual. The mountains seen on the horizon lie in repose in the fog. Everywhere one looks the greenery covers the land's rocky skeleton, which here in bony Castile reveals its hard skin.

Unamuno's description of the Galician landscape is important on two counts. First, it echoes characterizations made by writers of the *Rexurdimento*, as well as Emilia Pardo Bazán. These writers, like Unamuno, closely tied Galician identity to a Galician landscape understood to be lush, verdant, and feminine, which they counterposed to the Castilian *meseta* and its attendant ascetic and masculine qualities. In the prologue to her *Cantares gallegos*, Rosalía de Castro describes Galicia as "un xardín donde se respiran aromas puros, frescura e poesía" (a garden of pure air, freshness, and poetry) (10). And in the poems "Castellana de Castilla" (A Castilian Woman from Castile), "Castellanos de Castilla" (Castilians from Castile), and "Tristes Recordos" (Sad Memories), she contrasts the Galician landscape to that of a hostile, arrogant, and "seca Castilla" (barren Castile) (10). Or as Camilo José Cela put it decades later, in his article "Sobre el alma gallega y sus facetas, y algunas muestras de la morriña en su poesía" (On the Features of the Galician Soul, with Some Examples of *Morriña* in Galician Poetry), "Galicia, en el mundo español, no es el castillo roquero, sino la verde y dulce floresta" (Galicia, within the world of Spain, is not a castle of rock, but a green, sweet forest) (251). Pardo Bazán describes Galician nature in similar terms in her article "El olor de la tierra: Valentín Lamas Carvajal" (The Scent of the Earth: Valentín Lamas Carvajal, 1888), writing of "los horizontes, … las nubes, … la humedad, … la tierra gallega en suma, y … los árboles y plantas que nutre" (the horizon, … the clouds, … the humidity, … in fine, the Galician countryside, and … the trees and plants it nourishes) (3: 881). Tying the Galician landscape to Galician literature, she argues: "A falta de modelos reconocidos en el terreno literario, a falta de bibliotecas, el poeta gallego tiene la naturaleza – entendida esta palabra en el sentido algún tanto restrictivo de *campo*, de *vida rural* –. Solo allí encontrará el pensamiento formulado en dialecto, en el habla que maneja: sólo allí obtendrá, si la inspiración le ayuda, la difícil conjunción del fondo y de la forma, que eterniza la inspiración porque la hace nacer viable. (In the absence of established literary models, in the absence of libraries, the Galician poet has nature – if we apply to this word the somewhat limited meaning of *countryside*, of *rural life*. Only there will he find thought formulated in his dialect, in the language he speaks: only there will he achieve, if inspiration permits, the difficult meeting of meaning and form, which gives eternal shape to inspiration because it allows it to come into the world and survive) (3: 883; author's emphasis).

Let us return to Unamuno: as I will describe more comprehensively in the next chapter, Unamuno's description of the Galician landscape as feminine, soft, and fleshy, as opposed to the masculine, hard, and bony Castile, speaks to his dialectical view of Spain and of Iberia more broadly. According to this view, the peninsula's regional differences may ultimately be overcome through a process of mutual encounter and be resolved into a higher unity. In this way, Unamuno adds a temporal and teleological dimension to the hierarchy of loyalties affirmed by Pardo Bazán and Brañas. For Unamuno, the Spanish or Iberian *patria* attains its pre-eminence over the peninsula's regions precisely because these regions, led by Castile, have confronted one another, as in Hegel's account of interpersonal recognition. They have exchanged ideas, customs, and linguistic material, and been subsumed into a superior entity, alternately identified as *España*, *Hispania*, or *Iberia*. As Unamuno describes in his early essayistic volume *En torno al casticismo*:

> Pero si Castilla ha hecho la nación española, ésta ha ido españolizándose cada vez más, fundiendo más cada día la riqueza de su variedad de contenido interior, absorbiendo el espíritu castellano en otro superior a él, más complejo: el español. No tienen otro sentido hondo los pruritos de regionalismo más vivaces cada día, pruritos que siente Castilla misma; son síntomas del proceso de españolización de España, son pródromos de la honda labor de unificación. Y toda unificación procede al compás de la diferenciación interna y al compás de la sumisión del conjunto todo a una unidad superior a él. (*OC* 1: 802)

> While Castile has brought the Spanish nation into being, over time it has become ever more Spanish, consolidating its rich interior variety more and more each day, and allowing the Castilian spirit to be absorbed into a superior, more complex spirit: the Spanish spirit. This is the deep meaning

> of the regional pride that is felt more and more strongly each day, a pride which Castile herself feels. This is symptomatic of the process of Spain's *españolización*. These are the early signs of the deep labour of unification. And all unification is the result of internal differentiation and occurs through the subordination of the whole to a superior unity.

Unamuno, who on various occasions described the Portuguese language as "un castellano sin huesos" (a Castilian without bones), a statement he apocryphally attributed to Cervantes, viewed Iberia's Galaico–Portuguese Atlantic coast as the lush, soft, feminine, and graceful counterpoint to the dry, hard, masculine, and rough-and-tumble Castilian centre. Through the dialectical interaction of these regions, as well as Spain's Basque country and the Catalan–Valencian Mediterranean, Unamuno hoped that Spain would achieve a dialectical synthesis in which the still unfinished country would become authentically itself, and through which it might fully *españolizarse*. In this spirit, Unamuno declared in a letter to the Portuguese poet Teixeira de Pascoaes: "Portugal me interesa mucho porque me interesa España" (Portugal interests me so much because Spain interests me) (quoted in García 363). Further, Unamuno closed his essay "Por Galicia" (For Galicia, 1903), which he dedicated to his "buena amiga doña Emilia Pardo Bazán," by identifying Pardo Bazán with the feminine grace of Galicia, and himself with the masculine assertiveness of his adopted homeland of Castile, and by declaring to Pardo Bazán: "La más firme base de nuestra amistad es precisamente nuestra discrepancia en tendencias" (The firmest basis of our friendship lies precisely in our disparate tendencies) (1: 314).

Looking past Unamuno's essayistic production, the Basque writer provides one of his most substantive and fascinating descriptions of the Galician landscape and character in the long poem "Galicia" (1912), which he dedicated to the Pontevedra-based writers Torcuato Ulloa, Víctor Said Armesto, and Isidro Buceta, and which I transcribe here:

> Tierra y mar abrazados bajo el cielo
> mejen sus lenguas,
> mientras él entre montes de pinares
> tranquilo sueña,
> y Dios por velo del abrazo corre
> sobre sus hijos un cendal de niebla.
> Ondea palpitando el seno azul del novio,
> y a su aliento la verde cabellera

de la novia se mece; de castaños,
de pinos y de robles, de nogueras,
y rubio vello del maíz dorado
que a la brisa marina se cimbrea.
        Frunce el seño la novia en Finisterre,
que broncos mocetones alimenta:
yergue desnudo el cuello en el naciente,
espalda a espalda con Asturias recia,
y alza la frente blanca,
cimas de roca que las nubes besan
y que por ver el seno del amante
hacia el cielo se elevan.
        Vuelto él en nubes hasta el cielo se alza,
derrítese de amor, su jugo suelta,
y lenta de llovizna
va empapando a la tierra,
y corte por los ríos fecundantes,
ceñidos de alisedas,
nuevamente del mar al seno siempre joven,
henchido siempre de pujanza nueva.
        Por un resquicio azul desde la altura
se ríe el sol de fiesta,
e irisa con sus rayos la llovizna,
y la obra le completa.
        El mar que duerme en las tranquilas rías
buscando acaso olvido a sus tormentas,
se consume de sed del agua dulce
que de las cimas llega,
y mira al Ulla, al Lérez, y en las fuentes
que el bosque esconde sueña.
Sed es de la dulzura
que su amargor consuela;
sed de los besos húmedos
que ella le manda de sus hondas selvas,
sed de las fuentes que entre los castaños,
se la roca revientan.
        Como lenta caricia el Miño manso
desciende restregándose en sus vegas
y el Lérez, demorándose en "salones,"
en lecho de verdura se recuesta.

El Sar humilde, tras cortina de árboles
sus aguas cela,
cantando de la dulce Rosalía
cantos de amor y queja,
y en honda cama de granito pasa
el Sil asceta.
        Desde un verde rincón de la robleda
la verde melodía de la gaita
        como un arrullo avivadora se eleva,
y al reclamo de amor languidecidos,
Tierra y Océano más y más se aprietan.
Susurra gravemente a sus oídos
siempre la misma cántiga, la eterna,
para que olvide de sus duros partos
las repetidas pruebas,
y el dolor de vivir con su canturria
poco a poco le breza.
        Hormiguean los hijos de este abrazo
por valles, costas, montes, y laderas
y de sus nidos hacia el cielo sube
el humo del hogar como una ofrenda.
        Mozas con ojos que la vida encienden,
a la espalda mellizas rubias trenzas,
con las plantas desnudas
tibio calor prestándose a la tierra,
enhiestos senos que al andar trepidan,
firmes cual moldes y anchas las caderas,
y unos brazos rollizos,
que con la misma ciencia
ciñen el cuello a su hombre,
cunan al niño entre canciones tiernas,
o en los campos desiertos de varones
el azadón manejan.
Una raza de madres,
varonas que a sus hijos alimentan,
y a las veces, de colmo,
amamantan ideas,
o al lado de sus hombres
oficían de contienda.
Rinden culto a la vida

y entrambos mundos pueblan.
    Esta raza los árboles, las ánimas,
con pánico fervor venera,
y palpitan druídicos misterios
bajo sus oraciones evangélicas.
Pasan en estantigua los que fueron,
en larga noche negra,
y obedecen los santos a conjuros
de brujas y hechiceras.
    Trabajan rudamente
y zumban consolándose en las penas;
ríen y lloran a la vez, burlándose
por modo de defensa;
o acaso afilan de los "hermandiños."
en silencio y con trágica paciencia,
las hoces vengadoras.
    Allende el padre mar, más que pobreza
codicia o hambre de oro
les lanza a las Américas,
y como un dedo de herculina torre
un trabajoso "más allá" les muestra.
Por cima de la tumba de la Atlántida,
do acaso sus abuelos les esperan,
pasan soñando
y brezando con aires de la tierra,
mimosos, verdes,
la morriña céltica.
Se fundan sus canciones
con el manto del mar, de que salieron,
y al mar de olas celestes
sus almas van con ellas.
Y al mar, para consuelo, su terriña
apretada aguardándoles se queda.
    Desde su altar, ceñido de altas torres
de granítica piedra,
que ennegrecieron lluvias seculares,
fomento de leyendas,
Santiago peregrino,
penate de esta tierra,
con sus conchas marinas revestido,

sonriendo contempla
ese abrazo de amor que nunca acaba,
mientras en él se mezclan
de la madre de Cristo a los recuerdos,
los de la madre Venus, y remembra
su romería, cuando Pan y Cristo,
guiones a su vera,
por la vía de leche
que cruza las estrellas,
desde la Tierra Santa
le trajo Prisciliano de la diestra. (6: 509–11)

The land and sea, joined under the sky,
intertwine their tongues,
while the sky sleeps peacefully
among mountains and stands of pine,
and God covers his children's embrace
with a veil of mist.
The young man's blue chest tosses like waves,
and the green hair of the young woman
rocks with his breath; hair of chestnut,
of pine and of oak, of walnut,
and blonde vellum of golden corn
that sways in the sea breeze.
The young woman furrows her brow in Finisterre,
fed by rough waves:
she lifts up her bare neck in the East,
standing back to back with sturdy Asturias.
Her white brow is covered,
by mountain tops kissed by the mist,
which ascends to the heavens
because it has seen the young woman's breast.
He flies up to the heavens clothed in clouds,
melted by love, he looses his liquid,
and slowly the misty rain,
wets the earth,
and with swollen rivers,
cuts through the stands of black alders,
and returns to the sea, to the ever-youthful breast,
filled again with new strength.

The sun above laughs happily
Through a sky-blue window
and forms rainbows from the misty rain
and completes the work.
The sea that sleeps in the calm *rías,*
perhaps trying to forget the storms,
goes mad with thirst for the fresh water
that runs down from higher ground,
and he looks to the Ulla, to the Lérez, and he dreams
of the springs the woods hide within.
This is thirst for the sweetness
that consoles him in his bitterness;
thirst for the wet kisses
that she blows to him from her deep forest,
thirst for the springs that flow from the rocks
between the chestnut trees.
Like a slow caress the gentle Miño
flows down into the meadows it rubs up against
and the Lérez, tarrying in "anterooms,"
rests on a bed of green.
The humble Sar hides its water
behind a curtain of trees,
and sings of sweet Rosalía,
songs of love and mourning,
and the monk-like Sil flows
on a bed of granite.
From a green corner of the oak grove
the green melody of the pipes
intones a stirring sound,
and languid Land and Sea draw closer and closer,
heeding the call of love.
Her ears take in the same
grave, eternal song,
so that she forgets her hard labours,
the repeated trials,
and the pain of living with the song
slowly lulls her to sleep.
The children of this embrace scurry like ants
through valleys, coasts, mountains and trails
and from their nests the chimney smoke rises

to the sky like an offering.
Girls with eyes lit up by life
with twin braids of blond hair running down their back
their feet bare
lightly warming the earth,
with firm breasts that shake as they walk,
ample buttocks moulded in place,
and robust arms
that with the same skill
embrace the neck of their husband,
rock their children with tender songs,
and in fields deserted by men,
wield the mattock.
A race of manly women,
who nourish their children,
and what is more, sometimes,
suckle ideas,
or at their husbands' side,
officiate disputes.
They worship life
and populate both worlds.
This race venerates trees,
and souls with panicked fervour,
and druidic mysteries pulse
under their evangelical prayers.
The departed return as apparitions,
during long, dark nights,
and the saints obey
witches and sorceress' spells.
They work like dogs
buzzing around, consoling themselves with their suffering;
they laugh and cry at once, mocking themselves
as a form of self-defence;
and perhaps the vengeful sickles
silently and with tragic patience
file down the *hermandiños.*
More than poverty,
greed, or hunger for gold
Father Sea sends them beyond the horizon, to America,
with his herculean tower of a finger

pointing them toward a hardscrabble "farther beyond."
Dreaming, they pass,
over Atlantis's tomb,
where perhaps their grandparents await them
and they sing airs from their country,
of lovely, green,
Celtic *morriña.*
Their songs fuse
with the tossing of the sea, which birthed them
and their souls
follow the sea's celestial waves.
And in consolation for the sea,
their little *terriña* waits for them.
        From his altar, surrounded by high towers
of granite,
blackened by centuries of rain,
a source of legends,
the pilgrim Santiago,
penitent of this land,
adorned with sea shells,
contemplates with a smile
this unending, loving embrace,
while within him
memories of the mother of Christ
and those of mother Venus mix together, and he remembers
the pilgrimage he made, and when,
with Pan and Christ guiding him,
through the Milky Way
across the stars,
from the Holy Land
he led Priscillian with his right hand.

The poem, with its accumulation of images and plethora of intertwined Christian and classical references, presents Galicia as a space of natural and, in a rarity for Unamuno's poetry, openly erotic encounter between land and sea, humanity and the Earth, and Christianity and paganism.[33] Unamuno describes the Galicians, the people who issue from this originary encounter, as humble, hardworking, and generally effeminate (with the exception of Galicia's "manly women" at work in the fields). They are also marked by a hereditary melancholy and nostalgia, or *morriña,* and their popular Christianity retains a pagan element inherited from the Galicians' presumed Celtic forbearers. In all respects, Unamuno's Galicians (or more precisely, Galician–Portuguese) contrast sharply with Castilians, whom he describes as proud, aggressively masculine, and assertive, and whose relationship with God is mediated through a strict Catholic monotheism. Given Unamuno's dialectical vision of the Iberian Peninsula, it is easy to see how he would view these two populations in both contrasting and complementary terms, possessing qualities that with time, he believed, would fuse into a truly national Spanish personality. It is to this dialectical vision that we will turn in the following pages.

Chapter Four

Miguel de Unamuno: A Peninsula of Flesh and Bone

Miguel de Unamuno (1864–1936), the Basque-born Spanish writer, philosopher, critic, polemicist, professor and eventual *rector* of the University of Salamanca was known, among other things, as a great inventor of terms and manipulator of language. Over his long and very public career, Unamuno, who is arguably the most distinguished figure in Spain's storied *Generación del 98*, was responsible for a number of neologisms. In his early polemical volume *En torno al casticismo* (written 1895, published 1902), Unamuno coined the term *intrahistoria* (intra-history) to describe Spain's "deep" national history, a "history from below" grounded in the "tradición eterna" (eternal tradition) of the common people (Boyd 131). Unamuno located Spain's *intrahistoria* in his adopted homeland of Castile, the region he viewed as the driver of Spanish national unity.[1] As a fiction writer, Unamuno used the neologism *nivola* to describe the experimental narratives he wrote after rejecting the conventions of the realist novel (*novela*, for Unamuno) during the first years of his literary career.

Perhaps most famously, Unamuno returned repeatedly in his work to the phrase *carne y hueso* (flesh and bone), and in particular, to a figure he referred to as the *hombre de carne y hueso* (man of flesh and bone). Unamuno's *carne y hueso* recalls biblical tradition, and features at the opening of his volume of philosophical and religious inquiry, *Del sentimiento trágico de la vida en los hombres y en los pueblos* (On the Tragic Sense of Life in Men and Peoples, 1913). Here Unamuno affirms the "hambre de inmortalidad personal" (hunger for personal immortality) felt by living, breathing "hombres de carne y hueso" (men of flesh and bone) as "el íntimo punto de partida personal de toda filosofía humana" (the intimate, personal point of departure for all human philosophy) (*OC* 7:

109, 131). While Unamuno put the ideas of *carne y hueso* and *el hombre de carne y hueso* to a variety of uses, I will focus in this chapter on how he used the notions of "flesh" and "bone" to articulate a theory of Iberian identity and intra-Iberian relations in which the peninsula's constituent regions, and Castile and Portugal in particular, were strongly implicated. As such, Unamuno's descriptions of an Iberian Peninsula built, metaphorically speaking, of both "flesh" and "bone," provide a convenient means to explore his Iberianism in comparison to the Portuguese Iberianists Antero de Quental and Oliveira Martins, who both deeply influenced Unamuno, and his friend and epistolary partner, the Catalan writer Joan Maragall.

A deeply religious man with an impressive knowledge of the Bible, Unamuno grounds his references to *carne y hueso*, I argue, in the New Testament image of Christ's church as an integrated body, as described by St Paul: "For we are members of his body, of his flesh, and of his bones" (Ephesians 5:30). Unamuno follows Paul in describing the peninsular body as composed metaphorically of "flesh" and "bone," which must work together to ensure the health of the whole, and for which, as with the analogy between Christ's body and "the communal Body" of believers, "the relationship between parts is as important as that between parts and whole. Only when each part becomes a member of each other part," that is, when flesh and bone are inextricably bonded together, "is the communal Body whole" (Bryson 2). Evidence abounds for Unamuno's understanding of "flesh" and "bone" as images suggestive of mutual integration and dependence. In an untitled poem from his *Cancionero* (1928–36), Unamuno writes of the "arms" of the peninsula, here described as a living system, "desparram[ando] y acarici[ando] / sobre hueso, carne parda, / que sangre y sudor hostigan" (spilling and caressing / over bone, brown flesh / whipped by blood and sweat) (*OC* 6: 1097). And in another unnamed poem, Unamuno describes the inverse condition, writing of a "tierra descarnada, parda, / hueso ya tu corazón; / tierra descarnada, aguarda / tu final resurrección" (land without flesh, brown, / your heart turned to bone; / land without flesh, you await / your final resurrection) (6: 1219). Unamuno also explored these connotations of *carne* and *hueso* in his essayistic and critical writing, the segment of his written production that I will analyse in this chapter, and in which the vast majority of his reflections on intra-Iberian relations can be found.

Unamuno, like his colleagues in the *Generación de 98* and the writers of the Portuguese *Geração de 70* before them, wrote against the backdrop of protracted imperial decline, which for Spain reached its culmination in the country's military defeat by the United States in 1898, a national trauma popularly known in Spain as *el desastre* (the disaster). *Fin-de-siècle* Spain also experienced significant regionalist agitation, particularly in Catalonia, the growth of which is at least partially traceable to 1898. In responding to these crises, and to the perception that Spain was experiencing a period of profound instability, of "reajustes íntimos, vivaz trasiego de elementos, hervor de descomposiciones y recombinaciones" (deep changes ... a lively shifting about of elements, and stirrings of decomposition and recombination), as he wrote in an 1895 essay, Unamuno offered a vision of Spain (and by extension, Iberia) as a dialectical unity.[2] Unamuno's proposal that Spain or Iberia could be understood as an internally differentiated but ultimately unified whole, a position he began to stake out in the essays published as *En torno al casticismo,* was in keeping with the spirit of both the *Generación del 98* and the *Geração de 70.* Both the Portuguese and Spanish groups used essayistic prose to confront potentially destabilizing national and peninsular problems, and made clear in their writing their fear that their countries and perhaps Iberian civilization as a whole was faced with an existential crisis. Unamuno's dialectical vision of the Iberian Peninsula can be understood, in this sense, as an effort to reconcile the competing if not opposed values of fealty to an "authentic" peninsular culture, which he sometimes identified with the term *casticismo,* and openness to "modern" ideas emanating from Europe *más allá de los Pirineos* (beyond the Pyrenees).[3] In attempting through his dialectical vision of Iberia, or more bluntly, through Iberianism, to "square the circle" formed by the twin forces of Iberian authenticity and particularity, and European universality and modernity, Unamuno followed in Quental and Oliveira Martins's footsteps. He also echoed the calls made by Maragall for an Iberianism that would affirm Catalan nationhood while maintaining the integrity of the Spanish state, and anticipated the federalist proposals of twentieth-century peninsular intellectuals like Salvador de Madariaga.

Rather than glossing over Iberia's manifold regional differences and internal tensions and contradictions, Unamuno believed that these should be productively brought into relief, so as to be resolved into a higher unity. Unamuno's differentiated yet internally integrated view of Iberia, along with his penchant for biblical language and images, lent itself to the use of bodily metaphors. This helps explain Unamuno's repeated use of *carne y hueso* to counterbalance certain "bony" Iberian landscapes such as Castile, which he termed "una tierra en esqueleto" (a skeletal land) and languages like Castilian, which he considered assertive, masculine, and "rígida y ósea" (rigid and bony), against "fleshier" regions such as Iberia's Galaico–Portuguese Atlantic Coast, which he described as possessing "un paisaje carnal" (a carnal landscape), and tongues like Portuguese and Galician, which for Unamuno were characterized by the Galaico–Portuguese quality of demure, bewitching, feminine *meiguice* (1: 227–8, 383; 4: 332; 7: 557). For Unamuno, the Iberian "body" required both flesh and bone, rivers and mountains, *meseta* and meadow to function. Similarly, the Galaico–Portuguese and Castilian languages and literary traditions, in their push and pull of masculine assertion and feminine retreat, would in Unamuno's view necessarily benefit from exchange and eventual integration.[4]

Unamuno consistently presents *carne* and *hueso* as mutually dependent in his writings on Iberian identity and geography. Indeed, he describes the metaphorical condition of being "without flesh" or "without bones" in terms of a potentially fatal lack. Referring to language, in a 1929 poem Unamuno plays on the double meaning in Spanish of *lengua* as both a physical "tongue" and as "language," writing:

> Lengua, lengua, no lenguaje;
> lengua es que carne sin hueso;
> vendrá la letra, visaje,
> calavera para el seso (6: 1264)
>
> A tongue, a tongue, not a language;
> a tongue that is flesh without bone;
> the letter will arrive, a visual sign
> a skull to hold the brain

And in a 19 December 1907 letter to Maragall, Unamuno described an embattled Portugal cut off from the rest of Iberia as follows: "Ese pobre país está perdido; está purgando, a mi juicio, su independencia. Se desprendió del hueso y ahora en carne pura, en carne floja aunque sonrosada, empieza a marchitarse" (This poor country is lost; it is, in my view, throwing away its independent existence. It has fallen off the bone and now, all flesh, and now, loose but pink flesh, it is beginning to wither) (Unamuno and Maragall 78).[5] It is easy to understand Unamuno's poetic logic: a body composed of "all flesh" or "all bones" would necessarily die, whether we think in terms of human bodies or broader "organic" geographic, cultural, and linguistic systems such as the Iberian Peninsula.

Portugal, a country both geographically near to Unamuno's adopted home of Salamanca, and dear to his heart, played a privileged role in his articulation of a dialectical theory of Iberian identity and intra-Iberian relations, occupying one side of the flesh/bone divide and standing in counterpoint to Castile. As such, I will first describe Unamuno's relationship with Portugal, which is notable for its depth and capacity to illuminate the broader counters of his Iberianist program. I will then offer a more detailed analysis of Unamuno's dialectical understanding of the Iberian Peninsula, and will discuss his call for Portugal and Spain to be brought into geographic, cultural, and linguistic confrontation as a means to achieve eventual synthesis. In so doing, I will argue that despite the doubts voiced by some critics, Unamuno was an Iberianist. I will conclude by tying Unamuno's dialectical vision of Iberia back to the vocabulary of "flesh" and "bone" introduced in this preliminary discussion.

Miguel de Unamuno, *Lusófilo* and Iberianist

A good deal has been written on Miguel de Unamuno's relationship with Portugal.[6] Unamuno made numerous trips to the north of the country during the opening decades of the twentieth century, and befriended a number of prominent Portuguese intellectuals including the poets Guerra Junqueiro, whom he introduced to Maragall, and Teixeira de Pascoaes. João Medina describes Unamuno as the "emblema mesmo da lusofilia mais acentuada de quantas podíamos inventar [no] panorama de juízos espanhóis sobre o destino luso" (greatest lusophile of all those Spanish [writers] I inventoried who commented on Portuguese affairs) (*Ortega* 7). José V. de Pina Martins, in his introduction to the *Epistolário Português de Unamuno* (Correspondence of Unamuno with Portuguese Individuals, 1978) affirms that Unamuno is "um dos mais insignes lusófilos de todos os tempos" (one of the most distinguished lusophiles of all time) (vii). And the Azorean writer Vitorino Nemésio, who as a young man corresponded with and was a confessed "disciple" of Unamuno, wrote the following in a 14 May 1929 letter to the Basque writer: "Dos grandes intelectuais espanhóis é Unamuno o único de quem [os portugueses] podemos acercar sem receio de que nos olhe de lado e por favor. Consigo é possível, sem risco da nossa individualidade de povo, trocar ansiedades sobre o futuro e pactuar uma acção redentora"

(Of the great Spanish intellectuals you, sir, are the only one whom we [Portuguese] can approach without fearing that you might look at us askance or with pity. With you it is possible to speak of our fears and agree upon a redemptive course of action without compromising our individuality as a people) (quoted in Dios, 242).

While these judgments are marked by a certain tendency towards hyperbole that Unamuno appears to inspire in his commentators, they are basically sound. Portugal exerted a strong pull on Unamuno, inspiring him to write several travel pieces and critical reflections on its landscape, people, and literature. A series of these pieces, dating from 1907 and 1908, were collected in *Por tierras de Portugal y de España* (Through Portuguese and Spanish Lands, 1911), one of Unamuno's least appreciated but most elegantly written volumes.[7] Further, Unamuno read an appreciable amount of Portuguese literature (in the original, as per his advice to peninsular writers),[8] had nearly three hundred Portuguese or Portuguese-themed books in his personal library, and routinely praised Portuguese writers in Spanish-language publications.[9] Indeed, Unamuno inspired younger Portuguese writers, both the "disciples" with whom he corresponded, like Nemésio and Manuel Laranjeira, and others who did not have the opportunity to meet him, such as the noted Iberianist Adolfo Correia da Rocha (1907–95), who took the pen name Miguel Torga as a dual homage to Unamuno and Miguel de Cervantes.

Unamuno's readings in Portuguese literature skewed heavily towards the nineteenth and early twentieth centuries. With typical iconoclasm, Unamuno declared Luís de Camões "perfectamente insoportable, y a quien, si no fuese por un mal entendido patriotismo, declararían los portugueses cultos inferior a muchos otros escritores portugueses, sobre todo contemporáneos" (utterly unbearable, [a poet] who if it were not for a misguided patriotism, educated Portuguese readers would declare to be inferior to many other Portuguese writers, especially contemporary ones) ("Sobre la erudición y la crítica" [1905]; *OC* 1: 1265).[10] Unamuno drew on Portuguese Romanticism, as well as the critical and often pessimistic stance of the writers of the *Geração de 70*,[11] along with the *saudosismo* of his contemporary, the poet Teixeira de Pascoaes, in identifying the Portuguese character and national literary tradition with romantic melancholy, pessimism, and historical tragedy. For instance, in a 1907 article on the poet Eugénio de Castro, Unamuno declared: "La literatura portuguesa ... tiene dos notas dominantes, y son la amorosa y la elegíaca. Portugal parece la patria de los amor tristes y la de los grandes naufragios" (Portuguese literature ... has two dominant themes, and these are love and elegy. Portugal appears to be the country of mournful love and great disasters) (*OC* 1: 184). The funereal tone of Unamuno's depictions of Portugal circa 1907 and 1908, which is perhaps most succinctly expressed in his description of the Portuguese as a "pueblo de suicidas" (suicidal people) in the title of a 1908 article, might cause the reader to wonder at his confessed attraction to a country he painted in such sombre tones. Unamuno, always apt to embrace the contradictory and enigmatic, summarized his feelings on Portugal thusly: "¿Qué tendrá este Portugal – pienso – para así atraerme? ¿Qué tendrá esta tierra, por de fuera riente y blanda, por dentro atormentada y trágica? Yo no sé: pero cuanto más voy a él, más deseo volver" (What is it about Portugal, I ask, that attracts me so? What is it about this land, smiling and calm on the outside, and tormented and tragic on the inside? I don't know, but the more I travel there, the more I want to return) ("Guarda" [1908]; *OC* 1: 241).

Scholars interested in the Portuguese dimension of Unamuno's life and work have documented his relationships with Portuguese writers, have affirmed the intensity of his feeling for Portugal, and have speculated on Unamuno's possible Iberianism. Nonetheless, it is surprising that critics drawn to this topic have by and large failed to undertake an in-depth analysis of Unamuno's work in the interest of illustrating the thematic connections and disjunctions that existed between the Salamanca *rector* and the Portuguese writers and texts to which he devoted so much attention. One topic that has been particularly overlooked is the question of Portugal's place in Unamuno's understanding of Spain – and by extension, Iberia – as a category, or as a dialectical unity. This oversight is rather ironic, given the prominence in Unamuno's work of the *problema de España* (problem of Spain), and Unamuno's repeated assertions that Portuguese affairs had a direct bearing on Spain and the Iberian Peninsula. In short, for Unamuno the "problem" of Spain or of Iberia was also the "problem" of Portugal. Indeed, Portugal played a crucial role in Unamuno's understanding of "Spain" or "Iberia." In his late essay "Hispanidad" (1927), he categorized the former as a "categoría histórica, por lo tanto espiritual, que ha hecho, en unidad, el alma de un territorio con sus contrastes y contradicciones interiores. Porque no hay unidad viva si no encierra contraposiciones íntimas, luchas intestinas" (historical, and therefore spiritual category, whose earthy soul and whose internal contrasts and contradictions solidified its unity, because a living unity cannot exist without deep-seeded counterpositions and inner struggles) (*OC* 4: 1081). In passing, we should clarify Unamuno's use of the term "Spain." Like Quental and Oliveira Martins before him, and Madariaga after him, Unamuno gestures back to the Roman *Hispania* and the pre-1640 meaning of "Spain" and grants the term a dual meaning. On the one hand, Unamuno accepted though did not necessary celebrate the distinction, cemented with the Portuguese Restoration of 1640, between Portugal and Spain as politically and historically distinct nation states, which circumscribed the category of "Spain" to the post-1640 borders of the Spanish kingdom. Yet, on the other hand, he defended the extension of *España* – or more exactly, *Hispania* – to the whole of the peninsula, understood here as synonymous with "Iberia," as a means of acknowledging the deep historical and cultural ties that continued to bind Spain and Portugal, as well as the various "peninsular peoples," across political borders.[12]

At this point it behooves us to ask how Unamuno, as a *lusófilo* who was nonetheless deeply invested in the project of Spanish national renewal, and as a thinker who viewed the Iberian Peninsula as a dialectical unity, should be situated with regard to Iberianism. Further, we must ask what Unamuno's Iberianism implied for Portugal specifically. Unamuno never published an extended statement advocating political unity for Spain and Portugal, as did Quental in *Portugal Perante a Revolução de Espanha* (1868), or the young Oliveira Martins in "Do Princípio Federativo e Sua Aplicação à Península Hispânica" (1869). This lack of a sustained declaration of faith, along with statements that appeared to flirt with Spanish annexationism and that expressed hostility towards Catalan aspirations towards autonomy or independence, may account for the doubts of some critics regarding Unamuno's Iberianism. For instance, Joan Ramon Resina writes of Unamuno: "Su tantas veces prodigado iberismo tenía un pequeño inconveniente: no creer en él" (There is just one small problem with his much-attested Iberianism: he did not believe in it) (*Del hispanismo* 41). Notwithstanding these doubts, which are perfectly reasonable but ultimately misplaced, in my view, Unamuno's public statements and private comments suggest that he was at least theoretically open to Spanish–Portuguese political union, and certainly favoured some form of alliance between the two countries. Further, his views on the dialectical unity of the Iberian Peninsula and his support for linguistic and intellectual exchange between Iberian regions speak to his strong support for cultural or intellectual variants of Iberianism.

Unamuno, echoing the mature Oliveira Martins, lamented in his article "Sobre el criollismo: A guisa de prólogo" (On *Criollismo*: A Sort of Prologue, 1903) that "aquí al lado tenemos a Portugal, desgraciada nación que gime bajo el yugo inglés por culpa de su suspicacia, de su ridículo temor de que España se la agregue" (next door to us we have Portugal, an unfortunate nation that suffers under the English yoke because of its mistrust, because of its ridiculous fear that Spain wants to conquer it) (4: 579).[13] And in a 19 December 1907 letter to Maragall, written less than two months before the assassination in Lisbon of the Portuguese king and his heir apparent, Unamuno used the vocabulary of *carne y hueso* he perennially employed to discuss intra-Iberian issues to imply that Portugal could not long survive without some sort of rapprochement with Spain. Having "fallen off the bone," that is, disconnected itself from the rest of the peninsula, Portugal was little better than rotting flesh, and could not hope to survive as an independent state. Indeed, in a 5 October 1908 letter written to Eduardo Marquina, the Catalan playwright and eventual translator of Guerra Junqueiro into Catalan,[14] Unamuno builds on this pessimistic characterization, and explains how his recent trip to Portugal had alerted him to the specific relevance of Portuguese affairs for Catalonia, which in recent decades had experienced an upsurge in regionalist feeling and demands for greater autonomy. He explains:

> En Portugal se me ocurrieron muchas cosas que escribir a Maragall, a Zulueta, a usted, a cualquier catalán de sentido. Da pena aquel desdichado país de mendigos y de pedantes que ha vendido su personalidad étnica por una sombra de independencia nominal. La única redención de Portugal es ser conquistado por España – por Castilla más bien – ser *conquistado* y nada de unión ibérica. (*Epistolario* 247–8; author's emphasis)

> In Portugal a number of things occurred to me that I wanted to write about to Maragall, to [Luis de] Zulueta, to you, and to all other Catalans of intelligence. It pains me to see this unhappy country of beggars and pedants, which has sacrificed its ethnic personality for the spectre of nominal independence. The only possible redemption for Portugal is to be conquered by Spain – by Castile, specifically – to be *conquered* as opposed to enter into an Iberian Union.

It is difficult to determine to what extent Unamuno's statement here truly reflects his views on how Portugal's crisis might be resolved, and to what degree his argument that Portugal could not long survive except through incorporation into a Castile-centred Spanish nation state was designed to turn his interlocutors, including Marquina, away from the cause of Catalan independence. Indeed, Unamuno routinely paired his argument for Portuguese approximation to Spain, or integration into a peninsula-wide Spanish state, with his case for Catalonia to remain a part of Spain, even as Catalanism and Catalan pro-independence sentiment gained strength, leading to the bloody crescendo of the *Setmana Tràgica* in Barcelona in the summer of 1909. In the article "Desde Portugal" (From Portugal, 1908), written the same year as his letter to Marquina, Unamuno refers to Oliveira Martins's thesis on the artificiality of Portugal's political separation from the rest of the Iberian Peninsula in comparing Portugal's present state (formally independent but politically and economically embattled) with that of Catalonia (economically secure but desirous of greater autonomy, and even independence):

> Leo estas líneas [de *Portugal Contemporáneo,* de Oliveira Martins] y ... me pongo a pensar en la agorera suerte de esta nación tan poco naturalmente formada, y a la vez agólpanseme a las mientes dolorosos pensamientos sobre lo que en nuestra España está hoy ocurriendo. ¡Portugal y Cataluña! ¡Qué mundo de reflexiones no provoca en un español el juntar estos dos nombres! (*OC* 1: 211)

> I read these lines [from Oliveira Martins's *Contemporary Portugal*] and ... I meditate upon the unkind fate of that nation, which was so unnaturally formed, and at the same time painful thoughts on what is occurring today in Spain pile up in my mind. Portugal and Catalonia! What ideas occur to a Spaniard if he juxtaposes these two names!

In "Por la cultura: Las campañas catalanistas" (In Defence of Culture: The Catalanist Campaigns, 1907) Unamuno again cites Martins in noting that Portugal's renewed independence from Spain in 1640 precluded its merchants from prospering by barring their access to Spanish markets, whereas Catalonia (which launched its own unsuccessful independence revolt the same year) benefited economically from remaining within the Spanish empire:

> Lea usted la magnífica *Historia de Portugal,* de Oliveira Martins, y allí verá usted un sustancioso pasaje en que al tratar del demonio en Portugal de nuestros tres Felipes, el segundo, el tercero y el cuarto, dice el gran historiador que el anhelo de los portugueses era entonces la fusión de la patria con España, el que nuestras colonias estuviesen abiertas a sus mercaderes

> y las suyas a los nuestros, el que los portugueses pudieran ejercer todo cargo público en España, así como en Portugal los españoles … Lo que el gran Oliveira decía haber deseado Portugal lo consiguió desde luego Cataluña; las tierras descubiertas y conquistadas por Castilla fueron campo de sus mercaderes e industrials."
>
> Read Oliveira Martins's magnificent *History of Portugal*, and you will find a long passage in which, writing about the disastrous reign in Portugal of our three Philips, the Second, Third, and Fourth, the great historian states that the desire of the Portuguese people at that time was that their country might be incorporated into Spain, and that our colonies would be opened to their merchants and vice versa, and that the Portuguese would be allowed to hold any public office in Spain, and vice versa … What the great Oliveira stated as the desire of Portugal was achieved by Catalonia; the lands conquered by Castile were open to Catalan commerce and industry) (4: 524).

Unamuno's argument concerning Portugal and Catalonia is clear enough: Portugal has suffered through its "artificial" separation from Spain, whereas Catalonia has prospered. Therefore, Portugal should enter into closer relations with Spain, and perhaps even accept incorporation into Spain, while Catalonia, as an organic part of Spain, should avoid the mistake made by the Portuguese in 1640 and remain within the Spanish state.[15]

Curiously, the First World War seemed to prompt Unamuno to revise his views on the viability and desirability of Portuguese independence, and on the preconditions for Portugal and Spain to establish closer political relations. While, much to Unamuno's chagrin, Spain remained officially neutral in the conflict, with elements of the government supporting Germany, the young Portuguese Republic sent men and arms to fight with France and her allies, whose cause Unamuno enthusiastically supported. In the article "Portugal independiente" (Independent Portugal, 1917). Unamuno argued: "Hoy a España, si quiere convivir fraternalmente con Portugal, si quiere que haya una unión espiritual y de altura en la Península toda ibérica, no le queda sino ponerse resueltamente del lado mismo de que su hermana ibérica se ha puesto" (Today Spain, if it wants to maintain fraternal relations with Portugal, if it wants a high-minded, spiritual union to bind together the whole of the Iberian Peninsula, has no other option than to resolutely take the same side as its Iberian sister nation) (*Escritos* 246).

Beyond joining its "sister nation" Portugal in supporting France, Unamuno called on Spaniards in the article "Deber de España para con Portugal" (Spain's Obligation towards Portugal, 1917) to respect the self-determination of small nations, including Portugal: "Portugal ha ido a la guerra a defender la causa sagrada de la independencia de las pequeñas naciones. Sabía que si Alemania se anexionaba Bélgica y Austria se anexionaba Servia, no tardaría la España imperialista, agermanada, en tratar de anexionarse Portugal" (Portugal has gone to war to defend the sacred cause of the small nations' independence. She knew that if Germany succeeded in annexing Belgium and Austria succeeded in annexing Serbia, then a Germanized, imperialist Spain would not hesitate to try to annex Portugal) (249). No longer flirting with support for Spanish annexation of a decadent Portugal, as he had in his 1908 letter to Marquina, Unamuno called in "Deber de España para con Portugal" for Spanish Iberianists to work towards their goal while respecting Portuguese sovereignty and its national will. He declared: "La unión moral ibérica sólo puede establecerse bajo un régimen de voluntad nacional, de soberanía popular. Y a este régimen se opone la germanofilia española disfrazada de neutralidad incondicional" (An Iberian moral union can only be established on the basis of national will and popular sovereignty, which are antithetical to Spain's Germanophilia, which it disguises behind a façade of unconditional neutrality" (249). Further: "La República portuguesa sabe bien cuáles son sus verdaderos, sus únicos amigos sinceros en España. Y en Portugal saben bien cuál es el único medio de establecer sobre sólidas bases la unión moral, la suprema unidad acaso, la confederación de todas las naciones ibéricas" (The Portuguese Republic knows well who its true, its only friends are in Spain. And the Portuguese know the only way to solidly establish a moral union, and perhaps the supreme union, which would be through the confederation of all the Iberian nations) (249).

Unamuno's pivot from annexationist flirtation in 1908 to a more equitable Iberianist position in 1917, which recalls the federalism of Quental and the young Oliveira Martins, is remarkable. It is difficult to say if Unamuno retained these federalist views into his later years, given that he defended Castilian centralism with increasing assertiveness as he aged. But if Unamuno failed to articulate a coherent position on political Iberianism, he was much more consistent on questions of Iberian culture. Unamuno repeatedly affirmed the existence of an overarching "alma ibérica" (Iberian soul), "común espíritu ibérico" (common Iberian spirit), "patria común ibérica" (common Iberian country), and "génio peninsular" (peninsular genius) (*OC* 3: 946; 4: 536; 7: 1044; *Escritos* 230). Indeed, in a 1915 article, Unamuno described an unrealized project that Maragall had proposed to him to found a journal named *Iberia*, which would have been "escrita en las lenguas literarias de la península: castellano, catalán y portugués" (written in the literary languages of the peninsula: Castilian, Catalan, and Portuguese) (4: 536). Unamuno explained that *Iberia*, a project whose aims recall those of the short-lived *Revista Occidental* edited by Quental and Jaime Batalha Reis in 1875, was to have been

> un órgano de aproximación espiritual entre los pueblos ibéricos de distintas lenguas. Aproximarse espiritualmente es conocerse cada vez mejor. Y mi sueño y ahinco ha sido que nos conozcamos, aunque sea para disentir. Sé que conociéndonos mejor en nuestras diferencias mutuas, llegaremos también mejor a conocer nuestro común espíritu ibérico, lo que nos une frente a la diferencia común con los demás pueblos hermanos en humanidad. (3: 536)

> a vehicle for spiritual approximation between Iberian peoples who speak distinct languages. The closer one comes to another person in spiritual terms the better one knows him. And the dream that I have worked toward has been that we might know one another, if only to disagree. I know that the better we understand our differences from one another, the better we will also understand our common Iberian spirit, which defines us in contradistinction to all the other peoples to whom we are also brothers.

Unamuno's contention that part of his work as a public intellectual had been dedicated to bringing about greater mutual understanding between the Iberian peoples is borne out in his tireless efforts to promote Portuguese writers in Spain; indeed, one of his strategies in doing so seems to have been to affirm that writers like Quental, Oliveira Martins, and Guerra Junqueiro were just as "Iberian" as their Spanish counterparts.[16] Unamuno also acknowledged Portugal and Spain's historically close relationship, as in a 22 August 1914 speech given in Figueira da Foz, in which he declared: "Espanha e Portugal, *Hispania*, pois foi esta a denominação comum que tiveram no tempo dos romanos, levaram … uma vida se não comum, paralela, mais ainda na vida cultural do que na política" (Spain and Portugal, or *Hispania*, for this was the term used to describe them both during the time of the Romans, led … lives that, if not one in the same, were parallel, even more so culturally than politically) (*Escritos* 225). And as we shall see, Unamuno's view that Portugal and Spain were connected at the essential level was of a piece with his dialectical understanding of Iberian history and culture, which would find expression in the vocabulary of "flesh" and "bone" that he so often used to discuss intra-Iberian issues.

Iberia as a Dialectical Unity

Miguel de Unamuno's writing, both on Iberian issues and other topics, is profoundly marked by the idea of dialectic, a polyvalent term that is frequently invoked – and abused – in critical and philosophical discourse. As such, it behooves us to briefly explain how Unamuno understood the term, and how he applied it to the Iberian context. In the Hegelian sense, dialectic is predicated on the confrontation of two desires, ideas, or beings, leading towards the eventual overcoming or sublation (*Aufhebung*) of the contradictions that exist between the two. In this way, the dialectic presents us with, in Alexander Kojève's words, a "double Reality which is nonetheless one because it is equally real in each aspect" (174).

Unamuno openly identified as a dialectical thinker. He explained his affinity for dialectic in "La tradición eterna" (The Eternal Tradition, 1895), the opening essay of *En torno al casticismo*: "Es preferible, creo, seguir [el] método ... de afirmación alternativa de los contradictorios; es preferible hacer resaltar la fuerza de los extremos en el alma del lector para que el medio tome en ella vida, que es resultante de lucha" (It is preferable, I believe, to affirm both contradictory positions; it is preferable to emphasize the strength of the opposing, extreme positions in the reader's soul so that the middle ground can be granted life, as the result of struggle) (*OC* 1: 784). Further, Unamuno wrote in his article "Ni lógica, ni dialéctica, sino polémica" (Neither Logic nor Dialectic, but Polemic, 1915): "La dialéctica está llena de contradicciones íntimas, y por eso es fecunda. La dialéctica es el proceso de las antinomias y las antítesis. La dialéctica es lo menos dogmático que cabe, y por muy apasionada que sea, siempre, en el fondo, es escéptica. La dialéctica supone el diálogo" (Dialectic is full of deep contradictions, and for this reason is fruitful. The dialectical process is built upon antinomies and antitheses. Dialectic is the least dogmatic of methods, and though it is passionate, always, deep down it is skeptical. Dialectic presupposes dialogue) (*OC* 3: 747).[17]

Given the peninsula's conflicted, contradictory history and its tumultuous present, Unamuno viewed dialectical analysis as particularly useful for the study of Spain and Iberia. Unamuno clarifies this point in a comment on Portuguese Hispanist Fidelino de Figueiredo's book *As Duas Espanhas* (The Two Spains, 1932), taken from his late article "El soñar de la esfinge" (The Dream of the Sphinx, 1933). According to Unamuno, Figueiredo's study reveals a "profunda comprensión de que nuestra íntima historia espiritual estriba sobre nuestro carácter contradictorio, *o si se quiere dialéctico y dilemático,* en que somos un pueblo de contradicción" (deep understanding of the fact that our inner, spiritual history is grounded in our contradictory, *or rather dialectical and conflicted* character, which makes us a contradictory people) (*OC* 4: 1353; my emphasis). Further: "Esa dualidad – mejor: contrariedad – que es espíritu de lucha lo llevamos cada uno de los españoles dentro de nosotros mismos y cuanto más nos ensañamos con el adversario es que estamos peleando con el otro que llevamos por dentro" (We Spaniards all bear within us this this duality – or better yet, contrariness – which is our spirit of struggle. The more violently we struggle with our foe, the more violently we actually struggle against the other we bear within us) (1355).

Scholars broadly agree that Unamuno was a dialectical thinker, though the majority associate Unamuno's understanding of dialectical structures and processes with Søren Kierkegaard, for whom dialectical oppositions remain unresolved, and exist in perpetual, agonic tension, as opposed to G.W.F. Hegel, for whom oppositions are resolved through the overcoming, or sublation, of opposing forces.[18] Unamuno was a great reader of Kierkegaard, and drew on the Danish philosopher (along with Antero de Quental and others) in arriving at his understanding of human agony. Nonetheless, as I have argued elsewhere, Hegel, and the Hegelian dialectic in particular, were significant features of Unamuno's thought. The Hegelian stamp on Unamuno's thinking is particularly apparent in his analysis of peninsular affairs, in which he continually calls for regional, linguistic, and cultural distances to resolve themselves into higher unities identified with the Spanish or Iberian "soul," and linguistically, with a Castilian-based synthetic language he termed *sobre-castellano.*[19] As Gerhard Masur observes, "what Unamuno was striving for all his life was precisely the reconciliation of contradictions, the *coincidentia oppositorum*" (343). Unamuno's thinking shifted over time on the question of how best to bring about Spanish national regeneration, moving from a qualified support for regionalism and for the "Europeanization" of peninsular institutions and customs in *En torno al casticismo*, to a later defence of Castilian language and culture as privileged agents of peninsular unification, and an affirmation of Iberia's categorical difference from Europe.[20] However, Unamuno consistently insisted on the peninsula's overarching unity and on the existence of a "común espíritu ibérico" (common Iberian spirit), a sort of composite peninsular *Volksgeist* that he presented as the product of Iberia's various regional personalities – which included Portugal ("La literatura portuguesa contemporánea" [1907]; *OC* 1: 192).[21] Indeed, for Unamuno, the idea of *Volksgeist* not only allowed for, but presupposed contradiction, as he explained in *En torno al casticismo*: "Cuando se afirma que en el espíritu colectivo de un pueblo en el *Volksgeist*, hay algo más que la suma de los caracteres comunes a los espíritus individuales que lo integran, lo que se afirma es que viven en él de un modo o de otro los caracteres *todos* de *todos* sus componentes; se afirma la existencia de un nimbo colectivo, de una hondura del alma común, en que viven y obran todos los sentimientos, deseos y aspiraciones que no concuerdan en forma definida, que no hay pensamiento alguno individual que no repercuta en todos los demás, aun en sus contrarios, que hay una verdadera subconciencia popular" (When one affirms that a people's collective spirit, its *Volksgeist*, is more than the sum of the characteristics that are common to the individual members of that people, what one in effect affirms is that *all* the characteristics of *all* the people can be found in that collective spirit; one affirms that there is a sort of collective cloud, a depth to the common soul, in which all of these feelings reside and are acted out. These desires and aspirations may be opposed to one another, though all individual thoughts mark all other thoughts, even if these thoughts are opposed, for there exists a true popular subconscious) (*OC* 1: 867; author's emphasis).

Unamuno addressed the dialectical nature of Spain, or of Iberia more broadly, in *En torno al casticismo*, a volume concerned with locating and revivifying the bases of Spanish national identity. In "La casta histórica – Castilla" (Our Historical Lineage: Castile, 1895), the second of the essays collected in his 1902 volume, Unamuno opines that "toda unificación procede al compás de la diferenciación interna y al compás de la sumisión del conjunto todo a una unidad superior a él" (all acts of unification follow the rhythms of internal differentiation and submission of all parts to a superior unity) (*OC* 1: 802). Unamuno returns to this issue in his speech "Lo que puede aprender Castilla de los poetas catalanes" (What Castile Can Learn from the Catalan Poets, 1915), in which, referring to the First World War, he states:

> [La guerra] puede llevarnos a plantear de una manera más clara el problema de nuestra personalidad colectiva nacional, el problema de la personalidad de España. O más bien el de sus varias personalidades regionales en lucha unas con otras, *en lucha por integrarse* … Cada uno de nosotros ha sido varios, y una veces tuvo la hegemonía uno de nuestros yos y otras veces el otro. Y así en un pueblo, así en España. *Que es una personalidad colectiva compleja en interna lucha.* El alma común española, concebida y elaborada en controversia, en contradicción, en guerra civil, se está siempre haciendo. (*OC* 9: 318; my emphasis)

> [The war] grants us the opportunity to more clearly pose the question of our collective national personality, the problem of the Spanish personality, or rather, the question of its various regional personalities, which struggle against each other, *which struggle toward integration* … All of us have been many different people, and at times our I's have exerted hegemony over the others. This also holds for peoples, for Spain. *Spain is a complex collective personality marked by internal struggles.* The collective Spanish soul, which was conceived and formed amid controversy, contradiction, and civil war, is in a perpetual process of formation.

For Unamuno, the process of Spanish or Iberian integration, brought about through the dialectical confrontation of the peninsula's regional personalities, will necessarily lead to the supplanting of Iberia's regional languages – which for Unamuno included Portuguese, despite its status as the official language of a sovereign nation state – by *sobre-castellano*, a genuinely Spanish and thus truly Iberian composite language to be based in Castilian but which would incorporate linguistic contributions from other peninsular languages as well as the dialects of Spanish and Portuguese spoken in the New World. As Unamuno explained in his controversial "Discurso en los Juegos Florales celebrado en Bilbao el Día 26 de Agosto de 1901" (Speech delivered at the Floral Games held in Bilbao on 26 August 1901): "Del castellano, pronunciado y construído por distintos pueblos que habitan en ambos mundos dilatados dominios, surgirán, no distintas lenguas … sino el *sobre-castellano*, la lengua española o hispanoamericana, una y varia, flexible y rica, dilatada como sus dominios" (From the Castilian spoken and built by the various peoples that live over a wide swathe of both the New and the Old World, there will emerge not various languages … but *sobre-castellano*, the Spanish or Spanish American language, one and various, flexible, and rich, as wide as the lands in which it is spoken) (*OC* 4: 242; my emphasis). For Unamuno, the project of Iberian linguistic unification implied this only apparently paradoxical corollary: that all peninsular writers should familiarize themselves with Iberia's three principal languages – Castilian, Portuguese, and Catalan – and should follow his example and read broadly from "Iberian literature," which he defined as "castellana, portuguesa y catalana" (Castilian, Portuguese, and Catalan), always in the original (*OC* 1: 194). Despite his resolute defence of the long-term supremacy of the Castilian (or super-Castilian) language, Unamuno called on native speakers of Castilian to learn Portuguese and Catalan, which he termed "lenguas, hermanas de la nuestra castellana" (languages that are siblings of our Castilian) ("Diccionario diferencial catalán-castellano" [1916]; *OC* 4: 545).

Unamuno's argument is quite revealing of his broader view of the Iberian Peninsula, which in its reference to Castilian, Portuguese, and Catalan as the peninsula's three fundamental languages appears to have been informed by the tripartite Iberianism developed within Catalan Iberianist circles, and which he presumably absorbed from Maragall.[22] Moreover, Unamuno's comments demonstrate how he invested a high degree of dialectical potential in the oppositional (but also complementary) relationships between Castile and Catalonia, and Castile and Portugal – and on a broader scale, between Iberia and Europe.[23] In this respect Unamuno follows the examples of Quental and especially Oliveira Martins in affirming a common Iberian or peninsular spirit, consciousness, or "genius." For Unamuno, the Iberian *Volksgeist* would be strengthened by the efforts of intellectuals to overcome the peninsula's internal divisions, including the distinction between the Portuguese and Spanish languages – which, according to Unamuno, are "en rigor y en el fondo una misma" (in truth and deep down, the same), and whose differences were for him more superficial than genuine ("Español-portugués" [1914]; *OC* 4: 527). For this reason, Unamuno laments the Portuguese language's "absurda ortografía etimológica" (absurd etymological orthography) as a misguided effort, presumably by nationalistic Portuguese linguists, to "diferenciar la lengua portuguesa de la castellana mucho más de lo que se diferencian [en la realidad]" (differentiate the Portuguese and Castilian languages much more than they differ [in reality]). Further, he interprets the continued popularity of anti-Spanish jokes in Portugal (*espanholadas*) and anti-Portuguese jokes in Spain (*portuguesadas*) as symptomatic of the two peoples' mutual alienation ("Sobre el criollismo: A guisa de prólogo" [1903]; *OC* 4: 579; "El pueblo español" [1902]; 3: 716). In order to bring into relief Iberia's overarching language and personality, Unamuno argues, "los españoles debemos leer a los portugueses en su propia lengua, y no traducidos. El esfuerzo para ello necesario es pequeñísimo y se lo debemos a *nuestra común madre Iberia o Hispania*" (we Spaniards ought to read Portuguese [writers] in their own language, not in translation. The effort to do so is minimal and we owe it to *our common mother, Iberia or Hispania*) ("Prólogo a *Constanza* de Eugenio de Castro [1913]; *OC* 8: 1016; my emphasis). Unamuno would return to this theme in an article written shortly before his death, "Nueva vuelta a Portugal [IV]" (Another Trip to Portugal [IV], 1935):

> Hasta en lo escrito he propugnando que no hay por qué traducir del castellano al portugués y viceversa. El esfuerzo [de leer un texto en portugués] ... se compensa con que el portugués [los castellanoparlantes] encontraremos rincones y recovecos de nuestro idioma que no los descubrimos directamente. Aprender portugués es un buen recurso para enriquecer nuestro castellano. (*OC* 4: 1362)

> I have argued in writing that there is no need to translate from Castilian to Portuguese and vice versa. The effort [of reading a text in Portuguese] ... is compensated by the fact that in Portuguese, we [Castilian speakers] find hidden nooks and crannies of our language that cannot otherwise be directly perceived. Learning Portuguese is a good way to enrich our Castilian.

In sum, Unamuno argued that the Portuguese and Castilian languages should be brought into dialectical opposition, so that their differences might be subsumed into an eventual synthesis. In his article "Español-portugués" (Spanish-Portuguese, 1914), Unamuno characterized the future of Portuguese and Castilian as follows: "Todo choque entre ellas acabaría – o acabará, ¿quién sabe? – en una penetración mutua; el español se aportuguesaría más o menos, el portugués se castellanizaría. Sería una obra de integración" (Any clash between them would result – or will result, who knows? – in mutual penetration; Spanish would become more or less like Portuguese, and Portuguese would become like Castilian. It would be a case of integration) (*OC* 4: 528).

By this point the structural importance Unamuno granted to Iberia, understood as a dialectical unity, should be clear. By extension, the necessary participation of Portugal as Spain's counterpoint and mirror image in Unamuno's Iberianist project should be apparent. Referring obliquely to Portugal's role vis-à-vis Spain, Unamuno made an observation to Teixeira de Pascoaes in a 19 December 1905 letter that encapsulates his dialectical understanding of Iberia and his views on Spanish–Portuguese relations: "Portugal me interesa mucho porque me interesa España" (Portugal interests me a great deal because Spain interests me) (quoted in Morejón 363). I shall explore the nature of the Portugal/Spain binary, as conceived by Unamuno, presently, and will demonstrate how Unamuno utilizes a corporeal language to describe Portugal's dual function as a counterpoint and complement to Spain.

Portugal and Spain, Flesh and Bone

I have argued elsewhere that images of *carne y hueso,* or "flesh and bone," appear with such frequency in Unamuno, and have such resonance, that they can considered typifying features of his prose.[24] Unamuno's best-known usage of the term appears at the opening of *Del sentimiento trágico de la vida,* in which he affirms the centrality of the "hombre de carne y hueso" (man of flesh and bone). Beyond this example, references to "flesh and bone" appear throughout Unamuno's work, whether in combined form (*carne y hueso*) or in contraposition to one another (*carne/hueso*), as one of a chain of dialectically opposed terms in which the Spain/Portugal binary features as well.

For Unamuno, the word *carne* tends to suggest substance, that is, the materiality that gives meaning to the ideas it inhabits, as in the biblical image of the "Word ... made flesh" (John 1:14). For instance, in the opening pages of *En torno al casticismo* Unamuno declares: "Hay que mirarla [i.e., una idea] por de dentro, viva, caliente, con alma y personalidad" (you must examine [an idea] from within, while it lives and breathes, as having both a soul and a personality) (*OC* 1: 784). In contradistinction, for Unamuno *hueso* refers to the basic architecture of the individual or community, to man or mankind reduced, as one would say in English, to "bare bones." For Unamuno, who wrote that "el campo es una metáfora" (the countryside is a metaphor), Iberia's variegated landscapes serve as privileged terrain for illustrating the metaphorical interaction of "flesh" and "bone," with Unamuno identifying "bone" with the arid landscape of Castile, and "flesh" with Iberia's verdant Galaico–Portuguese Atlantic Coast.[25]

Beginning with "bony" Castile, Unamuno describes the inhabitants of this difficult, skeletal region as follows in "La casta histórica – Castilla," the second essay collected in *En torno al casticismo*: "Allí dentro [de la llanura castellana] vive una casta de complexión *seca, dura y sarmentosa*, tostada por el sol y curtida por el frío, una casta de hombres *sobrios*, producto de una larga selección por las heladas de crudísimos inviernos y una serie de penurias periódicas, hechos a la inclemencia del cielo y a la pobreza de la vida" (There lives there [on the Castilian plain] a tribe of *dry, hard, and gnarled* appearance, burnt by the sun and cut by the cold, a tribe of *sober* men, the product of a long process of selection carried out by the cold of the brutally harsh winters and by regular deprivation, men formed by an unkind sky and from the poverty of life) (*OC* 1: 811; my emphasis).

Significantly, the same qualities Unamuno attributed to the Castilian land and people also appear in his descriptions of the Castilian language. The following passage, taken from the suggestively titled text "Sobre la dureza del idioma castellano" (On the Hardness of the Castilian Language, 1899), demonstrates how Unamuno extended the "bony" qualities he ascribed elsewhere to Castile and Castilians to their tongue:

> Muchas veces se ha dicho que la lengua castellana es una lengua *rígida y ósea*, sin matices ni cambiantes ... una lengua que por su estructura misma propende a los vastos periodos oratorios, campanudos y resonantes, o a cierta concisión *angulosa y seca*; pero que resiste las caricias ondulantes, las veladuras penumbrosas, la sutil ironía ... Todo lo que el castellano toca se cristaliza al punto; todo lo que él dice se hace dogma. Como en los vastos páramos castellanos o como en los cuadros de Ribera, no hay en él medias tintas; todo es claroscuro, todo adquiere ese relieve *duro* que da el sol al separar, con las sombras que les hace proyectar, a los objetos. Cada uno de éstos adquiere una individualidad *decisiva y firme;* no hay envolvente nimbo que los una y armonice en superior conjunto. (*OC* 4: 332; my emphasis)[26]

> It has been said many times that Castilian is a *rigid and bony* language, lacking shades and colours ... a language whose structure predisposes it toward long, bombastic and resonant orations, or toward a certain *angular and dry* concision, and a language that resists soft caresses, shadowy regions, and subtle irony ... Everything the Castilian touches takes on a crystalline form, everything he says becomes dogma. As on the vast Castilian plains or in Ribera's painting, there are no half tones in Castilian things. Everything is black and white, everything acquires a *hardness* that

> shows in the play of sun and shadow. Each object acquires its own *decisive and firm* individuality. There is no cloud that takes all of them in, uniting them and bringing the overarching whole into harmony.

This passage makes clear that, notwithstanding the positive qualities Unamuno attributes to the Castilian language, landscape, and people (solidity, forthrightness, masculine strength, and so on), for him "Castilian things" lack subtlety of meaning, suggestiveness, and amorous softness, and therefore cannot be seen as self-sufficient. Hence the need for Castilian to reach out to other Iberian tongues and traditions in the interest of linguistic and spiritual completeness, an ideal that for Unamuno would find its ultimate linguistic expression in the synthetic language of *sobre-castellano*. For Unamuno, it is only through the dialectical confrontation of the Castilian language (and by proxy, landscape, and character) with the languages (and landscapes, and characters) of Iberia's other regions, and through their eventual resolution into a higher unity, that Castilian can become truly Spanish and therefore Iberian.

Summarizing my argument thus far, we find in Unamuno several connotations for the word *hueso*, or bone. These include the ideas of *essence*, *dryness*, *hardness*, *sobriety*, and *severity*. Unamuno locates these connotations within an identifiably Castilian natural, cultural, and linguistic landscape. Given the dialectical interdependence of "flesh" and "bone" in Unamuno, we may extrapolate a series of opposed but complementary connotations for the word *carne*: *substance*, *moisture*, *softness*, *flexibility* or *expansiveness*, and *mildness*. Considering Unamuno's significant emotional and intellectual investment in Portugal, it is not difficult to determine which portion of the Iberian Peninsula he identified with the notion of "flesh" and its connotations of substance, softness, and mildness. This was Portugal, the proverbial "país de brandos costumes" (country of mild customs).[27]

Let us turn, then, to the carnal side of Unamuno's dialectic of flesh and bone, which the Basque writer locates spiritually in the mild, verdant climes of northern Portugal and Galicia, which, as explained in this book's previous chapter, Unamuno viewed as intrinsically linked. In the 1908 article "Braga," later collected in *Por tierras de Portugal y de España*, Unamuno recounts his visit to this Portuguese city, and provides a suggestive description of the Minho region, which marks an implied contrast with the landscape of "bony" Castile: "Y allá fuí, atravesando tierras de esa *mimosa* provincia del Miño. Verdura por todas partes; las vides enlazadas a los chopos entre maizales; más allá *suaves lomas* cubiertos de pinos, y a lo lejos las colinas expirando entre niebla. Tierra de verdura y de niebla. *Tierra sin huesos*" (And there I went, journeying through this *tender* province that is the Minho. Green all around; the grape vines winding around the black poplars, placed between cornfields; farther on *gentle rises* are covered with pine trees, and on the horizon hills disappear into the mist. A land of greenery and mist. *A land without bones*")[28] (*OC* 1: 224; my emphasis).

Unamuno's descriptions of the Portuguese (or Galaico–Portuguese) landscape, people, and culture are nearly always presented in implied or explicit opposition to Spain, which Unamuno often presents as synonymous with Castile. For instance, one may cite Unamuno's politically incorrect, albeit positive, characterization of Portuguese women from the article "Braga." Unamuno muses, "tiene la portuguesa algo que sólo se expresa con una palabra, portuguesa también, y es *meigice*, blandura ... No es la rígida majeza de la española" (There is something about the Portuguese woman that can only be expressed in one Portuguese word: this is *meigice*, softness ... She lacks the rigid majesty of the Spanish woman) (1: 227–8; author's emphasis).[29] Similarly, in "Las animas del Purgatorio en Portugal" (Souls in Purgatory in Portugal, 1908), Unamuno describes Spanish Catholicism as more rigid, austere, and severe than the softer, more approachable variant practised across the border in Portugal, and invokes his friend, the Portuguese poet Guerra Junqueiro, in making this comparison: "El cristo español, me decía una vez Guerra Junqueiro, está siempre en su papel trágico: jamás baja de la cruz donde, *cadavérico*, extiende sus brazos y alarga sus piernas cubiertas de sangre; el Cristo portugués anda por costas y prados y montañas, y de vez en cuando, para llenar su papel, se cuelga un rato de la cruz" (The Spanish Christ, Guerra Junqueiro once told me, always plays his tragic role: he never steps down from the cross where, *skeletal*, he spreads his arms and legs, which are covered in blood; the Portuguese Christ walks along the coasts and through the meadows and mountains, and once in a while, in order to fulfil his obligation, spends some time on the cross) (*OC* 1: 213; my emphasis).

Turning to the issue of language, Unamuno makes several comparisons between Castilian and Portuguese, and often ties these comparisons to an apocryphal statement attributed to Miguel de Cervantes, to the effect that the Portuguese language could be described as "el castellano sin huesos" (Castilian without bones).[30] In the article "'Las sombras,' de Teixeira de Pascoaes" (1908) Unamuno writes: "Dijo Cervantes del idioma portugués que es el castellano sin huesos, y retrucándole, cabría decir que el castellano es el portugués osificado" (Cervantes said of the Portuguese language that it is a Castilian without bones, and in response, we might say that Castilian is ossified Portuguese) (1: 194).[31] Unamuno's characterization of Portuguese and Castilian phonology complements his views on the "spirit" of the Portuguese and Castilian peoples. While he describes Portuguese as "dulce" (sweet), mild, and feminine, he views Castilian as harsh, severe, and masculine (*OC* 11: 81). And in the article "Guarda" (1908), Unamuno contrasts the "dengosos acentos de la triste habla portuguesa" (coy sounds of the melancholy Portuguese language) with "los recortados de la recia habla castellana" (the clipped sounds of the hard Castilian tongue) (1: 242). While Unamuno's characterization of Portuguese as "dengoso" recalls the Galaico–Portuguese quality of *meigice* (in Portuguese, *meiguice*), his description of Castilian as "recortado" suggests a certain elevated, hard assertiveness or abruptness. Likewise in poetry, Unamuno contrasts his own Spanish-language compositions with the Portuguese verses of Teixeira de Pascoaes: "No hallaréis en sus composiciones esas estrofas densas, compactas, de espesísimo cristal, esculpidas, diamantinas, tales como se encuentran en [el poeta italiano] Carducci y como yo me he esforzado por hacer en mis propias poesías; las de Teixeira de Pascoaes se alargan y desvanecen como sombras de crepúsculo" (You will not find in his compositions the dense, compact, crystalline verses one encounters in [the Italian poet] Carducci and which I have tried to bring to my own poems; Teixeira de Pascoaes's poems stretch themselves out and fade away like shadows at dusk) (1: 195).

These examples should serve as sufficient evidence that Unamuno, in his prose pieces on Portugal and Castile, and in his essays on intra-Iberian relations, constructs two conceptual chains, identifying one with the "bone" side of the *carne y hueso* binary, and the other with the "flesh" side. Geographically, Unamuno identifies the first of these metaphorical chains with Castile or Spain, and the second with Galicia and Portugal. These chains may be represented as follows:

> **Bone**/Essence/Dryness/Hardness/Rigidity/Assertiveness/Severity/Masculinity/**Castile-Spain**
>
> **Flesh**/Substance/Wetness/Softness/Flexibility/Passivity/Mildness/Femininity/**Galicia-Portugal**

Our final step in this chapter will be to explain how Unamuno's corporeal language operates as a function of his dialectical understanding of the Iberian Peninsula, whose overarching unity he viewed as dependent on the demarcation and overcoming of its internal divisions and contradictions.

Dialectical Unity, Corporeal Ties

One of the principles of the Hegelian dialectic is that a superior or overarching unity (in this case, the Iberian Peninsula) is achieved through the sublation (*Aufhebung*), or overcoming, of the conflict between opposed desires, beings, or ideas. We can infer that terms placed into dialectical confrontation with one another necessarily maintain a relationship of mutual dependence or contamination, and that the two carry within them at least trace amounts of the Other, an idea that recalls the Thomistic notion of *mutua inhaesio* (mutual indwelling). If we apply this idea to the conceptual chains identified at the end of the previous section, it follows that we should be able to locate moments in Unamuno's writing in which the ideas of *carne* and *hueso*, linked respectively to Castile–Spain and Galicia–Portugal, are presented as mutually dependent or contaminated by one another, as evidence for Unamuno's utilization of a vocabulary of *carne y hueso* within a broadly dialectical analytical framework.

We might begin by citing Unamuno's late essay "País, paisaje y paisanaje" (Country, Landscape, and Human Landscape, 1933). Here Unamuno describes Spain as a human hand, with Spain's five principal rivers representing its "fingers": "Esta mano tendida al mar poniente … es la tierra de España. Sus cinco dedos líquidos, ¿Miño-pulgar? ¿Duero-índice? ¿Tajo-el del corazón? Guadiana y Guadalquivir … Y, sobre ella, sobre esa mano, la palma azul de la mano de Dios, el cielo natural" (This hand, facing the Western sea … is Spain. Its five liquid fingers: is the Miño the thumb? The Duero the index finger? The Tagus the middle finger? The Guadiana and Guadalquivir … And in the sky above it, above this hand, lies the blue palm of the hand of God) (1: 705). The immediate object of Unamuno's short essay, written during the tumultuous years of the Second Spanish Republic (1931–9), is the Spanish nation state, which he describes as united by a common "misión" (mission) and "historia" (history) irrespective of its political divisions or the government in power. Indeed, Portugal is not mentioned once in the text. Nonetheless, Portugal and the Portuguese people, culture, and language are strongly implicated in Unamuno's corporeal description of Spain. Four of the five rivers invoked by Unamuno flow through

Portugal. Most of Iberia's Atlantic coast, that is, the terrain on which the peninsula "fac[es] the Western sea," is Portuguese. The rest lies in Galicia, whose manifold historical, cultural, and linguistic ties to Portugal, explored in the previous chapter, were acknowledged by Unamuno. And Unamuno's closing descriptions of Spain as a "lengua de tierra en el extremo occidente de Eurasia" (a tongue of land on the extreme western edge of Eurasia) and a "mano que cogió a América" (hand that grabbed hold of America) make little sense unless Portugal is brought into Unamuno's understanding of the category of "Spain."[32]

In "País, paisaje y paisanaje," the divinely sanctioned, overarching unity of Spain (and by proxy, Iberia) is reflected both in its *paisaje* (landscape) and *paisanaje* (human landscape), which reinforce one another and contribute to the integrity of the whole, as do the peninsula's "flesh" (here, rivers) and "bones" (mountains):

> En esta mano, entre sus dedos, entre las rayas de su palma, vive una humanidad; a este paisaje le llena y da sentido y sentimientos humanos un paisanaje. Sueñan aquí, sueñan la tierra en que viven y mueren, de que viven y de que mueren unos pobres hombres ... El espíritu, el pneuma, el alma histórica no se hace sino sobre el ánima, la psique, el alma natural, geográfica y geológica si se quiere. (*OC* 1: 706)[33]

> Human beings live in this hand, between its fingers, between the lines of its palm: a human landscape fills in and grants meaning and human emotions to the landscape. Here a group of poor men dream, they dream of the land in which they live and die, and through which they live and die ... The historical spirit, *pneuma*, or soul can only be built atop the natural, geographic, or – if you like – geological spirit, soul, or psyche.

For Unamuno, Portugal's connection with the rest of the Iberian Peninsula is achieved both through "carnal" and "bony" forces, represented in his essay by the peninsula's rivers and mountains. In one of the last essays he wrote on Portugal, "Lisboa y Toledo" (Lisbon and Toledo, 1935), Unamuno stated that Portugal "está unido al resto de la Península Ibérica por sus espinazos rocosos en parte, mas sobre todo por los grandes ríos que enlazan ambos países, atravesándolos" (is joined to the rest of the Iberian Peninsula in part by rocky spines [i.e., mountains], but especially by the great rivers that, crossing both countries, tie them together) (*OC* 1: 717). This is not to say that Unamuno defines Portugal and Castile in equal proportion by their "carnal" rivers and "bony" mountains. Rather, as we have seen, the characteristic note of the Portuguese landscape and character in Unamuno is its carnality, while he understands Castile as particularly skeletal or bony. What Unamuno's language of mutual dependence and his dialectical understanding of the Iberian Peninsula imply is that Portugal is connected with its opposing term (Castile) through the encounter of two images, that is, flesh and bone. Moreover, Unamuno believed that Portugal needed to look east, beyond the "pequena casa lusitana" (little Lusitanian house), as Camões put it, outside of its corner of the peninsula, in order to find the compensatory Castilian qualities (hardness, rigidity, severity) that were the inverse of its own typifying characteristics (softness, flexibility, mildness). Likewise, Castile needed to look west, to Portugal, to seek out those qualities that would compensate for its own natural, cultural, and linguistic shortcomings – or put another way, would check its excesses.

By extension, Unamuno's application to the Iberian Peninsula of the Hegelian dialectic, in which opposed terms, desires, or beings confront one another as a precondition for mutual recognition and eventual synthesis, implies that a certain degree of mutual contamination should be present in the Portuguese and Castilian terrestrial and human landscapes. Thus, qualities that Unamuno attributes in the first instance to Castile should be found in residual form in his descriptions of Portugal's landscape and literature, albeit as discordant notes. One finds an example of this contamination of the Castilian into the Portuguese landscape in Unamuno's essay "O Bom Jesus do Monte" (The Good Jesus of the Mountain, 1908). Recalling the poet Tomás Ribeiro's description of Portugal in his epic poem *Dom Jaime ou a dominação de Castela* (Dom Jaime, or the Domination of Castile, 1862), as "jardim da Europa, à beira-mar plantado" (Europe's garden, planted by the sea), Unamuno remarks that Portugal's mountainous Serra do Marão, "recordaba, sobre todo, aquella astera, noble, huesuda y solemne Castilla, que es todo menos un jardín" (recalled, above all else, the austere, noble, bony, and solemn Castile, which is anything but a garden) (1: 232). And in the article "La literatura portuguesa contemporánea" (Contemporary Portuguese Literature, 1907), Unamuno remarked that the verses of Antero de Quental, one of his favourite poets, are "algo huesoso y duro con frecuencia: el elemento conceptual y abstracto aparece muy descarnado, no siempre bien recubierto por la fantasía" (often somewhat bony and hard: conceptual and abstract elements are presented in barebones fashion, and are not always covered with imaginative touches) (1: 190). Here

Unamuno's descriptions of the Serra do Marão and of Quental's poetry serve both to connect Portugal to Castile at the level of imagery, and to signal the exceptional or discordant quality of these "bony" characteristics in a Portuguese environment defined by the verdant softness of its landscape and the nebulous lyricism of its poetry, the latter quality being typified by Teixeira de Pascoaes.

In his 1908 prose piece "Braga," later included in *Por tierras de Portugal y de España* (1911), Miguel de Unamuno makes the following, revealing statement regarding his relationship with Portugal: "Yo no sé en qué consiste; pero en esta tierra portuguesa, casi todos aquellos con quienes cruzo me parecen antiguos conocidos: tienen caras que he visto en alguna otra parte" (I'm not sure why, but in this land of Portugal, almost everyone I meet seems like an old friend: I have seen their faces before, somewhere else) (*OC* 1: 227). To my mind, this declaration encapsulates both the promise and peril of Unamuno's attitude towards Portugal, and of his understanding of intra-Iberian relations and Iberianism more broadly. On the one hand, Unamuno's deep affection for Portugal, a land of "old friends" he has yet to meet, is obvious. This desire to actively engage with Portugal led Unamuno to make numerous trips to the country, build an impressive collection of Portuguese books, befriend Portuguese writers, both established and emerging, and serve as a sort of evangelist for Portuguese literature and thought in Spain. In short, Unamuno loved Portugal, and amassed the contacts, books, and first-hand and textual knowledge to prove it. But one also detects in Unamuno's statement the unifying impetus that underlay a good deal of his thought, and that when applied to peninsular issues, would see Portugal incorporated, if not politically then at least in terms of its language and culture, into an Iberia at least implicitly identified with the Spanish state and grounded in a Castilian language and culture that Unamuno understood as normative within the confines of the peninsula. In the next chapter we will turn to a writer who, though Unamuno's long-term epistolary partner, contested the teleological and normative dimensions of his friend's Iberianism. Instead, Joan Maragall looked to Iberianism as a means to advance the cause of cultural and perhaps political autonomy for his native Catalonia, while continuing to engage with Spain and reaching out to the Catalans' maritime cousins, the Portuguese.

Chapter Five

Joan Maragall: Iberian Hymns from Catalonia

In his study *El naixement de l'iberisme catalanista* (The Birth of Catalanist Iberianism, 1997), Víctor Martínez-Gil observes the following regarding Joan Maragall (1860–1911), the Barcelona-born poet, journalist, and translator whose popular, patriotic verses and public advocacy for Catalan language, culture, and nationhood transformed this "enamorado de Cataluña" (lover of Catalonia) into a symbol of Catalan identity and nation aspiration: "L'iberisme en Maragall és un punt d'arribada, una solució per a una qüestió crucial que el preocuparà des de sempre: les relacions entre Catalunya i Espanya" (Iberianism for Maragall is a point of arrival, a solution to a crucial problem that had long preoccupied him: the relationship between Catalonia and Spain) (204).[1] As Martínez-Gil explains, Maragall's early interest in articulating a distinct, self-sufficient *national* identity for Catalonia through poems such as "La Sardana" (The *Sardana*), "La Vaca Cega" (The Blind Cow), and "El Cant de la Senyera" (The Song of the *Senyera*),[2] and through his publicly-minded journalism, which he wrote in both Catalan and Castilian, was strongly impacted by Spain's 1898 military defeat by the United States. The *desastre* prompted Maragall, along with contemporaries from across the ideological spectrum of Catalanism,[3] including the left-leaning Valentí Almirall, author of *Lo Catalanisme* (1884), and the right-leaning Enric Prat de la Riba, author of *La nacionalitat catalana* (1906), to join their Castilian or Castile-identified counterparts in the *Generación del 98*, including Maragall's long-term epistolary partner Miguel de Unamuno and Azorín (*né* José Martínez Ruíz),[4] in addressing the crisis of the Spanish state and in assessing possible paths towards regeneration. In the Catalan case, these proposals included calls for greater Catalan autonomy within, or even independence from, Spain.

Concretely, Maragall proposed in his "Oda a Espanya" (Ode to Spain, 1898) and in his journalism from the same period that Catalan nationalism, language, and culture, which he identified with pragmatism and material prosperity, would grant a Spain stripped of its final American colonies access to European modernity, and might thereby serve as a "via regeneracionista" (path towards regeneration) for Spain in the wake of military disaster and economic disruption (Martínez-Gil, *El naixement* 205). As Robert Hughes puts it, poems like "Oda a Espanya" transformed Maragall into "the lyric and wounded voice of the desire for 'regeneration,' the poetic conscience of those who felt that Spain, morally speaking, had hit rock bottom" (447). In addition, these texts embodied Maragall's typically Catalanist frustration with the Spanish government, which, presumably acting on entrenched Castilian values, had failed to secure a place for the country in the modern political order by transforming Spain into an at least minimally representative and coherent nation state. In the opening stanza of the poem, written shortly before the culmination of Spain's military defeat, Maragall interrogates Spain as follows: "Escolta, Espanya, – la veu d'un fill / que et parla en llengua – no castellana; / parlo en la llengua – que m'ha donat / la terra aspra" (Hear, Spain, the voice of a son / who speaks to you in a language that is not Castilian; / I speak in the language that the rough land / has given me) (*OC* 1: 171).

There is considerable debate regarding how Maragall conceived of his relationship with Spain in the poem, and whether the "Oda a Espanya" can be read as a call for greater Catalan engagement in a beleaguered Spain, or for Catalan autonomy or even independence.[5] On the one hand, Maragall presents himself as a "fill" (son) of Spain, and he advises the country to "retornar-se" (return to itself) in the wake of disaster. Maragall's filial identification and solicitous stance imply both affinity with and concern for Spain as a *Mater Dolorosa*.[6] On the other hand, Maragall concludes the poem by suggesting that his loyalty is conditional, implying that if Spain fails to hear his message (i.e., if it fails to accept Catalanism as a regenerative path and insists on marginalizing Catalan language and culture), he is willing to go his own way: "No entens aquesta llengua – que et parla entre perills? / Has desaprès d'entendre an els teus fills? / Adéu Espanya!" (Can you not understand this language that I speak to you in this time of peril? / Can you no longer understand your sons? / Then farewell, Spain!) (172). Much as Maragall's Iberianism is not always easy to pin down, his position vis-à-vis Spain as presented in the "Oda a Espanya" likely lies somewhere between the Spanish regenerationism of Unamuno and his colleagues in the *Generación del 98*, and a Catalanist movement that was pressing Madrid in increasingly assertive tones for greater autonomy, and that featured adherents who viewed independence as a viable path forward for Catalonia. Martínez-Gil, for instance, offers that in the "Oda a Espanya," "Maragall opta ... per la separació, però, i això em sembla important, només després d'haver ofert el catalanisme com a via regeneracionista per a Espanya" (Maragall opts ... for separation, but – and this is quite important – only after having offered Catalanism as a regenerative path for Spain) (*El naixement* 205). And as Joan-Lluís Marfany remarks, Maragall's ambivalence in his "cants de la guerra" (songs of war) "correspon a una ambivalència essencial del nacionalisme català, migpartit entre la temptació de la independència essencial i una més pragmàtica política d'intervenció a Espanya" (corresponds to an essential ambivalence within Catalan nationalism, between the temptation of essential independence and a more pragmatic policy of intervention within Spain) ("Joan Maragall" 218).

Maragall's preoccupation with 1898, and his interest in regeneration and awareness of regeneration's resonance in *fin-de-siècle* Spain, along with, perhaps, his epistolary relationships with Unamuno and Azorín, have caused some scholars to follow Unamuno's lead and claim Maragall for Spanish letters and for the *Generación del 98*. For instance, Pedro Laín Entralgo terms Maragall "la insigne figura catalana de esa generación insigne" (the outstanding Catalan member of this outstanding generation) (13), and "el primogénito de la generación del 98" (the eldest member of the Generation of 1898) (26). Indeed, in his poetry and journalism Maragall bears certain hallmarks of the *Generación del 98*, among these his emotional reaction to Spain's military defeat, and his awareness of the need for profound change.[7] Maragall's anguish is apparent in his "Cant del retorn" (1899), which along with the "Oda a Espanya" and "Els adéus" (Goodbyes, 1896), comprise his three poetic "songs of war" written between 1896 and 1899.[8] Reflecting on Spain's loss of Cuba and Puerto Rico, which reinforced Catalan nationalism even as it negatively impacted commerce and employment in Catalonia,[9] Maragall declares: "Adéu, oh tu, Amèrica, terra furienta! / Som dèbils per tu" (Farewell to you, oh America, you violent land / We are too weak for you). Further, he characterizes the war – and perhaps Spanish colonialism on the whole – as "la trista lluita sense fe ni glòria / d'un poble que es perd" (the woeful struggle, without faith or glory / of a damned people) (*OC* 1: 173). In the article

"La regeneración política" (Political Regeneration, 1899), Maragall notes that "a la obsesión de la guerra ha sucedido la obsesión de la regeneración" (obsession with the war has given way to an obsession with regeneration), and he compares Spain in the diagnostic language of literary realism-naturalism to an ailing body: "La naturaleza es tan fuerte y tan misteriosa, que muchas veces la voz de la salud habla por boca de la enfermedad; es decir, que el enfermo, entre las extravagancias de su delirio, pide el remedio que realmente le conviene. Por esto hay que atender ahora al prolongado delirio de España para acoger cualquiera indicación provechosa que pudiera salir de sus desordenados discursos" (nature is so powerful and works so mysteriously that often health speaks through illness; that is to say, the sick man, in the middle of his delirium, sometimes calls for the treatment he really needs. For this reason we must pay close attention to Spain's prolonged delirium in order to extract some useful bit of information from its disordered soliloquies) (2: 575–6).[10]

Marfany pushes back against Entralgo's position, arguing that it would be "una greu distorsió" (a grave distortion) to include Maragall in the *Generación del 98*. He elaborates: "És cert que Maragall comparteix amb alguns dels seus contemporanis castellans alguns trets ideològics, entre ells el nacionalisme. També ho és, però, que entre d'altres coses, el separa una de fonamental: mentre que ells són nacionalistes espanyols, Maragall és un nacionalista català" (It is true that Maragall shares with his Castilian contemporaries certain ideological traits, one of them being nationalism. It is also true, however, that among those things that distinguish him [from them], there is this fundamental difference: while they are Spanish nationalists, Maragall is a Catalan nationalist) ("Joan Maragall" 216). This argument, which hinges on a too-simplistic distinction between Spanish and Catalan nationalism, and the notion that the two are mutually incompatable, fails to capture the nuances of Maragall's self-positioning as both a Catalan and Spaniard, and obscures his preoccupation with both Catalonia and Spain. The Catalan writer Gaziel (*né* Agustí Calvet Pascual) similarly rejected Maragall's possible affiliation with the *Generación del 98*, noting the optimism that underlies Maragall's view of Catalonia's future, and contrasting this to the pessimism evinced by writers like Unamuno, Ángel Ganivet, and Ramiro de Maeztu around the time of Spain's military defeat:

> Ell escollí un camí diametralment oposat al que seguien els escriptors de la *generación del 98*, resignats a acceptar com un fet la pàtria morta.

A pàtria morta, es digué Margall, pàtria nova. I la seva *Oda a Espanya*, que data justament de l'any fatídic, del 1898, és l'expressió perfecta d'aquell moment: l'adéu a l'ahir ominós, que s'enfonsa i es perd en la tenebra, i ensems el clam vers un demà ple de llum, que el poeta evoca amb fe de visionari. (146)

He chose a path diametrically opposed to that followed by the writers of the *Generación del 98*, who were resigned to accept the country's death as an accomplished fact. A dead country, Maragall said, means a new country. And his *Oda a Espanya*, which was written during that fateful year of 1898, is the perfect expression of that moment in history: it bids farewell to an ominous path, which sinks into and is lost in the darkness, and amid the clamour he can see a bright future, which the poet evokes with a visionary's faith.

While not entirely misplaced, Gaziel's distinction between Maragall's optimism and the *Generación del 98*'s apparently congenital pessimism strikes me, like Marfany's position, as an oversimplification. As we shall see, Maragall's assessments of Catalan and peninsular affairs were not without their melancholic or critical dimensions. Likewise, writers like Unamuno, Ganivet, and Maeztu presented the crisis facing Spain circa 1898 as an exceptional opportunity for renewal, and in this sense, were marked by a cautious or provisional optimism.

Nonetheless, Maragall made various statements that support the notion that he was primarily a Catalan rather than Spanish nationalist, and that ultimately he was not a Spanish regenerationist, as were Unamuno and company. In an unpublished 1897 article "La independència de Catalunya" (Catalan Independence), Maragall writes:

El pensament espanyol és mort. No vull dir que no hi hagi espanyols que pensin, sinó que el centre d'Espanya ja no té cap significació ni eficàcia actual dintre del moviment general d'idees del món civilitzat. Per això nosaltres, que tenim cor de seguir dintre d'aquest moviment general, hem de creure arribada a Espanya l'hora del *campi que puga*, i hem de desfer-nos ben de pressa de tota mena de lligam amb una cosa morta. (*OC* 1: 739)

Spanish thought is dead. I am not saying that there are no Spaniards who think, but rather that Spain's intellectual centre means nothing and can accomplish nothing within the general intellectual movement of the civilized world. For this reason, those of us who desire to accompany this

> general movement must conclude that the time for Spain's *campi que puga* has come, and that we must quickly cut ourselves off from all that ties us to this dead thing.

And in a 15 October 1898 letter to Joaquim Freixas, Maragall writes: "La qüestió per Catalunya és europeïtzar-se, tallant més o menys lentament la corda que la lliga a *la Morta*" (What Catalonia must do is Europeanize itself, and sooner or letter cut the cord that ties it to *la Morta*) (1: 978; author's emphasis). Here the deathly figure of *la Morta* might refer to Spain, or perhaps to Spain's politically, economically, and morally defunct Castilian centre and the government that represented its interests.[11] In this respect, Maragall echoes Valentí Almirall, who twelve years earlier in *Lo Catalanisme* had remarked on "la situació trista y vergonyosa de la nació en general; lo rebaixament del carácter castellá, incapás ja de dirigirla" (the sad and shameful state of the nation in general; the weakening of the Castilian character, [which is] now incapable of leading [the nation]) (93). Further, Maragall's views on the relationship between language and nation would seem to support the notion that his nationalism was fundamentally Catalan rather than Spanish. Maragall repeatedly declared, in terms typical of both Romantic nationalism and Catalanism, that "la nació és la llengua" (a nation is its language), as in a 12 July 1907 letter to Pere Coromines (*OC* 1: 959).[12] Or as Maragall would put it in his famous 1905 speech "Elogi de la paraula" (Eulogy for the Word): "Cada terra comunica a les més substancials paraules dels seus homes un sentit sentimental que no hi ha diccionari que l'expliqui ni gramàtica que l'ensenyi" (Each land imparts on its people's weightiest words an emotional meaning that cannot be taught by any dictionary or book of grammar) (1: 666). In other words, Maragall believed himself incapable of fully apprehending or conveying his sense of national identity except in Catalan, which he described as his native tongue.

The debate concerning Maragall's possible inclusion in the *Generación del 98* is ultimately academic as are, I think, most arguments on membership in literary "generations." However, the political subtext of this debate, and the question of Maragall's Spanish or Catalan nationalism, is worth noting: to present Maragall as a member of the *Generación del 98*, as did the *falange*-identified Entralgo, suggests that his regenerationism was fundamentally Spanish as opposed to Catalan in dimension. Further, it neutralizes Maragall's advocacy of Catalan autonomy and national consciousness by falsely implying that his Catalanism was nostalgic, cultural, and fundamentally apolitical. The counterargument, that Maragall's Catalanism differentiates him on some essential level from those Marfany terms his "Castilian contemporaries" in the *Generación del 98* (many of whom, including Unamuno, Azorín, and Maeztu, were not Castilian by birth), obscures the multiple layers of Maragall's regenerationist vision: while Maragall affirmed Catalan nationhood and worked to develop a Catalan national consciousness through his poetry, journalism, and public engagement, he was also concerned with problems facing Spain as a whole, and did not deny that Catalonia was implied in these problems. Like Unamuno, Maragall was aware of the complex interrelationships between the Catalan nation, the Spanish state, the Iberian Peninsula, and Europe – though as we shall see, Maragall in no way privileged or fetishized Castile, as did his Basque friend. Maragall's multiple, shifting engagements – with Catalanism, Spanish regenerationism, and Iberianism – make him a difficult figure to pigeonhole, and make questions of Maragall's relationship to the Catalan, Spanish, and Iberian literary and intellectual traditions at the *fin de siècle* all the more complex. As Krauel observes: "Maragall's thought is far too complex, far too nuanced, and far too contradictory to be pigeonholed into broad categories that have emerged from historical experiences different from that of Catalonia" ("Emotions" 198).[13]

Maragall's concern for Catalonia's role in Spain's regeneration, and its potential to spearhead the country's "Europeanization," would morph by 1906 – the year in which he authored a prologue to the Catalan Iberianist militant Ignasi Ribera i Rovira's book *Poesia & prosa* (Poetry & Prose), wrote his poetic "Himne ibèric," and published the article "El ideal ibérico" – into a broader interest in Catalonia's role in the Iberian Peninsula. There is debate as to what, or who, might have prompted Maragall's shift from a specifically Catalan or Spanish regenerationism towards a concern with the interrelationships between Catalonia, Castile, and Portugal, which Thomas Harrington refers to as "tripartite Iberianism."[14] Scholars have suggested Prat, whose long essay *La nacionalitat catalana*, published that same year, called for Catalan leadership within an expansionistic Iberia, or alternatively Ribera i Rovira, as influential in effecting what we might call Maragall's "Iberianist turn."[15] Though I do not dismiss these theories, there are deeper structural features of Maragall's Iberianism that recall Unamuno, and that speak to the reciprocal influence between Maragall and Unamuno. I will turn to Maragall and Unamuno's correspondence between 1900 and 1911 in the final section of this chapter.

Maragall may have failed to express his Iberianist views in the same systematic manner as Prat, Joaquim Cases-Carbó, and Ribera i Rovira, all of whom were more politically engaged than the reserved, gentlemanly, and independently wealthy Maragall.[16] Nonetheless, Maragall's embrace of Iberianism by 1906 is highly significant, given his iconic, patriarchal status in Catalan literary culture, and his capacity thereby to shape the views of later generations of Catalan readers and writers concerning Iberian affairs.[17] As Krauel notes, "Maragall has become one of those iconic cultural figures who combines literary excellence with moral dignity," such that today "Maragall is present everywhere in Catalan culture" ("Emotions" 195). Or in the words of Josep-Maria Terricabras:

> Joan Maragall és un dels grans poetes catalans. A ell es deuen alguns dels poemes patriòtics, religiosos i civils més celebrats i més repetidament citats i admirats de la literatura catalana contemporània ... Hagi estat generalment admirat: hi deu haver pocs pobles a Catalunya – si n'hi ha algun, per petit que sigui – que no li hagi dedicat un carrer o una plaça. (9)
>
> Joan Maragall is one of the great Catalan poets. He is responsible for some of the most celebrated and most frequently recited patriotic, religious, and civil poems in contemporary Catalan literature ... He has been widely admired: there can be few cities or towns in Catalonia – I know of none, however small – that have not dedicated a street or plaza to him.

Given his prominence, Maragall was elevated to the status of "spokesperson for the Iberianist movement" in turn-of-the-century Catalonia, where Iberianism took root in the fertile soil of the ongoing revival of Catalan language, culture, and political activism, and in the wake of the *desastre* (Harrington, "The Hidden" 154). And on substantive grounds as well, Maragall contributed to the intellectual development of Iberianism in *fin-de-siècle* Catalonia, being, in Martínez-Gil's words, "o seu maior definidor" (its greatest definer) ("A Visão" 60).

Further, Maragall's epistolary relationship with Unamuno, who translated some of Maragall's poems, including his "Oda a Espanya" and "Cant del hispans" (Song of the Hispanics), to Castilian and praised his Catalan friend to his fellow writers and to his readers,[18] has no doubt factored in Maragall's prominence both as a Catalanist and Iberianist. As Harrington notes:

> It would seem ... Maragall's ability to transcend the nearly complete anonymity of ... other [Catalan] Iberianists ... is due primarily to his reputation as a poet and, more importantly here, to the strong personal backing his ideas received over the years from two titans of the Castilianist cultural establishment: Miguel de Unamuno and Pedro Laín Entralgo. In this way, Maragall has functioned as a sort of "good savage" of Catalanism within the Madrid-based cultural establishment, and has been subject to all the attempts at co-optation that generally accrue to the "most civilized" representatives of an insurgent line of thought. ("Belief" 206)

Harrington's explanation for Maragall's prominence is logical, and his implied argument that scholars interested in Catalan Iberianism should focus less on the fragmentary, less overtly political Maragall in favour of more systematic and committed Catalan Iberianists like Ribera i Rovira is valid. However, I insist on the importance of Maragall's admittedly limited Iberianist production, given that it is the expression of Catalan tripartite Iberianism that, because of Maragall's prominence, would most decisively enter the scholarly record.

Maragall's overlapping interests in Catalan national consciousness and self-determination, in post-1898 Spanish regeneration, and in Iberianism would imply that he maintained a complex (or, less charitably, inconsistent or contradictory) sense of his Catalan, Spanish, and Iberian identities. Though as we have seen in previous chapters, in Antero de Quental's 1871 reference to his Lisbon audience as "nós Espanhóis" (we Spaniards) in *Causas da Decadência dos Povos Peninsulares*, and in Emilia Pardo Bazán's defence of her right to consider herself both Galician and Spanish in a passage from *La vida contemporánea* (1899), disentangling these overlapping self-identifications may be useful in illuminating the nuances of Maragall's Catalanist, Spanish regenerationist, and Iberianist programs. I will attempt to do so in the next section. I will then offer a detailed analysis of Maragall's Iberianism, and will conclude by analysing Maragall and Unamuno's correspondence and assess its impact on the deeper structures of Maragall's Iberianist thought.

The Prismatic Man: Maragall as Catalan, Spaniard, and Iberian

Maragall's writing offers ample evidence that he identified as Catalan, and that he understood that while Catalonia was a part of Spain, he also viewed Catalonia and Castile, and Catalans and Castilians, as fundamentally distinct. In his unpublished prose piece "La independència de Catalunya" (1897), Maragall speculates on Catalan–Castilian intellectual relations as follows: "I com que al mateix temps les condiciones naturals del *nostre* esperit ens fans absolutament inaptes per a assimilar-nos-la [la cultura castellà] i fer-la evolucionar en el sentit *nostre,* per això dic que avui tota promiscuïtat intel·lectual amb els castellans, siga per venir *ells* a *nosaltres* o siga per anar *nosaltres* an ells, no pot ésser sinó en detriment de la integritat i de l'evolució natural i pròpia del pensament català" (And given that the natural conditions of *our* spirit render us wholly incapable of assimilating [Castilian culture] or causing it to evolve in a direction that would be *ours,* for this reason I declare that any sort of intellectual promiscuity with the Castilians, whether *they* come to *us* or *we* go to them, can only be to the detriment of the integrity and the natural, independent evolution of Catalan thought) (*OC* 1: 740; my emphasis). Maragall's position in this piece is not representative of his mature views, which tended towards an Unamunian advocacy for Catalan–Castilian intellectual and cultural exchange, and advocated Catalan political engagement in Spain, and in Iberian affairs more broadly. Though as we shall see, even as Maragall acknowledged the achievements of the Castilian tradition and expressed interest in it, he consistently opposed what he viewed as historically or culturally ingrained Castilian traits of idealism, political unitarianism, and cultural provincialism, viewing them as antithetical to his fellow Catalans' congenital pragmatism and worldliness, and their traditional defence of individual and local or regional liberties.[19]

When Maragall refers to Catalan language and literature in his writing, he invariably terms them "ours," whereas his posture towards Castilian language and literature is more distant, albeit respectful. Moreover, Maragall acknowledged the historical privilege enjoyed by the Castilian corpus as the basis for Spain's "national" literature, an advantage that came at the implied expense of the Catalan language and tradition he and his Catalanist peers were working to revive and consolidate. For instance, in a 5 July 1881 letter to Freixas, which Maragall, rather ironically, wrote in Castilian, he explains:

> Participo de tu entusiasmo por la literatura castellana, si bien mis aficiones me llevan con preferencia al estudio de otra a la cual debo y profeso mayor cariño por ser la de la lengua en que balbuceé mis primeras oraciones y en la que expresaré sin duda mi amor a la primera *Carlota* o *Margarita* que algún ángel bueno ponga en mi camino; no menos que por ser el habla en que hemos expresado mutuamente nuestra amistad ... Sin embargo, no

llego al absurdo de negar mi admiración a la hermosa lengua y espléndida literatura de Castilla: tan espléndida como no podía menos de serlo habiendo disfrutado de privilegio en España, donde tantas inteligencias superiores se han desarrollado. (*OC* 1: 971–2; author's emphasis)

I share your enthusiasm for Castilian literature, though my sympathies incline me towards the study of another [literature], to which I owe and profess a greater affection, one written in the language in which I recited my first prayers, and in which I will declare my love to the first *Carlota* or *Margarita* who some good angel places in my path, and which finally, is the language in which our feelings of friendship towards each other have always been expressed … However, I would not go to the absurd extreme of denying my admiration for the beautiful language and splendid literature of Castile: a literature that could be nothing less than splendid given the privileges it has enjoyed in Spain, in which so many great minds have contributed to its development.

In two articles published in 1901,"Poesía catalana" (Catalan Poetry) and "Prosa catalana" (Catalan Prose), Maragall refers to "nuestra lengua catalana" (our Catalan language) and to Catalan literature as "nuestra literatura" (our literature) (2: 145, 158). In another article written the same year, "La joven escuela castellana" (The New Castilian School, 1901), Maragall underscores his distance from Castilian literature, writing: "De algún tiempo a esta parte van llegando a nuestras manos obras literarias de una nueva generación de escritores en lengua castellana; y cada una de ellas sucesivamente va afirmando en nosotros la idea de una evolución saludable en *aquella* literatura" (For some time now I have been receiving literary works written by a new generation of authors who write in the Castilian language, and each one of these works further impresses on me the fact that *that* literature is evolving in a healthy direction) (*OC* 2: 149; my emphasis). Curiously, Maragall refers in the same text to "la literatura española" (Spanish literature), though he does not clarify if he views this as synonymous with Castilian literature, or if it might also include texts written in Catalan, such as his poetry.[20]

On the other hand, Maragall also identified himself in writing as a Spaniard, and sometimes used the personal pronoun "our" (*nuestro/nuestra*) and related terms in relation to Spain. For instance, in his article "El pensamiento español" (Spanish Thought, 1893), referring to Spain's intellectual marginalization over the prior two centuries, he writes: "Como la evolución de làs ideas no había de detenerse por *nosotros*, siempre *nuestra cultura* resultaría un anacronismo" (Since the evolution of ideas would not wait for *us*, *our culture* became anachronistic) (*OC* 2: 396; my emphasis). Years later, in a 14 January 1909 letter to Valencian writer Gabriel Miró, Maragall refers to their shared homeland as "nuestra España" (our Spain) (2: 919). Though as in his comments on Catalan and Castilian literature, Maragall is careful to distinguish between Spain, with which he identified in print on various occasions, and Castile, with which he did not. Maragall alluded to this distinction, and the related problem of Castile's historical protagonism in Spain (which worked to blur the line between the two categories),[21] in his 1898 article "El discurso de Lord Salisbury" (Lord Salisbury's Speech), which concerns the infamous speech on "living and dying nations" given by the British prime minister to the conservative Primrose League:

> Pudiera muy bien ser que cualquier día, por los azares de la guerra presente, o por las consecuencias que la misma reportará a la vida interior de la nación, el antiguo espíritu español, que aún *nos* caracteriza y gobierna en pleno siglo XIX y que hace que los extranjeros llamen todavía a España con cierto tono de alabanza y con ciertos puntos de ironía la nación de los hidalgos, apareciera en completa bancarrota: entonces sería ocasión de medir la fuerza expansiva de aquellos elementos económicos, y de que demostrarán si tienen suficiente sentido político para asumir la dirección del Estado, dando a ésta una significación más europea y más moderna de la que hasta ahora ha tenido. En caso afirmativo, de ahí pudiera venir la regeneración de esta España que hoy parece moribunda a los ojos de muchos, porque quizás hay realmente en ella algo moribundo que no es ella misma. (555; my emphasis)

> It may be that one day before too long, due to the present war or its consequences for the inner life of the nation, the old Spanish spirit, which continues to characterize and govern *us* in this the nineteenth century, and which prompts strangers to call Spain, not without a certain tone and degree of ironic praise, the nation of noblemen, will reveal itself to be completely bankrupt. This will then provide the occasion for us to measure the expansive force of those economic elements [identified with Catalan industry and commerce], and to determine if they are politically capable of assuming command of the State, and if they can grant it a more European and more modern orientation than that which it has had until

now. If the answer is "yes," then this may bring about the regeneration of a Spain that appears dead in the eyes of many, for it will reveal that what is dead is not Spain itself, but rather something within it [i.e., moribund Castilian values].

And in his 1908 article "Visca Espanya!" (Long Live Spain!), Maragall defends the right of Catalanists and Europeanizing modernizers to identify with "aquesta Espanya nostra" (this, our Spain), and pushes back against the notion that Castilian centralists and other reactionary types enjoy a monopoly on Spanish patriotism: "El nostre 'visca Espanya' vol dir que l'Espanya visca – enteneu? –, que els pobles s'alcin i es moguin, que parlin, que facin per si mateixos, i es governin i governin; i Espanya ja no és un lloc comú de patrioterisme encobridor de tota mena de debilitats i concupiscències, sinó que Espanya és això que es mou i s'alça i parla i planta cara als que fins ara han viscut de la seva mort aparent" (Our cry of "Long Live Spain" means that Spain lives – do you understand? It means that the peoples [of Spain] raise themselves up and move, that they speak, that they act for themselves, that they are governed and govern themselves; it means that Spain will no longer be synonymous with an unthinking patriotism that obscures all manner of weaknesses and desires, but rather that Spain will move and raise itself up and speak and stand against all that which brought about its apparent death) (1: 767). Further, in a move reminiscent of Quental's contention in *Portugal perante a Revolução de Espanha* that Portuguese Iberianists were more genuinely patriotic than the dogged defenders of Portugal's independence, Maragall declares: "Espanyols? sí! mes que vosaltres!" (Spaniards? Yes [we are]! More so than you!) (1: 767).

Maragall returns to the idea that the Spain with which he identifies is a progressive country open to the benevolent modernizing and dynamizing influence of Catalanism in an evocative passage from his late essay "La espaciosa y triste España" (The Vast, Sad Spain, 1911). Here he describes a beggar, asking for alms in Castilian, as a means to explore the intertwined problems of intra-Iberian relations, language, Catalan and Spanish identity, class, and poverty:

> Ahora, mientras pretendía ir señalando a España sus destinos, mi conciencia de español se iba desdoblando en mí, de manera que hacía de la mía una España aparte que no se contentaba con la austera gloria señalada a la de solitarios y profetas, sino que se lisonjeaba con otra más mundana, con

una participación más directa en la vida civil de las naciones. Se ofrecían a mi memoria ciertos momentos políticos de mi tierra, ciertas actividades sociales de mi ciudad, ciertos acentos distintos de mi lengua, que me dieron la ilusión de no hablar ya conmigo mismo y con los míos más próximos, sino con unos hermanos más desgraciados en el mundo, entre los cuales no necesitaba yo contarme, a los cuales amaba de puertas afuera; que eran mis hermanos, sí, pero eran *otros*.

Pero he aquí que mientras tanto una salmodia se ha ido acertando por el camino a donde da mi ventana, una voz lastimera pregonando la miseria de una vida con ese arte refinado de pedir limosna que revela la mendicidad como una profesión nacional. Cierto que esa voz no hablaba en la lengua en que yo hablo, pero hablaba en esta misma en que estoy escribiendo; cierto que aquel hombre no era de mi tierra, pero por ella andaba y la gente le entendía como me entenderá a mí en estas rayas; cierto que delante de mi ventana hay un poste prohibiendo terminantemente la mendicidad en este pueblo, pero el hombre ha pasado imperturbable por delante del poste que ve desfilar cada día centenares de mendigos de otras tierras ante el cartel que sostiene, absolutamente ineficaz, verdadero símbolo de tanta ley escrita española. Ésta es, pues, tierra de España. He levantado los ojos y he visto los árboles raquíticos y las casas y los matorrales, y pitas y chumberas en la tierra rojiza y miserable, todo cubierto por el polvo que levanta en los caminos el paso de los mendigos trashumantes; y he olido el hedor de la basura recogida a la puerta del rico y del pobre indistintamente (con la sola diferencia de que en la del rico hay más) y paseada triunfalmente todo el día por toda la población a son de campanas; y he oído más allá el desfachado martilleo de un piano de manubrio de esos que las naciones civilizadas mandan a los países salvajes para recreo preliminar de su conquista, y que aquí ha venido a ser el instrumento favorito de este pueblo infeliz que en él estropea todo el gusto musical que Dios le tenía dado, jaleado por los que se llaman sus educadores; y he sentido, por fin, dentro de mí, como única reacción contra todo ello, un asco profundo e impotente. Era yo, pues, un español como tantos. (2: 758–9; author's emphasis)

Now then, as I was attempting to speak to Spain of its possible futures, my consciousness as a Spaniard expanded within me, converting my Spain into a different Spain, one that would not content itself with the austere glory of a Spain of solitary men and of prophets, but that would take pride in being more down-to-earth, and that would participate more directly in the affairs of nations. What came to my mind were memories of certain moments in the political life of my land, certain social activities from my city, certain distinct sounds of my language. All this created the illusion that instead of speaking to myself and to those closest to me, I was speaking instead to less fortunate brothers, among whom I do not include myself, but who I love nonetheless. Yes, these were my brothers, but they were *others*.

All the while a sound was approaching down the road that could be seen through my window. It was a pitiful voice recounting someone's misery, and it had the refined quality that betrays the fact that begging for alms is truly a national profession. It is true that this voice did not speak in my native tongue, but rather in the language in which I am now writing. It is true that this man was not from my land, but rather was travelling through it, though the people here can understand him just as they understand me. And it is true that there is a sign that can be seen just outside my window that explicitly prohibits begging in this town. But the man walked by the sign unconcerned, just as hundreds of beggars from other lands walk by this absolutely ineffective sign, which is truly a symbol of so much codified Spanish law. This, then, is part of Spain. I have looked up and seen the diseased trees, the houses and the brush, and the aloe and prickly pear growing from the poor, red soil, all covered in a dust that the itinerant beggars kick up with their feet. And I have smelled the stench of the garbage left outside the homes of the rich and poor alike (the only difference being that the rich produce more garbage); and I have marched triumphantly all day, through the entire town, to the sound of the bells; and I have heard from farther away the ugly pounding of a player piano of the sort that the civilized nations send to the savage countries for the amusement of those they have conquered, and which has become the favourite instrument of this unhappy town whose God-given musical taste it is busy destroying, while being cheered on by those who consider themselves the town's educators; and finally, I have felt as my sole reaction to all of this a profound and impotent disgust. I was, then, a Spaniard just like the rest.

Maragall describes the beggars who pass by his window as separated from him by their native tongue, social class, and homeland. That is, to Maragall they are "*otros*" (others). Nonetheless, he recognizes that he is bonded to them by their common condition as Spaniards, as individuals subject both to the beauty of Spanish folk culture (recall Maragall's image of his participation in a presumably religious procession) and the indignities of the country's underdevelopment (ineffective laws, poor soil, diseased trees, etc.). This prompts Maragall to acknowledge that he, like these beggars who have come to Catalonia from less prosperous regions of Spain, is "un español como tantos" (a Spaniard just like the rest).

Having described Maragall's self-identification as a Catalan and a Spaniard, I will turn in this section's final paragraphs to Maragall's late identification as an Iberian, which accompanies his turn towards Iberianism during the final years of his life. In his article "El ideal ibérico" (1906), Maragall provides a bridge between his self-identification as Catalan, and the Iberian Peninsula in which Catalonia is situated:

> Cuando hablamos del espíritu o sentido catalán, tampoco entendemos algo *nuestro* exclusivo, sino aquel elemento de *nuestro* carácter que, por oposición a aquella rigidez [atribuida por Maragall al "alma castellana"], pueda ahora, también por afinidad y nueva razón histórica, atraer y agrupar los instintos de variedad y de libertad de *todos los peninsulares*, incluso los castellanos, hasta constituirse en informador y representante de la política nueva.
>
> Estos sentimientos de libertad, variedad y armonía, dominados y ocultos por cuatro siglos, y por razones históricas, bajo el rígido unitarismo castellano, latieron, sin embargo, siempre vivos en el fondo de *la naturaleza peninsular*, y terminada ahora con la misión la fuerza de aquél, reaparecen como nueva y única fuerza reconstructiva de una política amplia y fecunda para *toda la Península*. (2: 725; my emphasis).

> When we speak of the Catalan spirit or way, we do not refer to something that is exclusively *ours*, but rather to that aspect of *our* character, that, in contrast to the rigidity [attributed by Maragall to the "Castilian soul"], might through affinity and new historical conditions attract and bring together the instincts toward variety and freedom that are present in *all of the peninsular peoples*, including the Castilians, and which in this way might become the guiding and representative element of a new politics.
>
> These feelings of freedom, of variety and harmony, which were repressed and hidden for four centuries, for historical reasons, by a rigid Castilian unitarianism, nonetheless still pulsed in the depths of *peninsular nature*, and with the historical mission of [Castilian unitarianism] now complete, they have reappeared as a new force, the only force capable of bringing about a broad and fruitful political reconstruction of *the entire Peninsula*.

And in the article "La integridad de la patria (diálogo trágico)" (The Integrity of the Country [a tragic dialogue], 1909), Maragall recounts a conversation with a Portuguese acquaintance António de Macedo Papança, the Count of Monsaraz – who was incidentally also a friend of Ignasi Ribera i Rovira – at a hotel in the French Pyrenees. Maragall first observes the irony that despite their common Iberian identity, the two men communicated in French for lack of a common language: "Entre un portugués y un catalán, tal conversación tomaba de sí misma un tinte ... ibérico. Sin embargo, habíamos de entendernos en francés; y este contrasentido, que comunicaba a la incorrección de nuestra palabras en lengua extranjera un tono deprimente, casi diría elegíaco, era ya por sí solo un severo juicio de toda la política peninsular en los siglos; era como el *inri* de un tremendo yerro histórico" (Between a Portuguese and a Catalan, such a conversation could only take on an ... Iberian tinge. However, in order to understand each other we had to converse in French. And this bit of nonsense granted our incorrect use of certain foreign words a depressing, almost elegiac tone. This itself amounts to a severe judgment of centuries' worth of peninsular politics; it was like the *inri* of a tremendous historical error) (2: 749; author's emphasis).[22] Despite Monsaraz's scepticism, Maragall argues in language that recalls the title of Enric Prat de la Riba's manifesto *Per Catalunya i per l'Espanya gran* (For Catalonia and a Greater Spain, 1916) for Catalan and Portuguese participation in "la gran patria ibérica común" (the great, common Iberian homeland), or "una patria mayor: la Península natural, íntegra, *nuestra*" (a greater country: a Peninsula that is natural, whole, *ours*) (2: 749, 751; my emphasis). Looking to an Iberianist future, Maragall declares: "¡Qué otra vida no fuera, qué alegría, qué orgullo, saber ser castellanos, portugueses, catalanes, vascos, todos libres y todos unos, y que de mar a mar no había extraños entre *nosotros*, sino una resultante común, una civilización ibérica!" (What other life there could be, what happiness, what pride would we feel, if Castilians, Portuguese, Catalans, [and] Basques were all free and united, and that from sea to sea there would be no strangers among *us*, but rather a common Iberian civilization?) (2: 751; my emphasis).[23] Maragall grounds his argument for Iberian federation in the unity of peninsular geography or "nature," and repeatedly describes this united peninsula as "ours": "*Nosotros*, en *nuestra* Península ibérica, tenemos una unidad geográfica tan precisa, que no podemos desentendernos de ella, que hemos de gobernarnos por ella, que es la condición de *nuestra* grandeza" (*We*, in *our* Iberian Peninsula, possess a clear, unavoidable geographic unity that should guide us, that is the key to our greatness) (750; my emphasis).

In sum, the Iberianist future projected by Maragall in "La integridad de la patria" is dependent on the "peninsular peoples" closing the distance between one another. Or put another way, the achievement of Maragall's goal requires that the Iberian peoples enlarge their idea of "we" or "us" beyond the borders of Catalonia, Castile, or Portugal such that there would be no "extraños" (strangers) among Iberians, as he wrote in "La integridad de la patria," or no "others," as he put it two years later in "La espaciosa y triste España." In this sense, Maragall's understanding of Iberianism depended on the same gestures of identification that he made throughout his career with Catalonia, Spain, and perhaps less frequently, with Iberia. I will now examine the broad contours of Maragall's Iberianist thinking.

Maragall's Fragmentary Iberianism

Maragall failed to make a definitive, public declaration of his Iberianist beliefs, in the manner of Quental's *Portugal perante a Revolução de Espanha* (1868) or *Causas da Decadência dos Povos Peninsulares* (1871), or Oliveira Martins's *História da Civilização Ibérica* (1879). Rather, he articulated his Iberianist views in fragmentary form, as did Unamuno. The corpus of Maragall's Iberianist texts is limited to two poems, "Himne ibèric" and "Or de llei" (True Gold), two articles, "El ideal ibérico" and "La integridad de la patria" (diálogo trágico)," and Maragall's prologue to Ignasi Ribera i Rovira's *Poesia & prosa.* Except for "Or de llei," an undated poem whose early estimated date of composition implies that Iberianism was at least a latent interest for the young Maragall,[24] and "La integridad de la patria," which was published in 1909, all his Iberianist texts date from 1906, though the "Himne ibèric" remained unpublished during Maragall's lifetime. Despite the fragmentary character of Maragall's Iberianist production, we can nonetheless identify recurrent themes that resonate with other writers considered in this book. In some cases, Maragall seems to have inherited his Iberianist ideas from or developed them in conjunction with a contemporary, while in others, Maragall represents a possible source for an idea that appears in the work of a later Iberianist writer. I will consider three such themes in this section: the tripartite division of the Iberian Peninsula, which Harrington refers to as "tripartite Iberianism"; Iberia's simultaneous unity and variety; and the precariousness of Portugal's continued independence from the rest of the peninsula.

Regarding Iberia's tripartite division, in his 1906 prologue to Ribera i Rovira, Maragall declares:

> En la península hispànica, per sobre o per sota de les fronteres o no fronteres polítiques, s'hi troben tres famílies nacionals ben definides pel seu parlar: la galaico-portuguesa, la castellana i la catalana, que ocupa també les illes Balears: son l'Espanya atlàntica, l'Espanya central i l'Espanya mediterrània. Són tres zones geogràfiques, tres faixes verticals i paral·leles de dalt a baix de la península hispana. Qui del reconeixement d'aquest fet natural en sabés i pogués arrencar tota una política peninsular, ben segur que donaria a Espanya la glòria i el benestar dels pobles que viuen en conformitat a la llei de la seva naturalesa. (*OC* 1: 827)

> In the Hispanic Peninsula, above or below political borders and non-borders, one finds three national families that are defined by their language: these are the Galaico-Portuguese, the Castilian, and the Catalan families. The latter also covers the Balearic Islands. They could also be called Atlantic Spain, Central Spain, and Mediterranean Spain. These three geographical zones are strips that run down the Spanish Peninsula from north to south. Recognition of this natural fact leads one to a political vision for the peninsula that would surely win for Spain the glory and well-being enjoyed by those peoples who live in accordance with the law of their nature.

Martínez-Gil contends that among his peers, it was Maragall who first articulated this tripartite scheme, which joins together Galicia and Portugal and silently subsumes the Basque Country within Castile.[25] Maragall would have then passed it along to Ribera i Rovira, a self-described "enamorat de l'Iberia" (lover of Iberia) whom Maragall endorsed in his 1906 review.[26] Indeed, a reading of Maragall's undated "Or de llei," which speaks of Spain as "una en tres, / perquè tres parles hi sentia, / i essent tres feien harmonia" (one in three, / for its are three tongues, / that speak in harmony), and whose composition Marfany dates between 1878 and 1883, would imply that Maragall had held to a tripartite vision of the peninsula from his earliest years as a writer. If Marfany's chronology is correct, Ribera i Rovira, twenty years Maragall's junior, would have been no more than three years old when "Or de llei" was written, and therefore could not have introduced Maragall to the idea of tripartite Iberianism (*OC* 1: 194).

Beyond the tripartite question, Iberianist ideas are present in Maragall's writing prior to 1906. In addition to "Or de llei," we may cite

Maragall's 1900 review of Azorín's *El alma castellana* (The Castilian Soul), in which he affirms the existence of a common, overarching Iberian "soul," an idea he shared with Oliveira Martins and Unamuno, and to which he would return in later years. Both affirming the Iberian soul and questioning its conflation with the Castilian soul, Maragall writes: "Como él [Azorín] ha sabido revelar el alma castellana, que indudablemente ha podido llamarse el alma española por muchísimo tiempo, se encontrara quien supiera buscar otras, ocultas siglos ha por los espacios de la Península ibérica, quizás, combinándolas, los españoles adquiriéramos conciencia de una alma nueva que buena falta nos hace." (Just as he [Azorín] has managed to reveal the Castilian soul, which for centuries now has been called the Spanish soul, would that there might be someone capable of finding other souls, which have been hidden for centuries throughout the Iberian Peninsula. Perhaps by combining them, we Spaniards could become aware of a new soul that we have sorely missed) (2: 608).

Harrington has argued against Martínez-Gil's interpretation, contending that in his 1906 prologue Maragall borrowed from – and later popularized – a way of thinking about intra-Iberian relations that had been developed by Ribera i Rovira.[27] Regardless of whether the idea was originally Maragall's or Ribera i Rovira's, what appears certain is that Maragall passed along to Unamuno the idea that the Iberian Peninsula was composed of three linguistically based "families." Indeed, months after his prologue to Ribera i Rovira was published, in a 3 January 1907 letter to Unamuno, Maragall wrote of a "composición, nunca aun realizada, [en que] está el secreto de la grandeza de España. ¡Ay! ya sé que V. no cree en eso; que empieza por no creer en la diversidad irreductible a simple unidad. Y, sin embargo: Portugal – Castilla – Cataluña – ¿no es innegable?" (Unamuno and Maragall 44) (arrangement, never before achieved, [but in which] lies the secret of Spain's greatness. Alas, I know that you do not believe in this, since it depends on the idea that diversity is not reducible to a simple unity. And yet: Portugal – Castile – Catalonia – how can this be denied?). Five years later, in a 5 March 1911 letter to Unamuno, written just months before his death, Maragall returned to the topic of Iberia's tripartite division, and proposed that he and Unamuno found "una Revista Ibérica, o Celtibérica, escrita indistintamente en nuestras lenguas, de modo que se acabase por leerlas y entenderlas ya indistintamente" (an Iberian, or Celtiberian journal, written in all [three] of our languages, so that our readers would end up reading and understanding all of them). Maragall argued for the journal, which would have followed in the footsteps of Quental and Jaime Batalha Reis's *Revista Occidental* and other short-lived Iberianist publications, as follows: "Esta alma ibérica que todavía somos tan pocos en sentir, hay que buscarla hacia adentro: hacia adentro de su Castilla los castellanos, hacia adentro de su Portugal los portugueses, hacia adentro de nuestra Cataluña los catalanes, hasta llegar a la raíz común: y de allí arrancará la España grande, la europea por invasión espiritual; y yo no entiendo otro europeísmo que este que V. ha predicado ya como un profeta, ni veo otro camino que este. Hacia adentro de cada modalidad hasta encontrar la causa única de las modalidades, su substancia única" (This Iberian soul, which so few of us feel within us, must be found within; the Castilians must find it within Castile, the Portuguese must find it within Portugal, and we Catalans must find it within Catalonia. In this way we will arrive at the common root, and from this will grow the great Spain, and it will become European through spiritual invasion. And I know of no form of Europeanism other than the one you have preached, like a prophet, nor do I know of any path other than this one. Each modality must look within itself in order to find the common cause of all of the modalities, their shared substance) (Unamuno and Maragall 97).[28]

Unamuno's initial response to Maragall's journal project was somewhat sceptical. In a fit of pique, Unamuno cast doubt in a 9 March 1911 letter to Maragall on the ability of peninsular intellectuals to feel the "Iberian soul," which both men defended, and which Maragall had proposed as the underlying impetus for the journal: "¡El alma ibérica! ¡Qué ensueño! Pero nos lo turban castellanistas, bizkaitarras, catalanistas, portuguesistas, andalucistas, etc., no que no castellanos, ni vascos, ni catalanes, ni portugueses, ni andaluces, etcetera" (98) (The Iberian soul! What a fantasy! Castilianists, *bizkaitarras* [i.e., Basque autonomists and nationalists], Catalanists, Portuguesers, Andalucists, etc., not to mention Castilians, Basques, Catalans, Portuguese, Andalusians, etcetera, are the problem). By 1915, when Unamuno wrote a retrospective article on Maragall's proposal, which had been pre-empted by Maragall's death on 20 December 1911, his doubts concerning the "Iberian soul" seem to have been alleviated. Unamuno states here that the unrealized journal was to have been written in Castilian, Catalan, and Portuguese, and would have been designed to foster "nuestro común espíritu ibérico" (our common Iberian spirit) (*OC* 3: 536).[29]

Despite Maragall's astute judgment that for Unamuno, diversity is ultimately reducible to a simple unity, as he alluded in his 3 January

1907 letter, Unamuno also advanced a tripartite, linguistically-based framework for understanding intra-Iberian relations in certain texts written in the years following Maragall's correspondence with him on that subject. In other words, Unamuno appears to have adopted Maragall's tripartite vision, presumably as a result of his correspondence with the Catalan writer. This strikes me as one of Maragall's principal contributions to Unamuno's thought, and by extension to the unifying, paradoxically "Castile-centric" brand of Iberianism that Unamuno advanced. In addition to his 1915 article on the unrealized *Revista Ibérica*, Unamuno, in his 1908 article "'Las sombras,' de Teixeira de Pascoaes" (*Shadows*, by Teixeira de Pascoaes), argued that despite his view that Iberia would eventually speak a common tongue (Maragall's intuition on Unamuno's teleological thinking was spot on), peninsular writers should nonetheless familiarize themselves with Iberia's three principal languages – Castilian, Catalan, and Portuguese – and read "Iberian literature" in the original. The tripartite structure of this argument is clearly derived from Maragall.

The impact of tripartite Iberianism, and Maragall's role in popularizing and transmitting it, would be felt by at least one other Castile-identified (though not actually Castilian) Iberianist, the Spanish federalist Salvador de Madariaga (1886–1978). Madariaga would frequently invoke the peninsula's tripartite geographic, cultural, and linguistic structure in making the case for a federal reorganization of post-Franco Spain. I will analyse Madariaga at length in this book's final chapter, but for the time being I will quote a passage from his 1930 preface to Aubrey F.G. Bell's English translation of Oliveira Martins's *História da Civilização Ibérica* (published as *A History of Iberian Civilization*), which betrays the influence of Unamuno, Madariaga's acknowledged intellectual mentor, and by implication, that of Maragall:

> Three languages (or groups of languages) embody these three spiritual modalities of the Spanish race. In the West, the Atlantic modality finds its expression in the Portuguese, of Latin languages the most tender and melodious. In the Centre, the Continental modality inspires that stately Castilian in which strength and grace are as harmoniously combined as tragedy and comedy in good drama. To the East, the Mediterranean modality shapes Catalan and its dialects, languages as supple and soft as clay, as vivid as painters' palettes, as receptive as the still waters of the clean sea that bathes the shores where they are spoken.

> In literature and the arts the character of each of these three modalities of Spain may be defined by the predominance of one particular aesthetic tendency. This predominant or specific tendency is in the West lyrical, epic-dramatic in the Centre, and plastic in the East. (148–9)

Let us now turn to the second recurrent theme of Maragall's Iberianism: the idea of Spain's – and by extension, the Iberian Peninsula's – simultaneous unity and variety, or as he put it in his article "El ideal ibérico," "la irreductible variedad de las poblaciones ibéricas dentro de la total unidad geográfica peninsular" (the irreducible variety of the Iberian populations within the Peninsula's overall geographic unity) (*OC* 2: 726). Though crucially, where Castile, as the embodiment of traditional Spanish values and as the agent of Spain's political and linguistic unification, plays a privileged role in Unamuno's conception of Iberia's overarching unity, Maragall inverts Unamuno's formulation: the dream of Iberian unity, if it is to be achieved, will be so in spite of Castile. For Maragall, the sea acts, at least poetically, as the peninsula's bonding agent, and the maritime nations of Catalonia and Portugal serve as the twin drivers of peninsular unification. Maragall addresses these ideas in his "Himne ibèric." The poem's first five sections describe Cantabria, "Lusitània" (i.e., Portugal), Andalusia, Catalonia, and Castile, and the text concludes with this gesture towards peninsular unity – albeit one that implicitly slights Castile for its lack of maritime access:

> Terra entre mar, Ibèria, mare aimada,
> tots els teus fills te fem la gran cançó.
> En cada platja fa son cant l'onada,
> mes terra endins se sent un sol ressò,
> que de l'un cap a l'altre a amor convida
> i es va tornant un cant de germanor;
> Ibèria! Ibèria! et ve dels mars la vida,
> Ibèria! Ibèria! dóna als mars l'amor. (1: 175)
>
> A land between seas, Iberia, beloved mother,
> all of your sons sing to you the great song.
> On every shore the waves sing,
> but inland one only feels the ever-present sun,
> which from one cape to the other invites us to love
> and the song becomes a song of brotherhood;
> Iberia! Iberia! Your life comes from the seas.
> Iberia! Iberia! Give back to the seas your love.

Access to the sea and its corresponding qualities (openness to European modernity, pragmatism, and cosmopolitanism) serve for Maragall as potential bonding agents between Catalonia and Portugal in his 1906 "Pròleg" to Ribera i Rovira. Here he writes:

> Nosotres amb els portuguesos gairebé no ens coneixen: i a fe que ens convé conèixe'ns perquè som els dels dos mars, i ben segur que ens hem de dir moltes coses. Uns i altres tenim els dos grans camins del món per a Espanya, i els dos llenguatges tenen una profunda semblança de dolcesa, amb la varietat que naix de les clares ones del Mediterrani per un costat i de les més obscures i dilatades de l'Atlàntic per l'altre. (1: 828)

> We and the Portuguese barely know each another, but we should get to know one another because we are both maritime peoples, and they surely have much to teach us. We each possess one of Spain's great paths to the world, and our languages are quite similar in their sweetness, though they differ from one another like the clear waves of the Mediterranean from the darker, larger waves of the Atlantic.[30]

And in a 19 December 1906 letter to Unamuno, Maragall underscored Catalonia and Portugal's maritime ties, and their corresponding distance from Castile: "Nunca los que hemos nacido de cara al Mediterráneo, nunca los hijos del húmedo Portugal, podremos acudir bajo su bandera [i.e., del prototípico héroe castellano]" (Those of us who were born facing the Mediterranean, likewise the sons of humid Portugal, will never rally to the flag [of the prototypical Castilian hero]) (Unamuno and Maragall 39).[31]

Maragall's treatment of Iberia's simultaneous unity and diversity also recalls the federalist tradition in which Quental and the young Oliveira Martins participated, and which was solidly rooted in nineteenth-century Catalan political culture.[32] In "Or de llei" Maragall makes the typically federalist statement that "els pobles lliures són els grans" (it is free peoples that are great) (194). And in arguing in "El ideal ibérico" (1906) for Catalanists to take up the intertwined federalist and Iberianist causes, he both invokes the former Spanish prime minister Francesc Pi i Margall's formula of Spanish "unity in variety," and offers an implicit critique of his pact-based federalism, as enunciated in his volume *Las nacionalidades* (1877): "Este ideal no puede ser sino el ideal federal, no encerrado en el abstracto doctrinarismo del pacto y de una forma exterior de Gobierno, sino abierto a un nuevo sentido en el que, precisamente por su reconocimiento del hecho, logra que las variedades naturales se integren espontáneamente en aquella fecunda unidad que es fondo natural también de todas; que viendo en todo organismo una federación de células deja libre el impulso al átomo social, al individuo, para lograr la unión de toda la raza humana en una sola hermandad de amor" (This ideal can be none other than the federal ideal, not reduced to the abstract doctrine of a pact or the exterior form of a Government, but rather open to a new orientation which recognizes natural variation, and allows natural variations to spontaneously join together in a fruitful unity that is the common ground shared by all. This ideal sees each organism as a federation of cells, and thus allows for the free initiative of each social atom, of each individual, in order to achieve the union of the entire human race in a brotherhood of love) (2: 726).[33]

Finally, Portugal provides the basis for a third recurrent theme of Maragall's Iberianism. In consonance with Unamuno, and anticipating Madariaga, Maragall argued that Portugal's political and historical separation from Spain was an aberration that could not be sustained indefinitely, and that if not corrected would impede the Iberian Peninsula from achieving a prosperous future. It is tempting to argue that Maragall came to this conclusion via Unamuno, who argued against the long-term viability of Portuguese independence and wrote in a 19 December 1907 letter to Maragall that Portugal "está perdido; está purgando, a mi juicio, su independencia" (is lost; it is, in my view, throwing away its independent existence) (Unamuno and Maragall 78). However, this argument does not make chronological sense: compare the date of Unamuno's letter (19 December 1907) and that of Maragall's first mention of Portugal's precarious independence, in "El ideal ibérico" (March 1906). In his 1906 article Maragall refers to Portugal in the context of his call for Catalonia to take the lead in integrating the Iberian peoples into a united whole. Maragall writes:

> Ha llegado, pues, la hora de que Cataluña ponga en el aire peninsular este ideal que llame a sí todas las libertades ibéricas agrupadas según las modalidades en que naturalmente se hayan manifestado o vayan manifestándose, desde el tímido pero profundo sentimiento particular de raza de los gallegos, desde el reducido pero vivaz fuerismo vasco, desde el vago regionalismo de las poblaciones que se contentarían ahora con una descentralización administrativa más o menos extensa, hasta el resuelto autonomismo catalán y que pueda también contener *la tanto tiempo ha consumada, pero no perdurable, separación portuguesa*, y aún los vislumbres del porvenir en África, o donde sea. (*OC* 2: 726; my emphasis)

> The time has come, then, for Catalonia to introduce to the peninsula the goal of bringing together all of the free Iberian peoples, which would be naturally grouped together according to the modalities they have adopted or are adopting, whether this be the Galicians' timid but deep feeling for their racial distinctness, the Basques' limited but resolute *fuerismo*, the vague regionalism of groups that would be satisfied with a more or less extensive administrative decentralization, or the Catalans' resolute autonomism, and including the separatism of the Portuguese, *which was achieved so long ago but which cannot continue indefinitely*, and even the visions of a possible future in Africa, or somewhere else).[34]

Maragall would return to the problem of Portuguese independence in "La integridad de la patria" (1909), a reconstructed dialogue with the Count of Monsaraz. While Maragall acknowledges Portugal's historical sovereignty ("Este derecho, esta libertad, Portugal tuvo fuerza para recabarlos a su tiempo"; "El problema catalán es el mismo problema portugués, retardado de unos siglos por circunstancias históricas, en pie ahora con nosotros. Los portugueses lo resolvieron; nosotros queremos resolverlo."),[35] he argues that Portugal's continued independence will prevent it – and Iberia – from achieving prosperity. Maragall asks: "¿Cómo pueden invocar los castellanos contra nosotros [los catalanes] la integridad de la patria, cuando ahí tienen Portugal, ese gran pedazo de ella, que no se llama España? ¿Y qué integridad viene a ser la de ustedes [los portugueses] fuera de ella?" (How can the Castilians use the argument for the integrity of the country against us Catalans when they have Portugal next door, this great piece of Spain that refuses to call itself Spain? And what kind of integrity can you [Portuguese] have outside of Spain?). More succinctly, he declares: "Sin Portugal no hay España; ... sin una federación acomodada a las patrias naturales no hay Portugal para nosotros" (Without Portugal there is no Spain, ... without a federation that respects the [peninsula's] natural peoples, Portugal cannot exist for us) (2: 750–1). Here Maragall fuses Unamuno's fatalism regarding Portugal's precarious independence with an argument taken from the Iberian federalist tradition. As both J.F. Henriques Nogueira and Quental contended, and as Maragall implies here, through federation, smaller nations like the Portuguese (or Catalans) can secure the "bem verdadeiro" (true good) of effective independence, as Nogueira put it, while casting off a debased form of nominal sovereignty (1: 165).

In passing, it is worth comparing Maragall's Iberianism, which he described as directed towards the goals of securing liberty for the peninsular peoples and allowing a federated Spain "una participación más directa en la vida civil de las naciones" (to participate more directly in the affairs of nations), as he put it in "La triste y espaciosa España," with that of his contemporary and sometime critic Enric Prat de la Riba.[36] Prat, in the concluding sentence of *La nacionalitat catalana*, which was published the same year as the bulk of Maragall's Iberianist production, stated that through federation, "podrà la nova Iberia enlairarse al grau suprem d'imperialisme: podrà intervenir activament en el govern del mon ab les altres potencies mundials, podrà altra vegada expansionarse sobre les terres barbres, y servir els alts interessos de l'humanitat guiant cap a civilisació els pobles enderrerits y incultes" (the new Iberia will be able to achieve the highest degree of imperialism. It will be able to actively intervene in governing the world, along with the other world powers. It will once again be able to conquer barbarian lands, and serve the lofty interests of humanity by bringing civilization to the backward and uncultured peoples) (128). Maragall's rhetoric occasionally approximates Prat's swaggering, expansive nationalism, as when he refers in "El ideal ibérico" to possible Iberian colonialism in Africa and to the irredentist idea of "la España grande" (the great Spain), in a 5 March 1911 letter to Unamuno. However, his rhetoric leans at least as heavily on the left-identified Iberian federalist argument and its concern for securing freedom and access to European modernity. Moreover, Maragall does not embrace imperialism as a value, as does the "anti-liberal" Prat.[37] In this sense, Maragall's position might be more appropriately compared to Quental's as enunciated in *Portugal perante a Revolução de Espanha* and *Causas da Decadência dos Povos Peninsulares*, whereas Prat's approximates the occasional aggression found in Oliveira Martins, in works such as *História da Civilização Ibérica*.

Maragall and Unamuno in Dialogue: Europeanization and "Another Spain"

Having outlined the broad contours of Joan Maragall's Iberianism, I will now turn to his correspondence with Miguel de Unamuno, and will assess its impact on the deeper structures of Maragall's Iberianist thought. Maragall and Unamuno's correspondence was carried out between 1900 and Maragall's death in 1911,[38] and has been described as a medium in which the two writers "attempt[ed] to grapple with the 'problem of Spain' and, for that matter, the 'problem of Iberia'" (Epps 98). Maragall and Unamuno's correspondence should also be viewed as an important vehicle through which Maragall and Unamuno exchanged ideas and influenced each other's thinking on Iberian issues. In the last section, I theorized that Maragall passed along his tripartite understanding of the Iberian Peninsula to Unamuno, and that this transmission was effected largely through their correspondence. Likewise, Maragall and Unamuno's epistolary exchanges may be credited with signalling or consolidating important shifts in Maragall's Iberianism. Admittedly, Unamuno's contributions to Maragall's Iberianism are less apparent than those of Prat or Ribera i Rovira, as Martínez-Gil, Harrington, and others have discussed. Nonetheless, they are important in that they seem to have impacted the deeper structures of Maragall's Iberianist thinking. I will focus in this section on two ideas that can be traced to Maragall's correspondence with Unamuno, and that bear directly on Maragall's Iberianism. These are Unamuno and Maragall's dialectical understanding of the relationship between Iberia and Europe, and Maragall's vision of "another Spain."

In passing, it is worth mentioning that Unamuno travelled to Barcelona during the Fall of 1906 to attend the *Primer Congrés Internacional de la Llengua Catalana* (First International Conference of the Catalan Language).[39] It was during this visit, Unamuno's first since 1899, that Unamuno and Maragall "se conoc[ieron] personalmente y la amistad, vertebrada hasta entonces por la correspondencia y el intercambio de obras, sal[ió] fortalecida" (met each other, and their friendship, which had been sustained until then through letter-writing and the exchange of publications, was strengthened) (Bastons 29). It seems plausible that Maragall's flurry of Iberianist writings during 1906 was at least partially inspired by the visit to his city of one of Spain's most polemical intellectuals, and one of its most prominent commentators on intra-Iberian relations.

In a 17 January 1907 letter to Unamuno, Maragall remarked that he had read his recent article "La cultura española en 1906" (Spanish Culture in 1906), and he described the lesson it had taught him regarding Spain's place in the world: "Es menester poder tomar perspectiva, poder situarse en Europa, para descubrir el África que en nosotros haya; y en nombre de ella revelándose contra Europa es entrar en Europa ... ensanchándola hacia nosotros, es decir, que Europa entre en nosotros a causa de la batalla" (We must see things in perspective, be able to situate ourselves in Europe, in order to uncover what is African within us. And by revealing our opposition to Europe, we will become part of Europe ... we will enlarge it in our direction, that is, allow Europe to penetrate us through the struggle) (50). This argument is exceptional, both for its degree of proximity to Unamuno's prior calls for Spain to "Europeanize," as in *En torno al casticismo* (written 1895, published 1902), and, moreover, for the fact that, Maragall's implication notwithstanding, Unamuno failed to address the topic of Europeanization in "La cultura española en 1906." Why, then, did Maragall mention Europeanization in reference to this particular article? It seems likely, barring a simple misreading, that in his letter to Unamuno he was using "La cultura española en 1906" as a kind of rhetorical springboard to signal his agreement with Unamuno's views on Europeanization and on the dialectical nature of the relationship between Iberia and Europe. In *En torno al casticismo* Unamuno had called on "Europeanized" Spaniards to "discover" Spain, and to thereby more closely and authentically tie Spain to Europe, by immersing themselves in the Castilian heartland's folk culture, traditions, and landscape. Just months prior to Maragall's 17 January 1907 letter, Unamuno made this assertion again in a 22 August 1906 address given at the Círculo Mercantil (Mercantile Circle) in Málaga: "Cuando se habla de la europeización de España, pienso siempre que es ella el mejor camino para españolizarnos, para descubrir lo nuestro propio permanente, quebrantando máscaras y postizos que una imperfecta europeización de pasados siglos nos ha impuesto. Y llego a creer que no debemos tampoco molestarnos de que se diga que el África empieza en los Pirineos, pues el espíritu africano, el que culminó en el ardiente Agustín de Hipona, es algo grande y fecundo" (Regarding the Europeanization of Spain, I have always said that this is the best way for us to become more Spanish, for us to discover our underlying, specific essence, for us to take off the masks and discard the falsehoods that the imperfect Europeanization of past centuries has imposed upon us. And I would even say that we should not be concerned by those who claim that Africa begins at the Pyrenees, for the African spirit, which culminated in the fiery Augustine of Hippo, is great and fruitful) (*OC* 9: 202).

The specific importance of Maragall's statement to Unamuno from his 17 January 1907 letter is not that he addresses Europeanization per se; indeed, Maragall had long been interested in this topic. Recall his 15 October 1898 letter to Joaquim Freixas, in which he declared: "La qüestió per Catalunya és europeïtzar-se" (What Catalonia must do is Europeanize itself) (1: 978). Rather, what is significant about this statement is that it signals a shift in Maragall's thinking about Europeanization, one that created the space for him to embrace an Iberianist future for Catalonia, Spain, and the peninsula as a whole. Whereas in the unpublished "La independència de Catalunya" (1897) Maragall had contended that Catalonia's entry into Europe was contingent on its cultural and perhaps political emancipation from a "dead" Castile,[40] in his 1907 letter, his argument is precisely the opposite: Catalonia – and Spain and Iberia by extension – can only become truly European by affirming its distinct peninsular "genius." This forecloses the option of Catalonia turning its back on the peninsula and positioning itself as an extension of Europe bordered by an "African" Castile,[41] as if it were a continuation of the Frankish *Marca Hispanica* of the eighth and ninth centuries. Maragall now believed that for Catalonia to "Europeanize" itself, it first had to affirm its Spanish or Iberian character and its ties with the other peninsular peoples. It would be an exaggeration to claim that Unamuno's dialectical view of the Iberia/Europe relationship should receive sole credit for effecting the "Iberianist turn" in Maragall's thinking. However, it seems plausible that Unamuno's analysis provided Maragall with a means of reconciling two potentially conflicting interests: his long-standing engagement with "Europeanization," and his more recent, or more recently intensified, preoccupation with the underlying commonalities of Iberian geography, culture, and civilization.

Let us now turn to a second feature of Maragall's Iberianist thought that is traceable to his correspondence with Unamuno. In his 7 March 1907 letter to Unamuno, Maragall comments on Catalonia's role in bringing into being an "otra España" (another Spain): "Siempre me parece que V. es el único español vivo ... en cuanto español, pues ya comprende V. que si algo hay aquí en Cataluña representa, al menos por ahora, una desintegración, aunque los más afectuosos la creamos precedente de una integración nueva. Pero aquélla ya sería *otra España*" (I have always thought of you as the only living Spaniard ... who is truly Spanish, for you understand that if for now Catalonia represents disintegration, those of who are more kindly disposed [towards Spain, presumably] believe it to be the harbinger of a new integration. But that would be *another Spain*) (Unamuno and Maragall 61; my emphasis). Superficially at least, the idea of Catalonia's role in fashioning "another" Spain was not new to Maragall. He had discussed it in his 1898 "Oda a Espanya," and he had held out Catalan values and achievements as possible drivers of Spanish regeneration in articles published in the years following the 1898 *desastre*, as in "El sentimiento catalanista" (The Catalanist Feeling, 1902), in which he wrote of the promise of a "nueva España" (new Spain) (*OC* 2: 631). However, Maragall's statement that the Spain with which he identified was "another" was more recent. In his 25 July 1905 article "Santiago, patrón de España" (James, Patron Saint of Spain), Maragall calls for "¡otra, otra España … la de ahora!" (Another, another Spain … the Spain of today!) (*OC* 2: 689). Maragall would expand substantially upon this discussion in "La espaciosa y triste España" (1911), in which he declared that the Spain with which he identified was "una España aparte" (a different Spain), but nonetheless one he would work to achieve.

What, then, is the specific importance of Maragall's 7 March 1907 comment to Unamuno on this "other Spain" which he hoped to achieve, and which he posited as a possible (though by no means certain) future for the country and for the Iberian Peninsula? First, Maragall's comment appears to signal his acceptance of Unamuno's Romantic-derived argument that countries (in this case Spain) incarnate a particular spirit, as enunciated in an address he gave on 25 February 1906 at the Teatro de Zarzuela in Madrid. Here Unamuno declares: "Hay dos patrias: una patria territorial y *otra patria espiritual*, y aquí casi todo el mundo habla de la patria territorial, sobre todo los que tienen territorios en ella; pero todavía si está esbozada la patria espiritual, apenas si nos hemos formado una idea de cuál ha de ser el espíritu de España en el mundo, y qué ideales, qué tono de cultura, le hemos de dar" (Two countries exist: a territorial country and *another, spiritual country*. Here almost everyone speaks of the territorial country, particularly those who are landowners, whereas the spiritual country has barely been sketched out. We have barely formulated an idea of what spirit, which ideals, and what sort of culture Spain wishes to contribute to the world) (*OC* 9: 177–8; my emphasis). The "other Spain" projected by Maragall would presumably integrate the "Europeanizing" Catalanist values of pragmatism, tolerance, and worldliness into the broader Iberian character. Second, in his 1907 statement Maragall puts Unamuno on notice, quite in the spirit of the "Oda a Espanya," that Castile-identified intellectuals (Unamuno, implicitly) must accept Catalonia's legitimate claims to linguistic and cultural recognition, and to greater political autonomy, if Spain is to benefit from Catalanism as the basis for "a new integration."

This in turn marks an important distinction between Unamuno and Maragall's Iberianist programs. Whereas Unamuno contended that Iberia's linguistic plurality would eventually give way to a single, synthetic *sobre-castellano*, and at times argued for Catalan intellectuals to write in Castilian as a means to lay the groundwork for this unification, Maragall believed that it was the maintenance and cultivation of the Iberian Peninsula's linguistic and cultural diversity that would prepare the way for an Iberianist future, and he resolutely defended the right of Catalans to express themselves in Catalan.[42] In one of his final articles, "'Catalunya i avant'" (1911), which he publicly addressed to Unamuno, Maragall responded to his Basque friend on this point: "No, mi admirado don Miguel de Unamuno; no, amigo mío muy querido; no puede ser, no podemos tomar la lengua castellana 'como lengua propia,' no podríamos hablar. Ahora nos damos a entender en ella porque la otra está dentro; y cuanto más firme y más fuerte la hagamos dentro, más nos daremos a entender en todas las lenguas" (No, my much-admired Miguel de Unamuno; no, my dear friend; it cannot be, we cannot view Castilian "as our own language," we cannot speak it in this way. Today we make ourselves understood in it because the other language [i.e., Catalan] is within us; and the more secure and the stronger we hold it within us, the more easily we will be understood in all languages) (*OC* 2: 760). Instead of taking up Unamuno's challenge that Catalan intellectuals should "impose" the Catalan character on the rest of Spain, just as Castile has "imposed" its language, laws, political rule, and culture on Catalonia, Maragall argues:

> la única [manera] eficaz [de efectuar "la gran obra nacional"] … es ir hurgando cada pueblo en su terruño, en su alma particular, hasta llegar a la raíz común, a la raíz ibérica que indudablemente existe. Allí hemos de encontrarnos, allí hemos de entendernos (y por cierto hablando cada uno en su lengua), allí hemos de unirnos valorando cada uno su elemento y su fuerza en la raíz común. Allí está la unidad; y por cierto más firme y armónica y definitiva que la que pudiéramos lograr – si alguna lográbamos – en la superficie. Allí está el imperialismo proporcionado a cada cual, allí la España grande – la castellana – catalana – vasca – portuguesa (porque, ¿qué importa la exterioridad política, pasajera, de los Estados?) – allí está el alma peninsular aún por descubrir, allí la gran civilización ibérica aún por hacer, y por la que seremos algo, mucho en el mundo. (2: 760-1)

> the only effective [means to bring about "the great national work"] … is for all of the peoples to delve into their own bit of land, their own particular soul, until they reach the common root, the Iberian root that no doubt exists. Here we will find and will communicate with one another (speaking our own languages, of course). This is how we will come together, by valuing each of our contributions to the common root. This is where

> unity lies, and it will be firmer and more definitive than any unity that could be achieved (if anyone is capable of achieving such a unity) at the surface. This is how we each gain access to an imperialism tailored to each one of us, how we will achieve the great Spain – which will be Castilian, Catalan, Basque, and Portuguese – (for what does the passing, external political form of states matter?). This is where we shall find the as-yet-undiscovered peninsular soul, the great Iberian civilization that remains unachieved, and this is how we will mean something, and mean a great deal, to the world.

In this way, Maragall had, at least to his own mind, squared the circle described by his potentially competing commitments to the Catalan nation, the Spanish state, and the Iberian Peninsula: by each people embracing its "particular soul," whether Catalan, Castilian, Galaico–Portuguese, or Basque, he argued, the peninsular peoples would together reach the common "Iberian root," which he would refer to elsewhere as the "Iberian soul." Would Maragall's more introspective brand of tripartite Iberianism or Unamuno's more expansive, dialectical variant carry the day in twentieth-century peninsular intellectual life? We will address this question in the following chapter, in the case of one prominent twentieth-century Iberianist, or as he would say, Spanish federalist: Salvador de Madariaga.

Chapter Six

The Iberianist Legacy: Salvador de Madariaga Reads Oliveira Martins

The Portuguese historian and polymath J.P. de Oliveira Martins (1845–94), who has appeared throughout this book, was a divisive but nonetheless influential figure in the intellectual life of late nineteenth-century Portugal. The historian Joel Serrão has observed that "a vida e a obra de Oliveira Martins foram, são e serão pomo de discórdia entre os seus concidadãos" (the life and work of Oliveira Martins were, are, and will continue to be a bone of contention for his countrymen) (52). This judgment could plausibly be extended to Spain, where prominent writers and intellectuals including Juan Valera (to whom Martins dedicated the second edition of his *História da Civilização Ibérica*), Marcelino Menéndez y Pelayo, and a young Miguel de Unamuno read and admired Martins's work. While Martins's sometimes aggressively pessimistic view of the peninsular past figured in his controversial reputation, so too did his declared Iberianism.[1] In terms of impact, Martins is unquestionably the most influential of the late nineteenth-century Portuguese Iberianists, with his ideas prompting reactions from peninsular writers throughout the twentieth century, and indeed up to the present.

As evidence for Martins's robust but contradictory legacy, Serrão cites the examples of early twentieth-century Portuguese intellectuals of opposing political views – António Sardinha, founder of the conservative *Integralismo Lusitano* movement, and the left-leaning writers associated with the journal *Seara Nova* – who found common ground in their appreciation for Oliveira Martins. Indeed, Martins was unique among the exegetes of the Portuguese *Geração de 70* and the more-or-less contemporary Spanish *Generación del 98* in that he both defended the distinctive value of Iberian civilization (which would appeal to traditionalists like Sardinha), and eviscerated the errors of Iberia's elites (which would appeal to Europeanizing progressives like the *Seara Nova* group). Comments made by prominent twentieth-century peninsular intellectuals bear out the notion that in the decades following Martins's death in 1894, his ideas continued to cross national, political, and disciplinary lines. Significantly, these reflections tended to gravitate towards the two conceptual poles of his affirmation of a distinct Iberian civilization, and his fierce criticism of the peninsular status quo.

The Portuguese poet, fiction writer, and diarist Miguel Torga, a noted Iberianist and opponent of the Portuguese *Estado Novo*, commented on Martins at least three times in his multi-volume *Diário* (1941–93). Torga recognized Martins's *História da Civilização Ibérica* as an important interpretation of peninsular culture, alongside works by Antero de Quental, Joaquín Costa, Unamuno, and Ángel Ganivet.[2] He also reflected on the severity of Martins's historical assessments. In a 28 February 1942 entry, Torga described Martins as "um homem a verrumar-nos, a analisar-nos colectivamente, sem poder fugir nenhum, a mostrar-nos à Europa com a alma ainda a escorrer sangue e façanhas, intolerância e fado" (a man who bores into us, analyses us collectively, without letting anyone escape, who shows us to Europe with our blood and deeds, our intolerance and fate still flowing from us) (2: 31). On 23 September 1953, Torga offered a less sympathetic view of Martins's critical approach: "Oliveira Martins, tão lúcido espírito, é um caso típico dessa incapacidade de consciencialização serena do que valemos. Enquanto a geração que mais ou menos lhe correspondia em Espanha escalpelizava a alma castelhana a procurar-lhe as linhas de força e de fraqueza, cobria ele de anátemas a da sua terra, errando ou acertando conforme o génio era servido" (Oliveira Martins, who was such a lucid spirit, is an example of someone unable to calmly appreciate our true worth. While the generation that more or less corresponded to him in Spain [i.e., the *Generación del 98*] probed the Castilian soul in search of its strong and weak points, Martins heaped curses on the soul of his land, missing or hitting the mark depending on what he was attempting to prove) (7: 58–9).

Torga's ambivalence speaks both to Martins's intellectual contradictions, and to those of Torga himself. On the one hand, Torga's opposition to the *Estado Novo* and his ceaseless critique of power would link him to the progressive, Europeanizing tradition in which Martins's friend and intellectual sparring partner Antero de Quental, along with Joan Maragall and, to a certain extent, the young Unamuno might be included. But Torga was also concerned with asserting the distinctiveness and specific value of Iberian civilization, a goal that underlies his collection

Poemas Ibéricos (1965). Further, he displayed a certain Euroscepticism, at least in his diary, especially once Portugal began its process of European integration following the *Revolução dos Cravos* (Carnation Revolution) of 25 April 1974, which overthrew the *Estado Novo* and placed Portugal on a democratizing path. Indeed, in an 11 November 1942 diary entry Torga warned against the "grande êrro ... [de] fazer da Ibéria uma terra de Europa" (great error ... [of] making Iberia a part of Europe) (2: 75).

Fidelino de Figueiredo (1889–1967), arguably Portugal's most prominent Hispanist scholar and the author of *As Duas Espanhas* (1932), an important interpretation of peninsular culture, wrote on Oliveira Martins on several occasions. In his *História d'um "Vencido da Vida"* (The Story of a "Vencido da Vida," 1930), a volume devoted to Martins, Figueiredo speculated on the causes of the Portuguese historian's popularity in *fin-de-siècle* Spain. Beyond stylistic factors such as Martins's "accentuada tendencia ensaista" (pronounced essayistic tendency) and "visão plastica e colorista" (visual, colourful approach), Figueiredo observed:

> Não é impossivel que contribuam para esta estima ainda dois factores moraes: o pessimismo hyper-critico do auctor português que acerta com essa descontentadiça tendencia da chamada 'europeisação de Hespanha'; e uma comprehensão inexacta do seu iberismo – que nunca implicou a renuncia á nacionalidade altiva, mesmo nos momentos de maior desalento ou de mais exaltada liberdade de linguagem. (*História* 144)

> It is possible that the esteem [in which Martins was held by Spanish readers] was the result of two additional moral factors: the Portuguese author's hypercritical pessimism, which spoke to the discontent that fuelled the so-called movement toward the "Europeanization of Spain"; and a misunderstanding of Martins's Iberianism – which never implied a renunciation of national feeling, even in his moments of greatest discouragement or in which he wrote with the least restraint.

In short, for Figueiredo, Martins's prominence in Spain was owed first to his pessimistic view of the Iberian past, which matched the critical mindset of Spain's *fin-de-siècle* regenerationists – at least one of whom, Unamuno, was a great reader of Martins. And second, the Spanish regenerationists' conscious or unconscious misreading of Martins's Iberianism led them to believe that Martins would have condoned Portugal's political reintegration into Spain. This was not the case, even in

Martins's early Iberian federalist period, though this misunderstanding made Martins a convenient name to cite in arguing for Portugal to rejoin the Spanish fold.

In a 1954 preface to Martins's *História da Civilização Ibérica*, Figueiredo again touched on the severity of Martins's judgments, though he dedicated the balance of his analysis to the appeal that Martins's integrated presentation of Iberian history held for Portuguese readers:

> O êxito da obra [a *História da Civilização Ibérica*] foi pleno. Os portugueses encontravam nela uma larga síntese ao gosto do tempo, síntese muito simplista e mnemónica, e corrigida quanto a excessos de abstracção por largas pinceladas de flagrante caracterização colorista. Era verdadeiramente cómoda aquela simbolização da história paralela dos dois povos irmãos nalguns sucessos e nalgumas figuras. Tinha a aparência de demonstração de coisa quase evidente, a que só faltasse a relevância sedutora, que lhe dava a magia da pena do escritor. ("Prefácio" 14–15)

> It [the *História da Civilização Ibérica*] was a great success. Portuguese readers found in it a broad synthesis of the sort that suited the taste of the time. The simplistic and mnemonic qualities of this synthesis and its excesses of abstraction were compensated by instances of quite colourful characterization. The symbolic presentation of the parallel histories of two sibling peoples, through a selection of events and figures, was truly appealing. It appeared to present something that was almost self-evident, lacking only the seductive relevance added by the magic of the writer's pen.

Decades later, Eduardo Lourenço (b. 1923), one of Portugal's most prominent literary and cultural critics (and also the founder of a Centro de Estudos Ibéricos in his hometown of Guarda), would elaborate on the peninsular dimension of Martins's analysis. Lourenço addressed this topic in his essay "A Espanha e Nós" (Spain and Us, 1988), and then in a 2005 interview with Maria Manuel Baptista. Addressing Portuguese–Spanish relations in "A Espanha e Nós," Lourenço wrote: "Os nossos destinos foram sempre, ou paralelos ou cruzados, nunca opostos enquanto *culturas*, pois, como o viu com nitidez Oliveira Martins, fazemos parte de uma única estrutura, criada séculos antes que os povos que constituem a Península se definissem como nação" (Our destinies have always been either parallel or crossed, and never opposed as *cultures*. As Oliveira Martins clearly saw, we are part of a single structure, formed centuries before the peoples of the Peninsula defined themselves as nations) (62; author's emphasis). Lourenço gave the following extended assessment in his 2005 interview:

> Oliveira Martins é um caso muito singular na historiografia portuguesa e, sobretudo, nessa consideração da visão da nossa História, incluindo nela a Espanha. Não é por acaso que Oliveira Martins é o autor da *História da Civilização Ibérica*. Quer dizer, concebeu a civilização ibérica como um todo de que nós fazemos parte. Nós somos um dos actores dessa civilização a que ele chama Ibérica, a qual não é só a civilização da Península que é europeia, mas é aquela que a Espanha e Portugal exportaram para o Mundo ...
>
> Oliveira Martins não vive obcecado por essa ideia de que nós perderíamos o nosso ser por uma aproximação com a Espanha. Pensa é que esse diálogo ibérico é constitutivo daquilo que nós somos e daquilo que eles são, mesmo se é um diálogo desequilibrado em função de uma das partes. Eu não sou historiador, mas não posso deixar de ter uma dívida para com Oliveira Martins por duas razões: a primeira, pelo olhar extremamente arguto, mesmo se toda a gente sabe que é um pouco apocalíptico, sobre a marcha da História Portuguesa. Mas pelo menos teve essa intuição extraordinária de não pensar a História de Portugal como uma coisa à parte, como uma ilha que só tem leitura no relacionamento consigo própria. Portugal não está só no mundo, primeiro tem a Espanha aqui ao lado e depois tem o mundo inteiro. Oliveira Martins tem muita consciência de que a História de Portugal não era só aquilo que aconteceu aqui, neste rincão da Península. (28–9)

> Oliveira Martins is a very unique case in Portuguese historiography, especially in terms of his vision of our history, which included Spain. It is not coincidental that it was Oliveira Martins who wrote the *História da Civilização Ibérica*. That is, he understood Iberian civilization as a whole of which we are part. We are one of the participants in this civilization, which he terms Iberian, and which refers not only to peninsular, European civilization, but also to the civilization that Spain and Portugal exported to the world.
>
> Oliveira Martins was not obsessed with the idea that we would lose ourselves by moving closer to Spain. He believed that this Iberian dialogue was constitutive of us, even if this was an unequal dialogue due to one of the two participants. I am not a historian, but I am indebted to Oliveira Martins for two reasons: first, for his extremely astute, though somewhat apocalyptic vision of the progress of Portuguese history. But he had the extraordinary intuition that the history of Portugal should not be

> viewed as something apart, as an island only capable of being understood in relation to itself. Portugal is not alone in the world. First it has Spain here at its side, and then it has the entire world. Oliveira Martins was quite conscious of the fact that the history of Portugal was not just what has happened here, in this corner of the Peninsula.

Spanish historian José Antonio Maravall (1911–86) wrote along similar lines in his prologue to a 1972 Spanish translation of Martins's *História da Civilização Ibérica*. Maravall praised Martins's understanding of Portugal and Spain's "correlación existencial" (existential correlation), and recommended his book as a means for readers to examine nation forming and the emergence of national consciousness – themes Maravall explored in his study *El concepto de España en la Edad Media* (The Idea of Spain in the Middle Ages, 1954) (9). However, Maravall parts company with Torga, Figueiredo, and Lourenço in viewing Martins's vision of the Iberian past in rather sunnier terms than is perhaps typical. For Maravall, Martins, animated by an "iberismo nuevo y dinámico" (new and dynamic Iberianism), looks to the peninsular past in order to locate collective myths that would be capable of inspiring change (14). While for Torga, Martins "bores" into the collective Iberian psyche with a perhaps excessive negativity, for Maravall, he tempers his sharp judgments of the Iberian past in order to stimulate reforms in which some form of Iberianism would figure.[3]

Having offered a selection of comments from some of Oliveira Martins's more prominent twentieth-century Portuguese and Spanish readers, in this concluding chapter I will look to another twentieth-century Iberian intellectual who was influenced by Martins, and who, perhaps more so than any other Iberian public intellectual of his time, can be productively brought into dialogue with him. This is the Spanish writer, historian, diplomat, and political exile Salvador de Madariaga (1886–1978). Madariaga elucidated his thoughts on the distinctiveness of Iberian civilization, on federalism both within and beyond Spain, and on Iberia's relationship to Europe in studies including *España: Ensayo de Historia contemporánea* (Spain: An Essay in Contemporary History, 1933), *Bosquejo de Europa* (Outline of Europe, 1951), and *Memorias de un federalista* (Memoirs of a Federalist, 1967).

Madariaga makes for a logical "bridge" between Iberianism's *fin-de-siècle* heyday and more contemporary debates on Iberian culture and identity for several reasons: first, his life spanned Spain's Restoration monarchy (1874–1931), Second Republic (1931–9), Francoism (1939–75), and the first years of post-Franco federal democracy. The problems he addressed, including the tension between Castilian centralism and Catalan, Basque, and Galician aspirations towards autonomy or independence, and the relationship of Spain to a federated Europe, remain highly relevant today. Second, as an international diplomat who wrote in Spanish, French, and English, Madariaga enjoyed significant international prestige. This gave his writings a broad projection unavailable to more strictly academic early to mid-twentieth-century Hispanists (Ramón Menéndez Pidal, Américo Castro, Claudio Sánchez-Albornoz, et al.).[4] And third, and most importantly for our purposes, Madariaga tied together and developed several strands of Iberianist thinking discussed in this book. Though Madariaga did not describe himself as an Iberianist – he preferred the term *federalist* – he nonetheless called for post-Franco Spain to reorganize itself as a federation, advocated European federalism more broadly, and affirmed the overarching unity of Iberian or "Spanish" civilization (a concept he viewed as inclusive of Portugal) even as he acknowledged internal differences within the peninsula.[5]

While one can locate points of contact in Madariaga's work with the ideas and proposals of *fin-de-siècle* Iberianists including Quental, Unamuno, and Maragall, it was to Oliveira Martins's *História da Civilização Ibérica* that Madariaga turned in 1930, when he was tasked with choosing the inaugural title for a series of Hispanic classics to be published in English translation by Oxford University Press. This chapter will first offer a biographical sketch of Madariaga, then summarize his written references to Martins, and will conclude by comparing Madariaga and Martins's ideas on Iberian history and culture.

Salvador de Madariaga: Iberian Federalist and Liberal Heretic

Salvador de Madariaga was born on 23 July 1886 in La Coruña to Colonel José Madariaga and María Ascensión Rojo. In his first volume of memoirs, *Memorias de un federalista,* Madariaga describes the La Coruña of his youth as a "país bilingüe" (bilingual country), and his childhood as one spent speaking both Castilian and Galician (17). Reflecting on his mixed ancestry (though born and raised in Galicia, Madariaga's paternal surname is Basque, and he had familial roots in other parts of Spain), he declared that, "si algo soy – [soy] gallego" (if I am anything, I am Galician) (13).[6] Madariaga went to great lengths in his memoirs to dispel what he viewed as the misconception, likely perpetuated by his commitment to Spanish federalism, his opposition to Catalan and Basque separatism (which he viewed as the mirror image of misguided Castilian centralism), and his association with the pre-Francoist Madrid political establishment, that he was Castilian by birth or affinity. Perhaps referring to the *casticista* attitudes diagnosed by the young Unamuno (who was also frequently described as a defender of Castile) Madariaga wrote that "aun los más humildes de mis impresiones infantiles surgieron lejos del casticismo castellano" (even my earliest childhood impressions were located far from Castilian traditionalism) (22). In a 17 March 1940 letter to Catalan intellectual and politician Josep Maria Batista i Roca, Madariaga declared with some irony: "Ya sabe usted que yo no soy castellano y que por mi nacimiento y formación he venido por mi desgracia a ser una de las encarnaciones del espíritu español integral" (You know that I am not Castilian but that because of my birth and education I have unfortunately become an incarnation of the spirit of all of Spain, which can content itself with nothing less than the whole of the peninsula) (quoted in Madariaga, *Memorias* 253–4).[7]

Madariaga's father, who believed Spain had been defeated by the United States in 1898 due to its "technological backwardness" (Preston 143), sent his adolescent son to study engineering in France, where he graduated from the School of Mines in 1911. Madariaga then took a position as a railway engineer in northern Spain, in this respect recalling the career trajectory of Oliveira Martins, who for a time worked as technical and economic director for the Porto–Póvoa line. Like Martins, Madariaga quickly gravitated toward political journalism and the intellectual milieu of the capital. And like Unamuno, one of his intellectual mentors, Madariaga supported the Allies during the First World War, and wrote propaganda for the British Foreign Office (144).[8]

After the war, Madariaga worked at the League of Nations, where he headed the Disarmament Section between 1922 and 1927 (144). This position gave him an international prominence he was to retain throughout his career. Madariaga's time at the League was also crucial in the development of his federalism. As Preston notes, "during these years he developed a truly international outlook. He was bitterly disappointed that the League never become a true world organization" (144).[9] Madariaga came to echo earlier Iberian federalists like Francesc Pi i Margall and Antero de Quental – and, by extension, Giuseppe Mazzini and Pierre-Joseph Proudhon. Pi i Margall and Quental argued that to secure local autonomy, democracy, and peace, the Iberian Peninsula and Europe as a whole should be reorganized along federal lines – though Pi, writing in *Las nacionalidades* (1877), was more sceptical than Madariaga that federalism on a global scale was possible.[10] Madariaga's federalism gained expression in texts like *Anarchy or Hierarchy* (1937), which he wrote after witnessing the fratricidal First World War and Spanish Civil War. Here he commented on the need for a "world-State," grounded in "world consciousness" or "world patriotism," which would be the capstone of a system of federal relationships (143, 200). Though disillusioned by the League's failure and Europe's descent by 1939 into a second world war, Madariaga would retain his federalist and liberal convictions, taking leadership roles in organizations like the Liberal International and the College of Europe.

In 1927 Madariaga became the inaugural Alfonso XIII Chair of Spanish Studies at Oxford, a position he retained until 1931, when he returned to Spain to serve the Republic. Crucial to our discussion, during Madariaga's time at Oxford he shepherded an English translation of Oliveira Martins's *A History of Iberian Civilization* to publication. We will return to this episode in this chapter's next section.

Following the establishment of the Republic in 1931, Madariaga represented Spain at the League of Nations, and held additional diplomatic positions. During this period Madariaga wrote a "Nota sobre la política exterior de España" (Note regarding Spain's Foreign Policy; dated 27 May 1932), in which he revealed his openness to an Iberian federation in which both Spain and Portugal would participate. However, he cautioned that this scheme might be compromised by Spanish overreach: "En sus relaciones con Portugal, sin abandonar el ideal de una posible Federación Ibérica, común hoy a las mejores inteligencias portuguesas, España habría de manifestarse con la mayor escrupulosidad y respetar ante todo el sentido de independencia que domina en Portugal, dejando más bien la iniciativa de todo movimiento de aproximación a los propios portugueses. Ello no obstante, convendría guardar ciertas distinciones que marquen en Portugal no es totalmente extranjero a España" (In her relations with Portugal, and without abandoning the goal of a possible Iberian Federation, which is shared by the best minds in Portugal, Spain should act with the utmost scrupulousness and above all respect the feeling of independence that prevails in Portugal, leaving it to the Portuguese to initiate any movement of mutual approximation. This said, certain details that show that Portugal is not totally foreign to Spain should be maintained) (quoted in Madariaga, *Memorias [1921–1936]* 613). Madariaga had referred to the possibility of establishing an Iberian federation some years earlier, in the article "¿Es España Estado o Nación?" (Is Spain a State or a Nation?), published in the reformist Madrid newspaper *El Sol* on 22 March 1923. Here Madariaga speculates that "de llegar a realizarse el ideal de la Federación Ibérica, habría como nexo entre las tres naciones peninsulares un Estado español" (the Spanish state would be the nexus around which the three peninsular nations [Galicia–Portugal, Castile, and Catalonia] would form a future Iberian Federation) (quoted in *Memorias* 208). This statement conveys Madariaga's openness to a federal reorganization of the Iberian Peninsula, as well as his insistence that such an Iberian Federation would be rooted in Spain, which implies that Portugal would "rejoin" the Spanish fold in forming a union with the other peninsular peoples – a position at odds with Quental and Oliveira Martins's arguably more equitable federalist proposals. Further, Madariaga's comment reproduces the tripartite division of the Iberian Peninsula promoted by Catalan Iberianists such as Maragall, and eventually adopted by Unamuno, who himself was one of Madariaga's principal intellectual influences.

While Madariaga represented Spain abroad, he confronted problems at home. His "liberal and cultured" personality and classical, even aristocratic[11] brand of liberalism have been credited with alienating more radical or populist Spanish Republicans (*Disinherited* 150). Like Ortega, his fellow contributor to *El Sol*, Madariaga was both anti-communist and anti-fascist, refused to take sides in the Spanish Civil War, and feared mass politics, which he once termed *populitis*.[12] This earned Madariaga "the hostility of both Right and Left" (289). Madariaga's fondness for irony and paradox – almost certainly learned from Unamuno – along with his anti-communism, may have further aggravated relations with his leftist peers.

Looking back in his memoirs, Madariaga described the tensions seething within the Republic as "un caso más, sólo que más trágico y feroz, del separatismo innato que a todos nos aflige" (one more example, albeit the most tragic and violent example, of the affliction of our innate separatism) (*Memorias* 72). With Francisco Franco's definitive victory over the Republic in 1939, Madariaga returned to Britain as an exile. Here he remained active in the Spanish opposition, though he frequently quarrelled with exiled Basque and Catalan leaders. These tensions seem to have been prompted by Madariaga's commitment to Spanish federalism, and his suspicion that certain prominent Basques and Catalans held separatist sympathies; these arguments are described in Madariaga's *Memorias de un federalista*, in which he affirmed the "necesidad de organizar el país de forma federal; conveniencia y aun necesidad de autonomías no sólo culturales sino políticas" (need to organize the country along federal lines; [and] the benefit and even necessity of the autonomous regions being defined not only in cultural, but in political terms). Madariaga also expressed his "temor de que se malogre este programa por el extremismo español, menos a causa del centralismo ... que por el ... separatismo" (great fear that this program might be undone by Spanish extremism, less the product of centralism ... than of ... separatism) (9).

Beyond his role as an internationally respected diplomat and leading member of the Spanish opposition, Madariaga continued during the Franco years to advance his federalist program for Spain and for Europe at large, and defended liberalism as he understood it. In 1947, Madariaga participated in the International Liberal Conference at Oxford, and between 1947 and 1952 served as first president of the Liberal International, an organization that advocated for free speech, free trade, multi-party democracy, and world peace.[13] In 1948, Madariaga proposed the creation of the College of Europe at The Hague (the college was founded the following year), and in his volume *Democracy versus Liberty? The Faith of a Liberal Heretic* (1958), Madariaga presciently called for a relatively decentralized European federation to be based initially in the capitalist, democratic West and eventually expanded eastward. Upon Franco's death in 1976, Madariaga returned to Spain, where he was elected to the Real Academia Española, before dying in Locarno, Switzerland, on 14 December 1978.

Madariaga and the Publication of *A History of Iberian Civilization*

Madariaga's work features several references to Oliveira Martins, the majority of which pertain to Oxford's publication in 1930 of Aubrey F.G. Bell's English translation of Martins's *História da Civilização Ibérica*. While I have not discovered when and under what circumstances Madariaga first read Martins, Madariaga was evidently familiar with the *História da Civilização Ibérica* as early as 1923, having referred to the Portuguese historian in passing in an article on the "Catalan problem" published on 31 January of that year in *El Sol*. It is possible that Madariaga may have come to Martins through Unamuno's writings, given his documented influence on Madariaga and effusive praise of Martins, and especially for his *História da Civilização Ibérica*. Madariaga gave various accounts of his motives for selecting the *História da Civilização Ibérica* as "one of the first books to appear under the auspices of the

Oxford Chair of Spanish Studies" ("Preface" v). In his preface to Bell's translation, Madariaga anticipated Lourenço's judgment of Martins, praising him as "an intuitive historian with the gift of vision" (v), and noting his ability to "[see] right through the maze of errors as well as his courage in putting before the Iberian peoples the general lines of a civilization and a culture which most of them had proved unable to see as one harmonious whole" (vi). Madariaga elaborated:

> For the first time an Iberian looks at Iberia as Iberia and reports to the world what the world has received and may still expect to receive from the peoples of the Peninsula. It is a singular good fortune that this bold Iberian should have been a Portuguese. For under his free and ardently patriotic pen, the Peninsular vision which animates his work can never be interpreted as impairing even by a shadow of a doubt the independent nationhood of Portugal. (vi)

For Madariaga, the fact that Martins was both Portuguese *and* a self-identified Iberian (and Iberianist) illustrated "the truth which our present age is beginning to realize ...: that spiritual unity may underlie political variety and give it strength without depriving it of liberty" (vi). This comment is in line with Martins's late view, as expressed in the article "Iberismo" (1889): "União de pensamento e acção, independência de governo; eis, a nosso ver, a fórmula actual, sensata e prática do Iberismo" (Union of thought and action, with independence of government. This is, in my view, the current, sensible, and practical formula for Iberianism) (*Dispersos* 2: 216).

Madariaga elaborated on Martins's understanding of the overarching unity of Iberian civilization in his own exegetic "essay" on Spanish civilization and culture, *Spain: A Modern History* (1930; Spanish trans. *España: Ensayo de Historia contemporánea*, 1933), which he published the same year as Bell's translation of Martins. Here Madariaga wrote:

> La misma idea de unión o federación política no llegó nunca a desaparecer ni en España ni en Portugal, sobre todo en el siglo XIX, al renacer por todas partes el interés en la mera política. Cosa curiosa, se siente más actividad en este terreno por parte de Portugal que por la de España, quizá porque el cambio producido por la unión hubiera sido más profundo en Portugal. No faltaron nunca portugueses penetrados de la idea de que para Portugal el dilema es: o ser miembro autónomo del cuerpo ibérico, o ser, con disfraz de independencia, miembro apenas más autónomo del imperio británico. Una de las voces elocuentes que en el siglo XIX resuenan para hacer renacer

a España, la España que comprende a Cataluña como comprende a Portugal, fue la del historiador portugués, Oliveira Martins. En su *Historia de la Civilización Ibérica*, dedicada a Juan Valera, Oliveira Martins penetra bajo los detalles históricos para extraer la unidad esencial de la civilización española ... Oliveira Martins tuvo poco éxito, y aun puede decirse que arriesgó su popularidad. Sus doctrinas ibéricas ofendían el sentimiento popular, vigorizado por el dispersionismo ibérico. El temor de una interpretación política rígida de la unión se alía en muchos portugueses con el recelo más concreto de una conquista española. (*España* 244, 246)

The matter of a political union or federation was never quite dormant, least of all in the nineteenth century when political thought became more general. Curiously enough, Portugal was the keener of the two, for the change it would imply looms larger in her future than in that of Spain. Some enlightened Portuguese realized that Portugal must be either an autonomous limb of an Iberian body or a disguised and hardly more autonomous limb of the British Empire. One of the more eloquent voices to call Spain back to life, that Spain which includes Catalonia as it includes Portugal, was a Portuguese historian, Oliveira Martins. In his *History of Iberian Civilization*, dedicated to the Spanish novelist and critic Juan Valera, Oliveira Martins endeavors to delve under historical details in order to draw out the essential unity of the Iberian civilization ... Oliveira Martins had but little following. His Iberian views, in fact, had injured his popularity with his countrymen. The fear of a rigid political interpretation of the union is, in many a Portuguese soul combined with the more concrete fear of actual Spanish conquest and occupation. (254, 256)

Madariaga's reference in *Spain: A Modern History* to Martins and his *História da Civilização Ibérica* is not surprising, given Madariaga's insistence, conveyed here and in numerous other works, that Portugal was an artificially and tragically disconnected part or "limb" of Spain, and that its future would necessarily be intertwined with a Spanish nation state organized along federal lines.

Moving forward, Madariaga referred to the publication of the English-language edition of *A History of Iberian Civilization* twice in his memoirs. He wrote the following in his *Memorias de un federalista* (1967):

Mi capítulo sobre Portugal [en *España : Ensayo de Historia contemporánea*] estaba todo él construido sobre esta definición: *el portugués es un español con la espalda vuelta a los demás españoles y los ojos en el Atlántico.* O dicho de otro modo, el portugués es un español separatista que, gracias a Francia e Inglaterra, se ha salido con la suya ...

> Para mí ... el hecho de que el portugués lograse realizar su separatismo y el catalán fracasara no constituía entonces ni constituye ahora una diferencia esencial, aunque desde luego se dé una diferencia histórica. Por lo mismo, me pareció de perlas la *Historia de la civilización ibérica*, de Oliveira Martins, uno de los portugueses que mejor han comprendido la unidad esencial de la península española. Como profesor de literatura española conseguí que la Universidad de Oxford emprendiera la publicación de una serie de textos hispánicos traducidos al inglés y, no sin cierto efecto de paradoja entre mis colegas, comencé la serie con el libro de Oliveira Martins. (54)

> My chapter on Portugal [in *Spain: A Modern History*] was built around this formulation: *the Portuguese is a Spaniard with his back turned to his fellow Spaniards and his eyes fixed on the Atlantic.* Or put another way, the Portuguese is a Spanish separatist who, thanks to France and England, has succeeded in breaking away ...
>
> For me ... the fact that the Portuguese were able to achieve their separatist aim and the Catalans were not does not make for an essential distinction, though it has entailed different histories. For this reason, I thought Oliveira Martins's *A History of Iberian Civilization* was fantastic. Among the Portuguese, he is one of those who have best understood the essential unity of the Spanish peninsula. As a professor of Spanish literature I arranged for Oxford University to publish a series of Hispanic texts in English translation, and I began the series with Oliveira Martins's book, which struck my colleagues as a bit paradoxical.[14]

The argument attributed here to Oliveira Martins – that Iberian civilization, transcending its political divisions, constituted an "essential unity," would have appealed to Madariaga on two counts. First, as a European federalist in the tradition of Mazzini, Proudhon, Quental, Pi i Margall, and indeed, the young Martins, Madariaga promoted the idea that individuals could – and should – maintain a hierarchy of mutually reinforcing loyalties to family, municipality, region, and nation state, and concluding with a supra-national federation.[15] In other words, Madariaga understood Iberian "regional" affinities (to Portugal, Galicia, Catalonia, Castile, the Basque Country, and so on) not as antithetical to a broader Spanish patriotism, but rather as a precondition for such patriotism under the federal system.

Second, Madariaga held to the core Iberianist tenet that Spain and Portugal were inextricably bonded by myriad historical, cultural, and geographic ties. And like Martins and Unamuno (but less so the "Europeanizing" Quental and Maragall), Madariaga viewed Spain's regions and Portugal as collaborating in the articulation of a distinctive and valuable Iberian civilization, which he did not hesitate to term "Spanish." Though Madariaga affirmed "Portugal's independent nationhood" in his preface to *A History of Iberian Civilization* (vi), he described Portugal elsewhere using the well-worn metaphor of an unnaturally and tragically severed limb of the Spanish or Iberian body, and seemed to follow Unamuno in believing that Portugal would not fully realize itself until it "returned" to a federated Spain. The reverse side of this argument, for Unamuno and Madariaga alike, was that Catalonia would fatally wound its (Iberian) self if it separated from Spain.

Given all of this, it was, as Madariaga admitted, "a singular good fortune" that the *História da Civilização Ibérica* had been written by the "ardently patriotic pen" of a Portuguese historian, for it allowed him to argue for Spanish–Portuguese approximation while drawing on Martins's authority as a Portuguese Iberianist, thereby inoculating himself against charges of Spanish annexationist intent towards Portugal ("Preface" vi). After all, if a patriotic Portuguese historian recognized the intertwined historical destinies of Portugal and Spain, then how could Madariaga's Iberian federalism be construed as a pretext for Castilian centralism or Spanish domination? Yet as Figueiredo observes, the mature Oliveira Martins's understanding of Iberia's historical or civilizational unity, as elucidated in the article "Iberismo" (1889), did not lead him to advocate peninsular political union, nor did it cause him to question the specificity of Portuguese history, culture, and identity – quite the opposite. To this extent, Madariaga's reading of Martins must be seen as partial and even self-interested in that it supported his program for reorganizing Spain as a federation in which Portugal, in fulfilling its historical destiny, might one day participate. In the following section I will attempt a more sustained comparison of Madariaga and Martins, analysing Madariaga's reflections on Iberian civilization and Portuguese–Spanish relations in comparison to Martins's views.

Iberian Unity and Variety: Madariaga and Oliveira Martins Compared

The most obvious commonality between Madariaga and Martins's views on Iberia is their shared belief in the overarching unity of peninsular civilization, a notion that coloured their vision of the Iberian past, and implied the common participation of the various peninsular peoples (the Portuguese included) in the ongoing development of this civilization. Both Madariaga and Martins recognized that Iberian unity was shot through with tensions and ambiguities, though they explained and resolved these tensions differently: Madariaga called for post-Franco Spain to reorganize itself as a federal democracy as a precondition for Portuguese reincorporation into a state that, while respectful of regional autonomy, would still be identifiably Spanish. Meanwhile, as a young man Martins advocated a decentralized Iberian federal republic, while in later years he called for Portuguese–Spanish intellectual exchange and a political and economic alliance, but explicitly rejected political union. Both men acknowledged the need to accommodate peninsular regional differences and recognized (though in Madariaga's case, did not condone) Portugal's political independence and Catalonia's autonomist and independence claims. Further, they both confronted 1640, a year that witnessed Portugal's restoration to independence and the beginning of Catalonia's revolt against the Habsburgs – events that would seem to directly undercut the prospects for Iberian unity. These shared preoccupations constitute the basis for the comparison between Madariaga and Martins undertaken in this section.

Madariaga made numerous affirmations of the overarching unity of Iberian civilization. In one of his first English-language volumes, *The Genius of Spain and Other Essays on Spanish Contemporary Literature* (1923), Madariaga contrasted Portugal and Catalonia's relationship to the entity he suggestively termed "the Spanish Peninsula":

> Seen in its entirety, above the historical and political contingencies which have obscured its intrinsic unity, the Spanish Peninsula appears as one well-defined spiritual entity. This fact the Portuguese critics are beginning to realize and the Catalan critics to forget. Both movements are historically logical, for, while Portugal has outlived the period of her affirmation as a separate sub-entity within the Spanish wider unity, Catalonia is on the contrary but beginning a struggle for asserting her own personality within the Peninsula and putting it beyond reach of attack from political prejudice. (148)

Martins would have agreed with the thrust of Madariaga's argument here, though probably not with the implications behind Madariaga's use of the term "the Spanish Peninsula." As Madariaga recognized, Martins also affirmed the "essential unity" and specific value of Iberian civilization. For Martins, the basis of this unity resided in the idea of a "génio peninsular," a collective "peninsular genius," spirit, or way of being shared by all Iberians, and that is apparent in the intertwined histories of the Spanish and Portuguese states. Madariaga's use of the term "genius" in the title to his 1923 study suggests that he, like Martins, subscribed to the idea, derived from Romantic-era ethnic nationalism, that Spaniards and Iberians more broadly were possessed of a shared *Volksgeist*. Further, Martins, like Madariaga, occasionally shifted in his discussions of Iberian unity from the rather nebulous terrain of collective "spirit" to the quasi-biological realm, by referring to Iberians as a "race."[16]

Despite Madariaga and Martins's affirmations of Iberia's "intrinsic unity," both men acknowledged regional differences, and subscribed to the notion – traceable to Pi i Margall, though prominent in Unamuno as well – that Iberian civilization is defined by the dialectical interaction of the forces of unity and variety, or as Pi put it "la unidad en la variedad" (unity in variety) (*Las nacionalidades* 96). Madariaga divided the peninsula in *The Genius of Spain* into "a trinity composed of a Western, a Central, and an Eastern modality, the norms of which respectively are Portugal, Castile, and Catalonia" (148). Madariaga evidently inherited this tripartite scheme from Unamuno (who, as I argued, took it from Maragall), and would reproduce it elsewhere. Madariaga affirmed the formula of Iberian "unity in variety" on various occasions, writing in his *Memorias de un federalista* that his travels through Spain had convinced him of "la variedad maravillosa de nuestro país y, por consecuencia, todavía más su no menos maravillosa unidad; porque no creo que haya en Europa pueblo y tierra de más rica y jugosa variedad y, sin embargo, pueblo y tierra que acusen una unidad más vigorosa" (the marvellous variety of our country and, by extension, its even more marvellous unity; because I do not believe that there is in Europe a people and land of such rich and colourful variety, nor a people and land that is more vigorously united) (29). Madariaga returned to the idea that Iberian variety existed within an overarching unity in *Spain: A Modern History* (1930), declaring of a "Spain" that included Portugal: "Varia, pero una, la tierra; vario, pero uno, el pueblo" (Varied but one is the land; varied but one the people) (*España* 26; *Spain* 11).

Martins too acknowledged differences between Iberians even as he insisted on overarching unity in his *História da Civilização Ibérica*. Madariaga, a twentieth-century Spanish federalist concerned with establishing a workable post-Franco political order, logically devoted a great deal of attention to relations between Castilians, Catalans, Basques, and Galicians. Martins, in contrast, approached Iberian history and culture from the vantage point of *fin-de-siècle* Portugal, and privileged binary comparisons between the Portuguese and a rather monolithic "Spain." In his *História da Civilização Ibérica*, referring to the early modern period, Martins observes: "O dualismo político da Península – Castela e Portugal – é o sistema sob que a Espanha aparece por fim no concerto das nações europeias, irmã na forma, acorde no pensamento, unificada na acção" (As two political nations, Castille and Portugal, the Peninsula finally took its place among the nations of Europe – two sisters of like thought and action) (*Civilização Ibérica* 209–10; *Iberian Civilization* 171). Further, in his discussion of Portuguese and Spanish maritime expansion, Martins affirmed the formula of "a unidade desta civilização [ibérica], expressa por um dualismo político" (the unity of this [Iberian] civilization, which finds expression in political dualism) (*Civilização Ibérica* 268). Martins would return to the notion that Iberian political dualism necessarily accompanied a deeper civilizational unity (a corollary of the "unity in variety" formula) in the opening paragraphs of his *História de Portugal*, published the same year as the *História da Civilização Ibérica*. Here he refers to Portugal and Spain as the "duas nações hespanholas: duas, porque a historia assim constituiu politicamente a Peninsula" (two Spanish nations: two, because history constituted the Peninsula politically in this way) (1: ix).

Reflecting the influence on his thinking of Romantic ideas of national "genius," Martins noted distinctions between the Portuguese and Spanish characters, and in lieu of objective or scientifically rigorous criteria for differentiation of these natural "types," he drew on artistic and literary metaphors. In "Os Povos Peninsulares e a Civilização Moderna" (The Peninsular Peoples and Modern Civilization, 1875), Martins writes of "os dois tons" (the two tones) of "idealismo peninsular" (peninsular idealism), one Spanish and the other Portuguese (81). And he opines: "O sentimento afectivo, o sentimento heroico, são mais suaves e tristes, mais graves e dignos, mais amplos, mais iguais, mais epicos nos portugueses; mais dramáticos e ruidosos nos espanhóis" (Affective tendencies and the heroic tendency are softer and sadder, more solemn and dignified, broader, more even-keeled, more epic in the Portuguese, and more dramatic and noisy in the Spaniards) (76). Finally, in his *História da Civilização Ibérica*, Martins affirms: "Cada um dos povos peninsulares desenvolve os recursos do seu génio, e, objectiva e històricamente, esses recursos são equivalentes: o que de um lado sobra em audácia, falta do outro em justiça. Há nos portugueses um melhor equilíbrio nas faculdades, como é próprio de um temperamento menos acentuado; e essa é a causa do carácter trágico da cena ultramarina portuguesa, ao lado da espanhola que é uma comédia" (Each of the peoples of the Peninsula develops the resources of its own genius, and from an objective and historical point of view these resources are equivalent: an excess of daring on the one side corresponds to a lack of justice on the other. The faculties of the Portuguese are better balanced, as was natural in their less emphatic temperament; and that is why the Portuguese scene beyond the seas is tragic whereas the Spanish is a comedy) (*Civilização Ibérica* 271–2; *Iberian Civilization* 229).

Madariaga proceeds along similar lines in *The Genius of Spain.* While he writes of Iberia's linguistic, cultural, and temperamental "modalities" (a term that recalls Maragall and, secondarily, Unamuno) as opposed to "tones," his point is substantially the same. Further, he follows Martins in using aesthetic tendencies and artistic genres (epic, drama, etc.) to differentiate what he views as the three principal strands of Iberian culture (Galaico–Portuguese, Castilian, and Catalan). Madariaga would grant historical context to what we might term his genre theory of Iberian culture in *Spain: A Modern History*. He writes:

> La poesía de España nació, pues, en galaico-portugués. En esta lengua permaneció mientas fue poesía lírica. Luego cambió el ánimo de la Península, pasando de lo lírico a lo épico. Habían cambiado las circunstancias. Ya no eran los españoles un pueblo de cristianos arrojados de su país por los moros, sino una raza que había reconquistado la tierra perdida y sentía en sus venas el vigor que más tarde iba a extender la civilización europea más allá de lo soñado por la imaginación medieval más desbordante. España (incluso Portugal) se hizo épica y dramática, y, por tanto, pasó a expresarse en castellano. (*España* 239–40)

> It [the language of Iberian poetry] remained Gallegan–Portuguese (to the point that the King of Castile himself, Alfonso X, wrote his poems in that language) as long as it remained lyrical. Then the mood of the Peninsula changed and from lyrical it became epic. The tide had turned. The people were no longer a race of Christians expelled from their country by the Moors; they were a race which had reconquered the land and was full of the marvelous vigor that, not very much later, was to expand European civilization beyond the dreams of the boldest medieval imagination. Spain

(including Portugal) became epic and dramatic. She had to express herself in Castilian. (*Spain* 249)

As I have alluded to previously, the status of Portugal and the Portuguese within Iberia proved central to both Madariaga and Martins's ideas on peninsular unity and diversity. Specifically, both men were compelled to confront the fact of Portugal's political independence from Spain, which was reasserted in 1640 after sixty years of dynastic union, along with Portugal's distinct historical trajectory, in which the early modern maritime voyages, Brazil, and the African colonies loomed large. Did these markers of Portuguese difference from Spain render the Portuguese something other than Spaniards? Madariaga and Martins arrived at distinct conclusions.

In *Bosquejo de Europa* (Outline of Europe, 1951), Madariaga resoundingly affirms the Spanish identity of the Portuguese: for Madariaga the Portuguese are Spaniards, no more and no less, regardless of what they themselves think. It logically follows that as Spaniards, the Portuguese should be incorporated into a single Iberian state, to be termed "Spain," and organized as a federal democracy in which the autonomy of the country's constitutive units, including Portugal, would be preserved. Madariaga viewed Portugal's continued political independence as unnatural, phantasmagorical, and tragic, and a form of separatism on a par with Catalan nationalism. He explained:

> Para darse cuanta de quiénes son los portugueses es indispensable partir del hecho esencial: que son españoles. Por haberlo dicho sin ambages se me ha tachado de nacionalismo, imperialismo y no sé cuántos crímenes más. Quienes así toman el rábano por las hojas olvidan dos puntos: uno, que los mismos portugueses se han considerado siempre como españoles hasta que la mayoría (pero no todos) dieron en cesar de hacerlo ya caduco el siglo XVII; otro, que la 'España' que incluye a los portugueses no sería ni es la que queda una vez amputado Portugal. Al decir que los portugueses son españoles se indica que lo son de la España que hasta el reinado de Felipe II trató de realizar su unidad, la España que comprende a toda la península. (209–10)

> In order to understand who the Portuguese are we must begin with this essential fact: they are Spaniards. I've been accused of nationalism, imperialism and who knows what else for putting this plainly. Those who get hold of the wrong end of the stick forget two things: first, that the

> Portuguese considered themselves Spaniards until the majority (though not all) of them stopped doing so at the end of the seventeenth century; and second, that the "Spain" that includes Portugal is not that same as that which remained once Portugal was amputated from it. To say that the Portuguese are Spaniards is to say that they belong to the Spain that up until the reign of Philip II was moving toward unity, that is, the Spain that includes the entire peninsula.

The fact that the Portuguese managed to achieve their "separatist" aims while the Catalans did not, Madariaga cautions, does not make Portuguese independence any more desirable or natural:

> Hasta ahora sólo los portugueses se han salido con la suya. Ello se debe a que sus tendencias separatistas hallaron más apoyo extranjero que las de Cataluña. El separatismo portugués pudo además apoyarse en un vasto imperio colonial de que Cataluña carecía. El señuelo de este imperio cegó a Portugal impidiéndole ver la ruta de sus verdaderos destinos. Era como un peso descomunal tirando de Portugal, descoyuntándolo de la España que no llegaría a realizar por faltar ellos. (213)

> Thus far only the Portuguese have managed to separate [from Spain]. This is because Portugal's separatist tendencies found greater foreign support than those of Catalonia. Further, Portuguese separatism was aided by a vast colonial empire, which Catalonia lacked. The lure of this empire blinded Portugal, dislocating it from a Spain that could not be built in its absence. Portugal's separation [from Spain], the act of its tearing itself apart from the Spain that could not come into being without the Portuguese, had a significant impact.

Madariaga had held these views for some time. In *Spain: A Modern History*, published in 1930, he commented on the phantasmagorical quality of Portugal's renewed independence in 1640, and on the negative implications of the *Restauração* (Restoration) for Portugal and Spain alike:

> Portugal lost her independence. English help was given her only under conditions which bound her destinies to those of the rising star of the North ... The secession of Portugal was the most important of downward events in Spanish history and, in a truer sense than the superficial one usually applied to it, of Portuguese history also. English political domination

> over Portugal is the last and perhaps the most important factor tending to separate Portugal from Spain. (248)[17]

Madariaga's view that Portugal only nominally recovered its independence in 1640, whereas it had for the most part been treated fairly under the Spanish Habsburgs (an interpretation squarely at odds with the conventional Portuguese view) led him to compare Portugal and Catalonia as follows:

> The mistake which Catalonia tried to commit several times in her history Portugal committed in 1662 [when English king Charles II married Catherine of Braganza]. Psychology, geography and history pointed to an Iberian evolution for Portugal. She chose a precarious life in the English alliance, forgetting that there is no alliance between the very weak and the very strong. And though England has been a good friend and even a generous one, and though Portugal, unlike Spain, has not lost her colonies, she has been melancholy ever since. For Portugal, three centuries of common life in Spain, even though cut about by civil wars, would have been more invigorating than peace and a nominal independence underpinned from abroad. (253)[18]

Madariaga blamed the failure of the Iberian dynastic union – which for him tragically shattered the dream of a politically integrated Iberian Peninsula – on two factors. First, he cited Portuguese and Catalan "separatism," which he blamed on what he saw as a constitutive tension within Iberian civilization between Castilian centralism and regionalist dispersion – which, following Unamuno and Ortega,[19] Madariaga viewed as two sides of the same identifiably Spanish coin.[20] He would return to this argument decades later. Referring to the Catalan and Basque cases in his *Memorias de un federalista*, Madariaga restates his views that separatism is "innate" to the Spanish character,[21] and that to indulge separatist tendencies amounts to an abrogation of one's historical responsibilities to Spain, given that "todos los españoles tenemos igual obligación y responsabilidad, y culpa y mérito en el vivir común, y en lo que hemos hecho, estamos haciendo y haremos con el país" (all Spaniards share an equal obligation and responsibility, are equally blame- or praiseworthy, as concerns our common life, and in terms of what we have done, are doing, and will do for our country) (47).[22]

Second, Madariaga blamed the failure of the Iberian dynastic union on the Castilian, Portuguese, and Catalan elites, and he refused to hold

Castile solely responsible. In *Bosquejo de Europa* he wrote: "El fondo del mal era la incompetencia política de los tres pueblos dirigentes de España – los catalanes, los castellanos y los portugueses –, y su incapacidad para, entre los tres, construir a España. Es inútil que los catalanes y los portugueses traten de echarle la culpa a los castellanos" (The root of the problem was the political incompetence of the three leading peoples of Spain – the Catalans, the Castilians, and the Portuguese – and their inability to work together to build Spain. It is useless for the Catalans and the Portuguese to place the blame on the Castilians) (210). Further, Madariaga confronted Castile's historical protagonism in peninsular affairs, which Unamuno had affirmed in *En torno al casticismo* and Ortega reasserted in *España invertebrada* (Invertebrate Spain, 1921). Madariaga declared: "Por paradójico que parezca, la leyenda de la superioridad política de los castellanos se debe al deseo de catalanes y portugueses de eludir sus graves responsabilidades en los desastres históricos de España, y en la común incapacidad de los tres pueblos para hacer una gran potencia en el territorio más estratégico del mundo" (As paradoxical as it might seem, the legend of the Castilians' political superiority has its roots in the desire of the Catalans and the Portuguese to deny their degree of responsibility for Spain's historical disasters, [and] in the common inability of the three peoples to create a great power in the world's most strategic territory) (210).

In his *Memorias de un federalista*, Madariaga would return to the culpability of the Portuguese and Catalan elites, invoking 1640 as the paradigmatic example of Spanish separatism and its negative consequences, namely, the destruction of "una España que sólo logró realidad histórica de 1580 a 1640" (a Spain that was a historical reality only between 1580 and 1640) (88), and the creation of a false sense of Portuguese nationhood that would compromise the Spanish nation state to which Portugal legitimately belonged. Once again equating Portuguese independence with separatism, Madariaga declared that "el separatismo portugués, *al lograr hacer una nación*, impidió que se creara la verdadera nación española, condenando así a sus dos muñones, Portugal y 'España,' a sus tristes destinos" (Portuguese separatism, *in creating a nation*, prevented the creation of the true Spanish nation, and condemned its two stumps, Portugal and "Spain," to their unfortunate destinies) (97; author's emphasis). Further, Madariaga theorized: "Seguro estoy de que el particularismo portugués y el catalán llevan en la historia tanta responsabilidad por las desgracias de España como cualquiera de las demás causas que se suelen enumerar; y de que, si Cataluña y

Portugal hubieran orientado sus esfuerzos hacia una coordinación creadora con los demás pueblos españoles, la historia de España hubiera sido mucho más estable" (I am certain that Portuguese and Catalan particularism share as much historical responsibility for Spain's problems as any other causes that might be cited. And I am likewise certain that if Catalonia and Portugal had directed their efforts towards creative collaboration with the other Spanish peoples, the history of Spain would have been much more stable) (125). Madariaga had gone further still in an 11 January 1966 letter to an anonymous Basque student:

> Subsiste el error capital de Portugal y de Cataluña: el de no haber sabido nunca *elevarse por encima* de un localismo miope y rezagado, hasta la concepción de la España peninsular como nación a nivel con Francia y con Inglaterra. Si vamos a acusar a Felipe IV y a Olivares de hablar como castellanos y no como españoles (lo que sería notoriamente injusto), ¿cómo hablaban los catalanes y los portugueses? De los tres grupos peninsulares, ¿quién se acercó más en sustancia (dejando aparte el modo) a lo que exigían el momento histórico y el sentido común?
>
> Y no va la pregunta a mero título polémico. En 1640, Cataluña y Portugal destruyen para siempre la España que pudo haber sido, federación monárquica de tres países cada uno con su lengua y parlamento; para caer la una al rango de provincia española y la otra al de colonia inglesa. Una política de federación exigente en cuanto a sus fines y modos por parte de catalanes y portugueses habría eliminado del plan de Olivares, sabio en sus fundamentos, las tendencias imprudentes que le inspiraban su temperamento y las tercas resistencias con que tuvo que luchar. Portugal y Cataluña son tanto como Castilla, si no más, las responsables de lo que fue después la historia de España. (quoted in Madariaga, *Memorias* 173; author's emphasis).

> The capital error committed by Portugal and Catalonia remains this: not knowing how to *elevate themselves above* a myopic and outmoded localism, and toward an idea of peninsular Spain as a nation on a par with France and England. If we are to accuse Philip IV and Olivares of speaking as Castilians and not Spaniards (which would be quite unjust), then how did the Catalans and Portuguese speak? Of the three peninsular groups, which came closest in substance (leaving aside the question of means) to what was demanded by the historical moment and by common sense?
>
> And this question is not merely polemical. In 1640, Catalonia and Portugal forever destroyed the Spain that could have been, a monarchical

federation of the three countries, each one with its language and parliament. Instead, the former was lowered to the status of Spanish province and the latter to that of English colony. A federal policy on the part of the Catalans and the Portuguese, one intelligent as to its ends and means, would have eliminated the plan of Olivares, whose intentions were good, but who was undone by imprudent actions inspired by his personality and the stiff resistance he encountered. Portugal and Catalonia are equally responsible, if not more responsible, than Castile for the history of Spain that followed.

Indeed, Madariaga argued that Spain could only be understood in its true sense, as the inheritor of the Roman *Hispania*, if it referred to the whole of an Iberian Peninsula united culturally, geographically, and politically. In Madariaga's view, separatists made a categorical error in "reduc[iendo] a España al rango de mero Estado" (reducing Spain to the status of a mere State," given that "un Estado puede no pasar de ser un mero mecanismo de gobierno" (a State is nothing more than a governing machine), whereas "la unidad de España no es sólo política, sino *vital*" (the unity of Spain is not merely political, but also *vital*) (50, 137; author's emphasis). Spanish unity, for Madariaga, ran deeper than politics or the "tragic" facts of Portuguese independence and Catalan separatism. Moreover, for Madariaga there existed an overarching "nacionalidad española" (Spanish nationality) to which Castilians, Catalans, Basques, Galicians, and Portuguese belong in common.[23] Madariaga followed Unamuno in reifying Spain as a "vital" unity, with an apparently self-evident claim to nationhood. This would have profound implications for his Iberian federalism, moving him to view an Iberian federation built from the existing Spanish nation state, and centred in Castile, as the only legitimate vehicle for federalism on the peninsula, and to discount alternative arrangements that would preserve Portuguese sovereignty and recognize Catalonia's aspirations towards true autonomy, and possible independence.

Given all of this, Madariaga argued that the territory that remained under the Habsburgs after the Portuguese Restoration of 1640, that is, modern-day continental Spain, was mislabelled when described as such:

Mientras que discutir si Cataluña es nación o región me parece ocioso y sin sustancia, y argüir sobre si el catalán es lengua o dialecto me parece grotesco, la insolubilidad del problema de cómo llamar a España menos

> Cataluña me parece responder a una realidad profunda, que es la hispanidad esencial de todas las gentes que habitan la península ibérica menos el puñado de desarraigados que ocupan Gibraltar. Bien es verdad que, por una necesidad debida precisamente a faltar también un vocablo para designar España menos Portugal, hubo que llamar España a lo que quedó. (49)
>
> While the question of whether Catalonia is a nation or region appears to me pointless and insubstantial, and while arguing whether Catalan is a language or dialect seems grotesque, the unanswered question of what to call Spain without Catalonia responds to a profound truth, which is the essentially Hispanic character of all of the peoples who inhabit the Iberian Peninsula except for the handful of foreigners who occupy Gibraltar. Lacking a word that would describe Spain without Portugal, what remained [after 1640] was of necessity called "Spain".

Or more succinctly: "El caso es que lo que queda de España cuando se le arrancan Cataluña, el País Vasco y Galicia no tiene nombre" (The fact is that what remains of Spain once Catalonia, the Basque Country and Galicia have been torn from it does not have a name) (48).[24]

Oliveira Martins approached the mutable character of the term "Spain," and the questions it raised concerning intra-Iberian relations, from a distinct perspective. Rather than marshalling the Roman provenance and peninsula-wide application of *Hispania* as a piece of nomenclatural evidence to argue in favour of the unified destiny of the Iberian or "Spanish" peoples, Martins in his article "Iberismo" (1889) interpreted the use of "Spain" by Ferdinand and Isabel as evidence of an "pensamento da unificação peninsular, que Felipe II julgou ter consumado: êsse reino tem de-certo o ideal da unidade: tradição não a pode ter" (agenda of peninsular unification, which Philip II thought that he had achieved: this kingdom [i.e., Spain] certainly holds to the ideal of unity, though tradition belies this notion) (*Dispersos* 2: 206). In other words, Martins approached the drive towards peninsular unification not as a transcendental fact, but as a policy consciously pursued by the Spanish monarchy, and a policy that, despite its failure and being fundamentally misguided, is nonetheless rooted in Iberian "tradition." While Martins rejected the notion that Iberia was destined for political unity, he, like Madariaga, affirmed the overarching unity of Iberian civilization and believed that Spaniards and Portuguese alike possessed a common peninsular "genius," albeit one that manifested itself with a certain degree of difference in the two nation states. Did this mean that Martins considered the Portuguese to be Spaniards in the same categorical sense as Madariaga? And like Madariaga, did Martins view Portuguese incorporation into the Spanish state as necessarily following from the recognition of the Portuguese people's Spanish ties and the peninsula-wide dimension of Spain as a historical, cultural, and geographic unity? While Martins's thoughts on these matters were somewhat inconsistent (or more kindly, evolved over time), they were on the whole more nuanced than Madariaga's views. Indeed, examination of Martins's statements reveals that Madariaga's assertion that for Martins, "las expresiones 'España' y 'Península Ibérica' son intercambiables" (the terms "Spain" and "Iberian Peninsula" are interchangeable) is simplistic at best, and misleading at worst (quoted in *Memorias* 192).

Granted, in the opening pages of his *História de Portugal*, Martins referred to the adjectives "iberico" (Iberian), "peninsular" (peninsular), and "hespanhol" (Spanish) as having an "alcance equivalente" (identical meaning). Though a mere two paragraphs later he announced that his book would be dedicated to "caracteris[ando] o que ha de particular na historia portugueza" (characterizing the particularities of Portuguese history) (1: ix). This implies that Portugal, though unquestionably Iberian and peninsular, was not for Martins exactly or exclusively Spanish. A letter dated 18 April 1884, written by Martins to the Spanish novelist Juan Valera, provides a good illustration of his equivocation on the question of whether Portugal was part of Spain, and if the Portuguese were Spaniards. In certain passages from the letter Martins, like Madariaga, invokes Spain and the Spanish people as categories that are inclusive of Portugal and the Portuguese, referring to "o [povo] hespanhol (deixe-me incluir, como portuguez, na conta)" (the Spanish [people] (allow me, as a Portuguese, to include myself on this list) and to "a nossa Hespanha" (our Spain) (*Correspondencia* 42–3). Elsewhere, however, Martins utilizes biblical metaphor in attempting to explain the lingering complexities of the Spanish–Portuguese relationship, which preclude him from univocally stating that the Portuguese are Spaniards, as did Madariaga. Martins writes: "Estreitem-se as relações com Portugal ao ponto de, a não fazermos um só povo, ser-mos *dois n'um só corpo*, conforme dizem as letras sagradas" (Let [Spain] strengthen its relations with Portugal such that, while we might not become a single people, we may be *two in one body*, as the holy scripture states) (43; author's emphasis). Martins seems to refer here to Ephesians 2:16 ("And that he might reconcile both unto God in one body by the cross, having slain the enmity thereby"), which describes Christ's dual nature as both human and divine – a logical impossibility which Catholic doctrine understands as a holy mystery. Through this biblical metaphor, Martins asserts that the Portuguese both are and are not Spaniards, as if to say that the Portuguese–Spanish relationship, defined alternately by proximity and distance, identity and difference, eludes easy or logical explanation. If the Portuguese–Spanish relationship is to resolve itself, Martins implies, it will be through an Unamunian dialectical confrontation in which in the words of one critic, "a vivência ibérica [é] uma outra forma, mais profunda, mais completa, de reviver a própria nacionalidade" (the Iberian dimension becomes another, deeper, more complete form of [Portuguese] nationality) (Magalhães 170).

At any rate, as early as 1869, Martins seems to have denied that recognition of Portugal's ties to Spain, or the terming of the Portuguese as "Spaniards," necessitated that Portugal be absorbed politically into Spain. Even as Martins argued on pragmatic grounds in "Do Princípio Federativo e a Sua Aplicação à Península Hispânica" (On the Federative Principle and Its Application to the Hispanic Peninsula, 1869) for Spain and Portugal to together form a federal republic, he rejected the idea, championed by Madariaga, that the 1580–1640 dynastic union anticipated the sort of Iberian federation he hoped to see established. Indeed, Martins followed Pi i Margall in making precisely the opposite argument: Habsburg misrule in Portugal had perhaps fatally compromised the possibilities for long-term unity between the two Iberian nation states.[25] Martins referred to the dynastic union as "o nosso cativeiro" (our captivity), and as "anos da decadência e dos piores da crueldade" (years of decay and of the worst cruelty) (33, 35). In his *História de Portugal*, Martins offered a more nuanced assessment, differentiating between the more positive reigns of Philip I (r. 1556–98) and Philip II of Portugal (r. 1598–1621), and Philip III (r. 1621–40), whose minister the Count-Duke of Olivares was a "homem de *hespanholadas*, creou embaraços e levantou conflictos que o perderam" (man who inspired anti-Spanish jokes, [who] created problems and conflicts that led to his demise) (2: 109). In his three-volume *Portugal Contemporâneo* (1881), Martins returned to his more uniformly negative characterization, referring to "a deplorável história da anexação de Portugal, e a da ocupação castelhana, mais deplorável ainda" (the deplorable story of Portugal's annexation [by Spain], and of its occupation by the Castilians, more deplorable still) (3: 244).

If Martins's descriptions of 1580–1640 ranged from partially negative to decidedly pessimistic, his characterization of the Portuguese Restoration was no sunnier. In this respect at least, Martins largely agreed with Madariaga. In his *História de Portugal*, Martins used frankly jaundiced language to describe the Portuguese rebellion against Olivares, begun in 1637, as the action of a "animal ofegante, extenuado. A vista, pervertida, mostrava-lhe cousas extravagantes; e a terra andava-lhe á roda, diante dos olhos espantados e vitreos de moribundo" (breathless, haggard animal. With its poor eyesight, it saw the strangest things; and the world spun around it, before its frightened, glassy, dead eyes) (2: 116). In addition to questioning the vitality of a Portuguese national body that would at least nominally recover its independence in 1640, Martins anticipated Madariaga's critique of post-1640 Portugal's alliance with England as an abrogation of national sovereignty, terming his country in the *História de Portugal* an English "protectorate," and writing: "Era impossivel descer mais fundo, baixar mais, abdicar de um modo mais completo a independencia, que se debatia contra o hespanhol, e se sacrificava, assim ao inglez" (In sacrificing itself in this way to the Englishman, [Portugal] could not have fallen any further, gone any lower, or more completely abdicated the independence it had fought for against the Spaniard) (2: 139). In his article "Alianças" (Alliances, 1890), Martins, riding the wave of anti-English sentiment felt in Portugal following the British Ultimatum of 11 January 1890, was more succinct: "Explorando a nossa fraqueza, a Inglaterra, como um vampiro, sugou-nos" (Taking advantage of our weakness, England, like a vampire, sucked us dry) (*Dispersos* 217). Further, Martins critiqued the collective Portuguese "odio a Castella" (hatred of Castile) that became one of the bulwarks of Portuguese nationalism after 1640, noting that unlike Great Britain, Castile "nem nos opprime, nem nos odeia" (neither oppresses nor hates us).

In his article "Desde fuera: el problema catalán. 1. Factores psicológicos" (From the Outside: the Catalan Problem. 1. Psychological Factors), published on 31 January 1923 in *El Sol*, Salvador de Madariaga makes what is possibly his first written reference to Oliveira Martins, and in so doing, commits his first misreading of the Portuguese historian. Madariaga notes that for Martins, "las expresiones 'España' y 'Península Ibérica' son intercambiables" (the terms 'Spain' and 'the Iberian Peninsula' are interchangeable) (quoted in *Memorias* 192). Madariaga's point, which he makes in the context of an argument against Catalan independence, is that the Iberian Peninsula and its peoples are inextricably linked to Spain as a geographic, cultural, and political reality. Hence the folly, for Madariaga, of Portugal's renewed independence in 1640, and of more recent Catalan pro-independence agitation. Indeed, Madariaga mused in the 1 February 1923 instalment of the "Desde fuera: el problema catalán" series that a "Cataluña independiente sería algo así como un brazo que se va de paseo dejando en casa al resto del cuerpo" (independent Catalonia would be like an arm that goes for a walk, leaving behind the rest of its body) – an image of a disconnected limb that recalls his (and Quental, Martins, Pardo Bazán, and others') organicist descriptions of a Portugal unnaturally and tragically amputated from the Spanish body.

Madariaga's reference to Martins in his 1923 article is symptomatic of his misunderstanding, whether careless or wilful, of the Portuguese historian, and speaks to broader distinctions between the Iberianist programs of the two men. As we have seen in this chapter, Martins viewed the terms "Iberian Peninsula" and "Spain," along with their adjectival forms "Iberian," "peninsular," and "Spanish," as interchangeable – but only up to a point. Further, over the course of his abbreviated but remarkably productive public life Martins embraced a variety of Iberianist proposals, ranging from the Iberian federalism of his youth to the proposed Portuguese–Spanish alliance of its later years. While Martins can be taken to task for numerous aspects of his historiography (including sloppy treatment of sources, narrative liberties, and historical judgments more hyperbolic than dispassionate), he did not commit Madariaga's error of reifying Spain such that Portugal or Catalonia's "Spanish-ness" would render their participation in the Spanish nation state self-evident. As Madariaga wrote in a 28 December 1959 letter to Basque leader José Antonio de Aguirre: "Si, en efecto, vascos y catalanes no fueran españoles, su separación de España me parecería objetivamente necesaria y beneficiosa. Por lo grave de la actitud separatista es que no es conforme a la realidad. Los vascos y los catalanes son españoles" (If, in effect, the Basques and Catalans were not Spaniards, then their separation from Spain would seem to me both objectively necessary and beneficial. But the separatist position is misguided in that it does not reflect reality. The Basques and Catalans are Spaniards) (quoted in *Memorias* 142). Even as Martins, like Madariaga and so many other Iberianists, insisted on the overarching unity of Iberian civilization, he carved out ample space for the particularities of Portuguese history, and at least in his early federalist years, for regionalist aspirations across the peninsula. Madariaga, as a convinced Spanish federalist, vociferously defended autonomy for Spain's regions – Catalonia included – provided their political leaders denounce separatism.[26]

Madariaga's insistence on the political implications of Iberia's shared "Spanish-ness" may read as somewhat jarring, and it no doubt appeared a Faustian bargain to at least some of Madariaga's Basque and Catalan interlocutors. This said, Madariaga's line in the (peninsular) sand points towards one of the two principal currents of Iberianist thinking in late twentieth- and early twenty-first century peninsular political and intellectual life. These are, first, the centre-left federalism enshrined in Spain and to a lesser extent in Portugal's post-dictatorial constitutions, both of which promise regional autonomy in exchange for recognition of what the 1978 Spanish constitution terms the "indisoluble unidad de la Nación española, patria común e indivisible de todos los españoles" (indissoluble unity of the Spanish Nation, the common, indivisible homeland of all Spaniards);[27] and second, more frankly radical proposals for intra-Iberian approximation that bypass the authority of Madrid and Lisbon and the dualistic political model they uphold. Here José Saramago's novel *A Jangada de Pedra* (1986), which depicts the coming together of Iberians from both sides of the Portuguese–Spanish border in the aftermath of the peninsula's cataclysmic physical separation from Europe, serves as an example. In one scene, the characters Joaquim Sassa and José Anaiço look over a map, which in the wake of natural disaster and the Spanish and Portuguese governments' failure to effectively respond has been transformed so as to depict the full range of Iberia's regional variety. This mentally transformed Iberian Peninsula is free of the state borders and dualistic political organization that Iberia's new situation as, quite literally, an island unto itself has rendered artificial and obsolete:

> O mapa desdobrado mostrava as duas pátrias, Portugal embrechado, suspenso, Espanha desmandibulada a sul, e as regiões, as províncias, os distritos, o grosso cascalho das cidades maiores, a poalha das vilas e aldeias, mas nem todas, que muitas vezes é invisível o pó a olho nu, Venta Micena foi apenas um exemplo. As mãos alisam e afagam o papel, passam sobre o Alentejo e continuam para o norte, como se acariciassem um rosto, da face esquerda para a face direita, é o sentido dos ponteiros do relógio, o sentido do tempo, as Beiras, o Ribatejo antes dela, e depois Trás-os-Montes e o Minho, a Galiza, as Astúrias, o País Basco e Navarra, Castela e Leão, Aragão, a Catalunha, Valência, Estremadura, a nossa e a deles, Andaluzia onde ainda estamos, o Algarve. (*Jangada* 90)

> The open map showed the two countries, Portugal indented, suspended, Spain unhinged to the south, and the regions, the provinces, the districts, the thick rubble of the major cities, the dust of the towns and villages, but not all of them, for dust is often invisible to the naked eye, Venta Micena being merely one example. Their hands smooth and stroke the paper, they pass over Alentejo and continue northwards, as if they were caressing a human face, from right to left, following the hands of the clock, the direction of time, the Beiras, Ribatejo before them, and then Trás-os-Montes and Minho, Galicia, Asturias, the Basque country and Navarre, Castile and León, Aragón and Catalonia, Valencia, Estremadura, both the Spanish and the Portuguese, Andalusia where we still find ourselves, the Algarve. (*Stone* 79–80)

While the geological separation of the Iberian Peninsula from Europe is the stuff of fantasy, and serves Saramago as a potent literary metaphor for the Iberianist future he advocated, it nonetheless recalls the intimate relationship between Iberianism and crisis introduced in this book's opening chapter. Today, the Spanish and Portuguese states confront serious political and economic challenges in the wake of events such as the 2008 economic crash and ensuing sovereign debt and unemployment crises, and the 9 November 2014 and 1 October 2017 Catalan referenda, in which large majorities of Catalans voted in favour of independence from Spain despite Madrid's insistence on the illegality of the independence vote. Leaders and observers alike would do well to recall José Félix Henriques Nogueira's prophetic 1855 statement concerning Iberianism's capacity to periodically re-emerge in times of crisis:

> É uma ideia diversamente interpretada, diversamente compreendida, diversamente aceite, mas é uma ideia de magnitude, de futuro, de vitalidade … A ideia ibérica tira a sua força principal dos homens novos, dessa mocidade filha da revolução, que a pretende completar, erigindo-lhe um templo condigno dos seus majestosos alicerces. O iberismo é de ontem; mas invade tudo. (2: 67)

> It is an idea that is interpreted, understood, and accepted in diverse ways and to varying degrees, but it is an idea of magnitude, with a future, and with vitality … The Iberian idea draws its strength primarily from young men, the youth who are the children of the revolution, and who seek to bring it to fruition, by building it a temple that is worthy of its great foundation. Iberianism is of the past, but it invades everything.

Without the benefit of hindsight, it is difficult to assess the degree to which Iberianism in its various manifestations may appear on the margins of the current public outcry over the Iberian Peninsula's latest period of acute though perhaps not quite existential crisis. Where "the Iberian idea" *has* made itself felt in recent years has been in the world of academic Hispanism. Here an emergent "Iberian studies" has issued a serious challenge to the ways in which peninsular literary and cultural studies have traditionally been researched and taught. We will turn to this lively debate in the conclusion to *Iberianism and Crisis*, and will attempt to bridge the Iberianist past with the possible disciplinary futures of Iberian studies.

Conclusion: Iberianism's Lessons

In recent years a number of scholars have issued proposals aimed at radically reconceptualizing the discipline of peninsular literary and culture studies. Many of these scholars, who are based at both North American and European universities, have presented their proposals as interventions in an emerging field termed "Iberian studies." Briefly, Iberian studies seeks to reimagine – and reinvigorate – scholarship and teaching in peninsular studies by placing the Spanish and Portuguese literary canons into critical dialogue with each other, and with Catalan, Galician, Basque, and other peninsular traditions.[1] Meanwhile, Iberian studies have gained a certain institutional traction in the form of academic centres, departments, and publishing initiatives.[2] Key features of Iberian studies that differentiate it, at least in theory, from academic Hispanism, which proponents of Iberian studies present as the field's prevailing disciplinary paradigm, include (1) an embrace of multilingualism; (2) comparativism across borders and between peninsular states, nations, and regions; and (3) an inclusive, non-hierarchical approach to literary and cultural materials.[3]

In this conclusion, I will first offer a critical summary of the ongoing Iberian studies debate – a debate that is highly relevant to the sort of multilingual, cross-border, and intra-Iberian analysis I have undertaken in *Iberianism and Crisis*. I will then attempt to bridge the Iberianist past described in this book with the disciplinary futures projected by the proponents of Iberian studies. Concretely, I will look to three Iberianist writers with whom the reader will now be familiar – Antero de Quental, Joan Maragall, and Miguel de Unamuno – to provide lessons to the emerging field of Iberian studies.

From Hispanism to Iberian Studies

While Iberian studies and the critique of Hispanism have important antecedents (see Maragall and Unamuno's comments regarding peninsular multilingualism and intellectual exchange, for example), José del Valle and Luis Gabriel-Stheeman made one of the first substantive contributions to the current Iberian studies debate in "Nationalism, *Hispanismo*, and Monoglossic Culture," the introduction to their edited volume *The Battle over Spanish between 1800 and 2000: Language Ideologies and Hispanic Intellectuals* (2002). Here Del Valle and Gabriel-Stheeman define Hispanism as follows: "*Hispanismo* can be said to consist of at least the following ideas: The existence of a unique Spanish culture, lifestyle, characteristics, traditions and values, *all of them embodied in its language*; the idea that Spanish American culture is nothing but Spanish culture transplanted to the New World; and the notion that Hispanic culture has an internal hierarchy in which Spain occupies a hegemonic position" (6; authors' emphasis). They note that academic Hispanism emerged at the end of the nineteenth century from conditions of crisis – incidentally, the same conditions that gave rise to the Iberianist proposals analysed in this book. For Del Valle and Gabriel-Stheeman, Hispanism responded to Spain's "sustained identity crisis ... a crisis that culminated with the questioning of the nation's integrity by the development of nationalist movements in the peripheral areas of the Peninsula. In this context, the notions proposed by *hispanismo* provided the much-needed signs of identity which Spain could display in front of those who questioned its integrity and viability as a modern nation" (7).[4]

With Hispanism's guiding principles (Spain's cultural cohesiveness, Spanish cultural transplantation to Latin America, and Spain's primacy within the Hispanic world) thus defined, contemporary scholars have moved to identify its academic, if not more broadly cultural or political sins. These include Hispanism's alleged complicity in Spanish cultural and linguistic neo-imperialism, and its marginalization or outright exclusion of non-Castilian languages, literatures, and identities from the peninsular studies canon. In the introduction to her edited volume *Ideologies of Hispanism* (2005), Mabel Moraña charges Hispanism with endorsing "enforced [Castilian] monolingualism" and with "suppression of diversity and particularism" (x, xii). In his contribution to Moraña's volume, Joan Ramon Resina, director of Stanford University's Iberian Studies Program and one of the US academy's fiercest critics of Hispanism and most vociferous defenders of Iberian studies, makes this same point. He writes that Hispanism "has never been free from ulterior motives," chief among these being the promotion of a "phantom imperialism" in the service of the Spanish state ("Whose" 161, 167). And in Resina's *Del hispanismo a los estudios ibéricos: Una propuesta federativa para el ámbito cultural* (From Hispanism to Iberian Studies: A Federal Proposal for the Cultural Realm, 2009) – probably the single most influential text in the Iberian studies debate – he charges Hispanism with having "amputado amplios segmentos de la imagen cultural de la Península" (amputated large segments of the Peninsula's cultural profile). This seems a reasonable judgment, if one considers academic Hispanism's paucity of scholarship on non-Castilian writers and texts in comparison to the reams of paper it has devoted to the giants of Castilian literature. However, Resina also declares that "el hispanismo ... no es sino nacionalismo cultural posimperial" (Hispanism ... is nothing more than post-imperial cultural nationalism) (29). Here he risks oversimplification by failing to account for the intellectual and ideological diversity of self-identified Hispanists, both historically and in the present.

Hispanism, in definition and more so in practice, is somewhat broader and more inclusive than is implied by many defenders of Iberian studies. Indeed, the amended, twenty-second edition of the Real Academia Española's *Diccionario de la lengua española* defines *hispanismo* as "afición al estudio de las lenguas, literaturas o cultura hispánicas" (interest in the study of Hispanic languages, literatures, or culture).[5] This definition is more pluralistic than might be expected from one of academic Hispanism's most conservative institutions. I should make my position clear: I firmly believe that Iberian studies, in its challenge to academic Hispanism's tendencies towards Castilian monolingualism and the reification of Spanish national unity and cultural primacy over "peripheral" peninsular groups (to say nothing of Spanish-speaking Latin America), offers a more vibrant and intellectually honest account of peninsular literatures and cultures than is provided by monolingual study of Spanish or Portuguese (or for that matter, Catalan, Galician, or Basque). Further, by embracing multilingualism and comparativism, Iberian studies participates in a broader, salutary movement within humanistic scholarship away from the study of self-enclosed "national" traditions located within apparently self-evident and internally consistent geo-cultural categories (Iberia, Latin America, etc.) towards self-consciously reflexive or "criticial" approaches that are specifically relational and cognizant of the mutual contamination and dependence of traditions, geo-historical regions, and discourses: one thinks, for instance, of the rise in recent decades of the fields of Transatlantic and Transoceanic studies, inter-American studies, border studies, and the like.

This said, Hispanism's critics and Iberian studies' proponents (who are often one and the same) are at times too categorical in their descriptions of Hispanism and its practitioners. My late colleague at the University of California, Davis, Samuel G. Armistead (1927–2013), serves as a counterexample. A distinguished medievalist who trained in Spanish philology at Princeton under Américo Castro and who was a corresponding member of the Real Academia Española, Armistead nonetheless satisfies the three criteria for Iberian studies I have enumerated above. His work on medieval balladry ranged over a variety of peninsular languages, including Judeo-Spanish, his research was eminently comparative, and his approach to texts and canons was radically inclusive.[6] While Armistead was exceptional, and swam against the tide of what was once termed medieval Spanish studies, it is nonetheless crucial for the Iberian studies debate that we recall examples of self-identified Hispanists, like Armistead, who rejected Castilian "linguistic monism" and Spanish cultural supremacy, and who, in this sense, practised a form of Iberian studies decades before its principles and aims were defined (Resina, "Whose" 169).

Nonetheless, as Sebastiaan Faber and Resina have both observed, and as senior peninsularist colleagues have attested, US Hispanism has, whether implicitly or explicitly, endorsed Castilian monolingualism and affirmed Spanish cultural precedence over its former colonies. Resina argues: "El hispanismo norteamericano contribuye a la reproducción de una imagen homogénea de la Península; una imagen cuya capacidad de persuasión se sostiene gracias a la obstrucción de perspectivas y lugares alternativos para la práctica del hispanismo" (North American Hispanism contributes to the reproduction of a homogeneous image of the Peninsula, an image whose persuasive capacity is kept intact thanks to the foreclosure of alternative perspectives and sites for the practice of Hispanism) (*Del hispanismo* 91). And making substantially the same point, Faber cites a letter by the eminent Spanish philologist Ramón Menéndez Pidal, published in the inaugural February 1918 issue of the journal *Hispania,* in which Pidal affirmed that "toda la civilización hispano-americana descansa principalmente en su base española" (all of Spanish American civilization rests primarily upon its

Spanish base) (9). This said, Pidal argues in the same open letter that "las otras lenguas que se hablan en la Península [además de la castellana], son ciertamente españolas también, pero no son *'el español'* por antonomasia" (the other languages spoken in the Peninsula [other than Castilian] are of course Spanish as well, though they are not *"Spanish"* as such) (3; author's emphasis). Despite Pidal's valorization of Castilian as "the" Spanish language, his statement also speaks to a shared interest on the part of Pidal, Castro, and other key figures in early twentieth-century Spanish philology in Iberian linguistic and regional variation.[7] If Hispanism has tended to promote Castilian monolingualism and Spanish cultural primacy, it has not done so monolithically, nor to the complete exclusion of other peninsular languages and literatures.

Critics have noted that Hispanism's resistance to change makes it ill suited to confront the widely acknowledged "crisis" currently facing peninsular studies, and the humanities in general. Among the causes of this crisis we may cite the rise of cultural studies and, particularly, the "hegemonía creciente de la literatura latinoamericana" (growing hegemony of Latin American literature) (Resina, *Del hispanismo* 158), both in academic Spanish departments and in the global readership for Hispanic literature. Joseba Gabilondo goes as far as to claim that: "Peninsular literature and culture is taught in the USA only as an effect (and even affect) of the geopolitical juncture of Latin America vis-à-vis the USA" ("Spanish" 31). Together these factors have led to lower student enrolments in peninsular literature courses (especially in comparison with courses in Latin American literature), and decreased institutional support for peninsular studies. Exacerbating these problems are the ongoing financial difficulties facing the Spanish and Portuguese states, which were triggered by the 2008 global financial crisis. These budgetary woes have led to cuts in peninsular state, regional, and quasi-governmental (i.e., Instituto Cervantes, Instituto Camões) support for peninsular studies programs and research abroad. Román de la Campa has perceptively observed that "the era in which Hispanism stood as an organic principle governing the study of Spanish and Spanish American letters seems like a dim and distant memory" (300). Once again risking hyperbole, Gabilondo claims that "Hispanism no longer has a future at the [North American] university" ("Spanish" 32). If taken at face value, Gabilondo's prediction is excessively dire. Even in the most pessimistic of scenarios, the study of Spanish or Portuguese literature, history, and culture would retain at least a vestigial importance at more elite US universities, as well as those that serve local communities willing to support these programs, such as the University of Massachusetts Dartmouth in the case of Portuguese Americans and the University of Nevada, Reno for Basque Americans. However, Gabilondo's statement nonetheless reflects the pessimism that in recent years has come to pervade the field of peninsular studies, and the humanities as a whole.[8]

Hispanism's beleaguered state might be demoralizing to some. Though as we have seen, crises, for all their apocalyptic connotations, can also provide opportunities for renewal. This renewal may be civilizational, as was proposed by Iberianism in the late nineteenth and early twentieth centuries, or disciplinary, as in the case of Iberian studies today. As Brad Epps and Luis Fernández Cifuentes observe in "Spain beyond Spain: Modernity, Literary History, and National Identity," the introduction to their 2005 edited volume of the same name: "If some wax nostalgic for a putatively self-evident notion of Spanish critical authority, others celebrate the displacement as a sign of vitality in which Spanish literary history is *mixed up* in other histories, indeed other stories and other subjects" (19; authors' emphasis). I share Epps and Fernández Cifuentes's more hopeful view. In substantiating this cautiously optimistic position, I would cite the dynamism of the current Iberian studies debate, which has already borne fruit in the form of important scholarship by Resina, Gabilondo, Faber, and others, as well as curricular innovations, and the creation of Iberian studies working groups in the United States and Europe.

Beyond its potential to revive the fortunes of peninsularism, Iberian studies, as a multilingual, multipolar, and comparative alternative to Hispanism, promises scholarly and pedagogical benefits that are broadly analogous to those opened up by approaches that apply similarly self-conscious critical and relational approaches to other regions and canons.[9] In describing these benefits, the champions of Iberian studies have tended to describe the Iberian Peninsula, in language perhaps unintentionally reminiscent of structuralism, as an internally variegated system. Here meaning is generated, in Saussurian fashion, through the differential relations established across linguistic and literary traditions, and between Iberian writers, texts, and cultural productions. Resina offers that

> el sistema cultural de la Península Ibérica, concebido por el hispanismo como un *continuum* homogéneo de tradición "española," puede ser estudiado ventajosamente como un proceso de diferenciación de culturas que

> constituyen el ambiente interior del sistema. Desde el punto de vida de este modello, es obvio que el sistema no puede ser comprendido a través de uno solo de sus componentes, y que deforma la comprensión de la totalidad convertir uno de esos componentes en el punto de vista rector de todo el entramado sistémico" (54; author's emphasis).

> the cultural system of the Iberian Peninsula, which Hispanism understood as a homogeneous continuum of "Spanish" tradition, may be profitably studied as a process of differentiation between the cultures that comprise the system. Following this model, it becomes obvious that the system cannot be adequately understood through only one of its components.

More recently, Santiago Pérez Isasi and Ângela Fernandes have described Iberian studies in "Looking at Iberia in/from Europe," the introduction to their edited volume *Looking at Iberia: A Comparative European Perspective* (2013), "as the methodological consideration of the Iberian Peninsula as a complex, multilingual cultural and literary system" (1). Putting aside the limitations of structuralism, I find both of these formulations reasonable, and as a comparatist, quite appealing. However, I would note the perhaps obvious point that the Iberian Peninsula is far from a closed system: just as Portuguese literature, culture, and intellectual history can be profitably studied in relation to Spain, it also participates in other necessary, extra-Iberian dialogues – with Brazil, and Portuguese-speaking Africa, for example.

Iberian studies have not been exempt from criticism, even from academics who would seem to sympathize with its stated goals. In recent years Joseba Gabilondo has emerged as one of Iberian studies' most serious sceptics – or sceptical practitioners. In his 2013 article "Spanish Nationalist Excess: A Decolonial and Postnational Critique of Iberian Studies," Gabilondo cautions that comparativism and multilingualism, in the absence of broader theoretical contextualization, are not sufficient to differentiate Iberian studies from the Hispanism it aspires to displace. After all, Hispanism has traditionally accommodated at least a degree of comparativism and has evinced some interest in Spain's "peripheral" languages and literatures, even as it has affirmed the overarching unity of a Spanish civilization solidly rooted in Castilian tradition. On this score we may cite the case of Menéndez Pidal, and in a less overtly academic sense, those of Miguel de Unamuno and Salvador de Madariaga. To this extent, Hispanism might not be so different from less radical formulations of Iberian studies – and this seems to be the crux of Gabilondo's objection. Gabilondo contends: "As long as the situation of Hispanism or Spanish studies is approached atheoretically, without a clear articulation of the theoretical reasons for a shift to Iberian studies, such an atheoretical approach will only reinforce the status of Peninsular/Spanish/Hispanic studies as 'object' and/or 'area of study' to be analysed according to theories originating elsewhere, predominantly in English in the USA. Iberian studies obscure the problem of the nationalist excess that defines the Spanish/Portuguese fields" ("Spanish" 28). Gabilondo argues that peninsular literatures and cultures can only be decoupled from Hispanism's "master signifier" of Spanish nationalism through contextualization within a broader theoretical field, which he suggests might draw on post-colonial and subaltern studies. Barring such theorization, Iberian studies risk reproducing Hispanism's "nationalist excess," and becoming Hispanism by another name (23). I do not share Gabilondo's opinion that Iberian studies must, or even can, make a clean break from Hispanism, which Gabilondo follows Resina in viewing as synonymous with Spanish nationalism. Indeed, the constraints imposed by prevailing departmental configurations (i.e., departments of Spanish, Spanish and Portuguese, Hispanic Studies, and so on) foreclose this possibility in all but the most fluid, resource-rich, and progressive of university environments. In most cases, what seems necessary is an evolution away from traditional Hispanism and toward an Iberian studies that is inclusive of both the Castilian canon and other Iberian languages, traditions, and cultural expressions. Rather than the break Gabilondo proposes, a "methodological" or "paradigmatic shift" from Hispanism towards Iberian studies, as signalled by the title of Resina's book, or a Zizek-inspired "parallax shift" as proposed by William Viestenz, seem more feasible courses of action (Viestenz 17, 19). Nonetheless, Gabilondo's argument that Iberian studies must find a raison d'être beyond the recognition and celebration of peninsular linguistic, literary, and cultural diversity is compelling. Further, I concur with Gabilondo that it is highly desirable for Iberian studies to "help create a fruitful exchange and dialogue with other disciplines and areas," though I do not share his concern that unless a theory of Iberian studies is adopted a priori, the field will necessarily fall back on an apparently untheoretical Cold War–era "area studies" model, or indeed, on Hispanism ("Spanish" 29).

Moving to a distinct critique, in a 9 January 2015 presentation at the Modern Language Association convention in Vancouver, entitled "¿De qué hablamos cuando hablamos de Estudios Ibéricos?" (What do we talk about when we talk about Iberian studies?), Jorge Pérez called attention to Resina's apparent hostility to cultural studies in *Del hispanismo a los estudios ibéricos*.[10] Pushing back, Pérez argued that "el cine es una plataforma ideal para llevar a cabo estudios comparativos sobre la riqueza multicultural y multilinguística de la península que además, debido al impacto internacional de algunas de estas películas, permite que la perspectiva cultural ibérica sea accesible desde otras latitudes y perspectivas culturales" (cinema provides an ideal platform for undertaking comparative studies on the rich multiculturalism and multilingualism of the peninsula. Further, due to the international impact of certain [Iberian] films, it allows an Iberian cultural perspective to be accessed across continents and cultural perspectives). He concluded by arguing that "si pretendemos reconfigurar el campo, no podemos conceptualizarlo sobre la base única de la literatura, y asumir que más adelante podemos ampliar el archivo adaptando la misma metodología a otros productos culturales que son considerados solo a posteriori" (if we hope to reconfigure the field, we cannot allow our understanding of it to derive exclusively from literature, and assume that later on we can expand the archive by applying the same [literary-critical] methodology to other cultural products, which are only considered *a posteriori*). Further, Pérez warned that Iberian studies risks obsolescence if, by privileging literature over film, it reproduces in terms of genre the emphasis on hierarchy that prevailed under Hispanism. Pérez's point is well taken, and especially relevant for Iberian studies as its proponents debate guiding principles, work towards institutional recognition, and, especially, define their corpus of study. This corpus need not, and should not, limit itself to literary texts, to the exclusion of other forms of expression, such as film. Further, it should avoid an unnecessarily restrictive definition of literature, and embrace genres such as the essay and other forms of literary non-fiction, in which intra-Iberian relations have so often been explored, questioned, and theorized.

Having elucidated some of the principal features of Iberian studies, as well as some of the lingering questions surrounding this emerging academic approach, I will now briefly return to the topical terrain of *Iberianism and Crisis* and to Iberianism, and will revisit the work of three writers examined in this book: Quental, Maragall, and Unamuno. The purpose of this closing exercise will be to illustrate three lessons from their work that, in my view, can be productively applied to Iberian studies.

Iberian Studies and the Shadow of Iberianism

"Iberianism," as we have seen in this book, refers to a minority intellectual current that advocates closer political and intellectual relations between Spain and Portugal, and a generally more equitable relationship between the Spanish state's constituent parts, which are sometimes expanded to include Portugal. Iberianism, then, is evidently not the same thing as Iberian studies, and it would be an example of academia's all-too-common tendency to think that it can re-enact the great geopolitical and cultural debates of the past to claim that we, as scholars interested in Iberian studies, can somehow "do" Iberianism. Nonetheless, there is a compelling symmetry to be observed between Iberianism, which flourished during a period of exceptional political, economic, and cultural crisis on the peninsula, and Iberian studies, which have emerged in response to an assumed disciplinary crisis in peninsular literary and cultural studies. Further, Iberianism, in its interrogation of the peninsular status quo and seemingly intrinsic comparativism and multilingualism, provides a logical area of study for Iberian studies and, as I will argue in this section, a source of instructive lessons for the emerging Iberian studies project. Let us begin with Quental.

In the opening sentences of his 1871 speech on the *Causas da Decadência dos Povos Peninsulares*, Quental identifies his predominantly if not entirely Portuguese audience as *peninsulares* (peninsulars) and even *nós Espanhóis* (we Spaniards) (7–8, 12). What does it mean for Quental to give the Portuguese the name of "Spaniards," who are frequently presented in Portuguese historiography and national imagination as Portugal's great rivals? As I argued in chapter 2, I suspect that despite Quental's penchant for rhetorical flair and scandalous declarations, his statement aims to enlarge the idea of "nós" (we/us) to include all of the "peninsular peoples," and thereby suggest that the Portuguese are *Iberians*. In so doing, Quental gestures towards an understanding of the category of "Spain" that prevailed prior to 1640, the year Portugal recovered its independence after an eighty-year period of dynastic union. This event cemented the modern, political meaning of "Spain" as referring only to those portions of the peninsula under Habsburg (and later, Bourbon) control. As Oliveira Martins, Miguel de Unamuno, Salvador de Madariaga and numerous other commentators have observed, "Spain" in its older sense, which dates back to the Roman *Hispania*, refers to the whole of the Iberian Peninsula, irrespective of political boundaries. The Portuguese could, therefore, in Quental's opinion, legitimately refer to themselves as "Spaniards." For Quental, the idea that the Portuguese could recover this older, pre-1640 definition of Spain *as Iberia*, and that they could identify as Spaniards, transgressed one of the core tenets of the Portuguese national story: that the Portuguese *are not* Spaniards, and that Portugal is not Spain.

This binary logic of Portuguese versus Spaniard, Portugal versus Spain depends on an ultimately reductive and univocal understanding of "Portugal" and "Spain" as categories. While treating Portugal and Spain as an either/or proposition may hold a certain nationalistic appeal, or an attraction borne of simplicity, as Quental suggests, these categories are in fact plural, historically contingent, and responsive to internal and external power dynamics. Whereas prior to the Iberian dynastic union a writer like Luís de Camões could refer to the Portuguese as Spaniards, and to Portugal as a part of Spain in his epic poem *Os Lusíadas* (1572) without appearing to compromise Portuguese sovereignty, after the 1640 Restoration, the changed relationship between Portugal and Spain (and the terms "Portugal" and "Spain") would render such a gesture suspect. Given the amount of ink spilled by proponents of Iberian studies in criticizing Hispanism's monolingual, hierarchical, and Castile-centred understanding of the field, it behooves us to begin our interrogation of peninsular literary and cultural studies with a serious look at the terms we use when describing our field of inquiry, with the aim of questioning their ontological value and historicizing their usage. Quental's *Causas da Decadência dos Povos Peninsulares* provides us with one platform for doing so, though the textual corpus addressed in *Iberianism and Crisis* provides us with several alternatives. These include Oliveira Martins's denaturalizing of the medieval *Portucale* in his *História de Portugal* (1879), and Maragall's rich interrogation of Catalan and Spanish identity, as well as language and class in essays like "La espaciosa y triste España" (The Vast, Sad Spain, 1911).

Moving ahead to 1898 and across the peninsula to Barcelona, in his "Oda a Espanya" (Ode to Spain), Maragall makes a public declaration of sorts that in its subversive potential recalls Quental. In the opening stanza of his poem, written shortly before the culmination of Spain's disastrous military defeat by the United States, Maragall interrogates Spain as follows: "Escolta, Espanya, – la veu d'un fill / que et parla en llengua – no castellana; / parlo en la llengua – que m'ha donat / la terra aspra" (Hear, Spain, the voice of a son / who speaks to you in a language that is not Castilian; / I speak in the language that the rough land / has given me) (*OC* 1: 171). As was discussed in chapter 5, there is considerable debate regarding how Maragall understands his relationship with Spain in this poem, and whether the "Oda a Espanya" should be read as Maragall's appeal for Catalan engagement in a beleaguered Spain, or rather as a call for separation from it. Regardless of the poem's ambiguity, the lesson we can take for Iberian studies is found in Maragall's insistence that Spain listen to his message, delivered in Catalan as opposed to Castilian, and therefore recognize his claim to be a son of Spain, albeit one whose native language is Catalan, and who is not culturally Castilian. Similarly, Iberian studies must recognize and insist on the multilingualism of the Iberian Peninsula and of many of its writers, and on the plurality of its interconnected literary and cultural traditions and identities, which should be evaluated in a spirit of inclusivity and egalitarianism. The case of Maragall is especially relevant, given that his writing is divided on a roughly equal basis between texts written in Catalan and Castilian. In order to be properly understood as a writer and critic, Maragall must be seen in light of his contributions to both Spanish–Castilian and Catalan letters as distinct albeit related literary traditions. To ignore Maragall's poetic and critical production in Catalan, or his criticism and journalism in Castilian, is to "amputate" one half of his literary and intellectual personality, as Resina might say. In pedagogical terms, this is as artificial and shortsighted as assigning to students, for example, only Gil Vicente's Castilian plays in a course on medieval Spanish theatre on the assumption that the many Portuguese-language works of this Portuguese-born playwright fall outside of the course's linguistic scope. And yet this and similar "amputations" – some of which are frankly antihistorical – are all too common when multilingual Iberian writers are taught in literature-focused programs in Spanish, Portuguese, Catalan, and so on, which have been organized monolingually.[11] Iberian studies must not make the same mistake.

By extension, Iberian studies must relentlessly challenge the persistent assumption that languages like Catalan, Portuguese, Galician, and Basque, along with their attendant literary and cultural expressions, are somehow less peninsular, less Hispanic, and yes, less Spanish than Castilian. On the other hand, it would be foolish for Iberian studies to ignore the fact of Castilian linguistic and cultural predominance within the Spanish state and in Latin America (Brazil excepted), and within peninsular and Latin American literary and cultural studies. Maragall, though a champion of Catalan language and literature, was well aware of this disparity, noting in his "Oda a Espanya": "En'questa llengua," that is, Catalan "– pocs t'han parlat; / en l'altra, massa" (in this language, few have spoken to you; / but in the other, so many) (172). Recognition of the equal dignity of Iberia's languages and literatures should not blind us to disparities between Spanish, Portuguese, Catalan, Galician, and Basque in terms of number of speakers, degree of international projection, and level of institutional support.

Let us turn finally to Unamuno. In a 19 December 1905 letter to the Portuguese poet Teixeira de Pascoaes, Unamuno declared: "Portugal me interesa mucho porque me interesa España" (Portugal interests me so because Spain interests me) (quoted in Morejón 363). It is tempting to view this as a rather pithy statement in which Unamuno once more indulges his fondness for mirroring effects and apparent paradox. In reality, the statement encapsulates Unamuno's dialectical understanding of the Iberian Peninsula, in which Spain, and Iberia by extension, appears as a differentiated yet internally integrated whole. We should attempt to put aside the political implications of Unamuno's dialectical view of Iberia, which suggests a teleological movement towards linguistic and perhaps political unity under the aegis of Castile, along with some of Unamuno's questionable statements regarding Portugal and its precarious political independence. Instead, let us focus on Unamuno's more basic, quite sensible point: Portugal, whatever its political status, cannot be properly understood in isolation from Spain, and likewise, and perhaps more radically given the power dynamics at play, Spain cannot be properly understood in isolation from Portugal. As Maragall put it in a 1909 article, "sin Portugal no hay España" (without Portugal there is no Spain) (*OC* 2: 751). Broadening Unamuno's observation beyond the Portugal–Spain relationship, we might borrow from the subtitle of Resina's recent edited volume *Iberian Modalities* and argue that Iberian studies aspires to offer a relational approach to peninsular literary and cultural studies, in which none of the Iberian canons or traditions (Castilian, Portuguese, Catalan, Galician, Basque, etc.) can be fully understood in isolation from its neighbours.

This, to my mind, is perhaps the most powerful argument in favour of Iberian studies. Iberian studies, properly understood, should not aspire to dismantle an outmoded model of Castilian or Portuguese linguistic and cultural supremacy only to attempt to replace it with a competing Catalan, Galician, or Basque monolingual or mono-cultural hegemony. Such attempts would be quixotic at best, except in very specific regional or academic environments, given the much more limited global projection of the Catalan, Galician, and Basque languages relative to Spanish or Portuguese. Rather, Iberian studies, in embracing the principles of comparativism, multilingualism, and inclusivity, should affirm that Spain, Portugal, Catalonia, Galicia, the Basque Country and so on – as well as their attendant literary and cultural traditions – only mean something in dialogue, both with each other and with the world beyond the Pyrenees.

Notes

1. Iberianism in a Time of Crisis

1 See Saler, and Laqueur on the semantic ambiguity of the term *fin de siècle* and its suggestions of "morbidity, decline, decadence, cultural pessimism" (Laqueur 5).
2 For anti-Iberianism in Portugal, see Catroga ("Nacionalismo" 437–44); Mascarenhas (32–6); Matos (*Historiografia* 285–304).
3 Novelist Eça de Queirós wrote in the 1890 article "O Ultimatum": "Durante o desagradável mês de Janeiro, Portugal atravessou uma crise – que é incontestàvelmente a mais severa, talvez a mais decisiva que esta geração tem afrontado" (During the unpleasant month of January, Portugal experienced a crisis – unquestionably the most severe, and perhaps the most consequential, that this generation has faced) (*Obras* 942). On crises in Portugal and Spain, see Matos ("A Crise" 99); Del Valle and Gabriel-Stheeman (7).
4 See Krauel (*Imperial*).
5 All English-language biblical quotations included in this book are from the King James Version.
6 In Turgenev's *Fathers and Sons* (1862) the dying protagonist Bazarov (himself a medical doctor), refers to his death throes as a "crisis" (191). See also Galdós's novels *El doctor Centeno* (1883) and *Halma* (1895). See Galdós (*El doctor* 1: 131, 2: 237; *Halma* 205).
7 See also Clarín's reference to "crisis del ánimo" in his novel *La Regenta* (1884–5) (1: 15).
8 On Almirall's *regeneracionismo*, see Harrington (*Public Intellectuals* 34).
9 The "Sexenio Democrático," also referred to as the "Sexenio Revolucionario," refers to a six-year period that began with the overthrow of Spain's Queen Isabel II. The throne was then granted to Amedeo, Duke of Aosta (r. Amadeo I, 1871–3). With Amadeo's abdication, the First Spanish Republic was declared (1873–4). With the collapse of the republic, Isabel II's son was installed as King Alfonso XII, marking the beginning of the Restoration.
10 For a dissenting view, see Catroga ("Política" 26–31).
11 Biographical details on Martins are largely taken from Serrão.
12 Martins reserved some of his most colourful descriptions for his correspondence, as in an 1892 letter to Eça, in which he characterized Portugal and its national politics as a "pastelaria merdosa em que nos havemos de

afogar e morrer" (shitty pastry shop in which we'll drown and die) (*Correspondencia* 141).

13 The term *casticismo* resists translation, though here it refers to adherence to or respect for national tradition, the apparent inverse of "Europeanization." Valentí Almirall described the conflict as between *españolismo* and *extranjerismo* in an 1877 article. See Almirall (*OC* 1: 617). Martins commented in an 18 April 1884 letter to Spanish writer Juan Valera on a similar divide in Spanish letters between *estrangeirados* and *nacionais*. See Martins (*Correspondencia* 41).

14 Harrington provides an alternate reading, arguing: "For Quental, Portugal is not a backward country in need of reform, but rather a fatally flawed nation enslaved by its own aberrant historical trajectory" (*Public Intellectuals* 84).

15 These ideas are commonplaces of peninsular exegesis. See Unamuno (*OC* 1: 824); Pidal (*Los españoles* 33–8); Quental (*Causas* 11); Ganivet (68).

16 See, for instance, Matos ("Iberismo" 361).

17 These are the Castilian, Galician and Portuguese, Catalan, and Basque spellings. For examples of this argument, see Unamuno (*Escritos* 225; *OC* 4: 1081, 1357) and Cases-Carbó (7).

18 Here I refer to Sabaté and Fonseca's edited volume, *Catalonia and Portugal: The Iberian Peninsula from the Periphery* (2015).

19 The memory of the 1580–1640 dynastic union served as a rallying cry for Portuguese anti-Iberianists, and an obstacle for Portuguese Iberianists. See Catroga ("Nacionalismo" 441–4); Mascarenhas (33); Matos ("Iberismo" 362); Rocamora ("Causas" 632–3).

20 Harrington defends the latter position. Invoking Spain and Portugal's nineteenth-century crises, he observes: "It might more accurately be said that these events did not so much create a feeling of Iberian solidarity, but rather that they encouraged the re-emergence of an already existing sense of shared, but simultaneously diverse, cultural patrimony between the culture-nations of Spain (Catalonia, Castile, and Galicia) and their Portuguese brethren" (*Public Intellectuals* 13).

21 The balance of Iberianist scholarship has been produced by Portuguese academics, and focuses on Iberianism in Portugal. Notable exceptions include Rocamora's *El nacionalismo ibérico: 1792–1936* (1994) and Martínez-Gil's *El naixement de l'iberisme catalanista* (1997). Iberianism has generally merited greater attention in Portugal than in Spain. I suspect that its transgression of a key component of the Portuguese national story (that Portugal is not Spain) may play a role in its prominence among Portuguese scholars.

22 See also Abreu (53); Martínez-Gil (*El naixement* 40, 43); Rocamora ("Causas" 636).

23 Rocamora explains: "El nacionalismo ibérico, aunque distinto al español y al portugués, estaba en íntima relación con ambos, de forma que si los dos últimos eran incompatibles entre sí, separadamente eran compatibles con el ibérico" (Iberian nationalism, though distinct from Spanish or Portuguese nationalism, was intimately related to both, such that if the latter two were mutually incompatible, separately, they were each compatible with Iberian nationalism) (*El nacionalismo* 18). Further, Rocamora notes the influence on Iberianism of nineteenth-century European nationalism, and observes: "El nacionalismo ibérico resultó del deseo de alcanzar un estado viable e internacionalmente prestigioso, coincidiendo con tendencias predominantes en el nacionalismo liberal" (Iberian nationalism was the product of the desire to achieve a viable and internationally respected state, and it coincided with the dominant tendencies of liberal nationalism) (183).

24 See also Harrington (*Public Intellectuals* 2).

25 See also Williams.

26 See Matos ("Iberismo" 355).

27 See Matos (*Historiografia* 280).

28 See Catroga ("Nacionalismo" 419, note 2).

29 See Nogueira (1: 260–3).

30 See Martins ("Do Princípio Federativo" 39–40).

31 Martins initiated an epistolary relationship with Valera, and dedicated the second edition of this *História da Civilização Ibérica* to him. In response, Valera wrote a series of articles, "Historia de la civilización ibérica" (1887), ostensibly about Martins's book, but largely dedicated to Catalanism. On 7 August 1887, Marcelino Menéndez y Pelao wrote the following to Valera concerning Martins: "En todo lo que va de siglo no ha habido portugués tan español como él" (In this century there is no Portuguese who is more Spanish than he) (quoted in Serra and García Martín 166).

32 "Tripartite Iberianism" is Harrington's term. He uses it to describe "the rich vein of decentralizing thought [in early twentieth-century Catalonia] which presumes the existence of three distinct but mutually dependent culture-nations within the Iberian Peninsula: Catalonia, Castile, and Portugal" ("Belief" 226, note 3). Martínez-Gil refers to this as "Catalanist Iberianism," and notes that while the tripartite division of Iberia was a popular notion at the *fin de siècle*, its intellectual roots ran deeper, at least to the eighteenth century. See Martínez-Gil ("A Visão" 58, 60).

33 For detailed readings of Prat's *La nacionalitat catalana*, see Harrington (*Public Intellectuals*); Krauel (*Imperial* 147–74).
34 For a historical overview, see Harrington (*Public Intellectuals* xviii–xxiv).
35 Despite his differences from the fictional Ega, Quental called in *Portugal Perante a Revolução de Espanha* for the Portuguese to "renounce [their] nationality" and embrace Iberianism.
36 For instance, Joaquín Costa argues against union with Portugal and for North African expansion in *Reconstitución y europeización de España* (1900). See Costa (33).
37 See Rocamora (*El nacionalismo* 110).
38 See Harrington ("The Hidden").
39 See Pi y Margall (*La reacción* 270).
40 Catalan Iberianist and Lusophile Ignasi Ribera i Rovira alludes to this passage in his study *Iberisme* (1907). See Ribera i Rovira (70–1). Ribeiro wrote the popular anti-Iberianist poem *Dom Jaime* (1862).
41 See also Berkowitz (16); Brobjer (302).

2. Antero de Quental, *Iberista*

1 Eça (1845–1900) was a writer who became Portugal's most prominent proponent of literary realism-naturalism. Ortigão (1836–1915) was a journalist and writer who collaborated with Eça on a long-running series of satirical chronicles, *As Farpas*. Braga (1843–1924) was a writer and politician of positivist and republican sympathies.
2 See Pires (53, 60); Eça de Queirós ("Um Génio" 484–5); Reis (11).
3 See Eça de Queirós ("Um Génio" 485).
4 As Catroga notes, fifty-eight Iberianist texts were published in Portugal between 1867 and 1871, while only forty-five were published between 1852 and 1867. See Catroga ("Nacionalismo" 443).
5 See Saraiva (18) for the impact of 1868 on the *Geração de 70*, and Mascarenhas (41–3) on its impact on Quental and Portuguese Iberianists.
6 See Quental (*Obra Completa, Cartas 1–2* 834; *O Que É a Internacional* 334; *Prosas* 1: 314, note 1; *Portugal* 116).
7 See, for example, Maragall (*OC* 2: 551–5).
8 See Rocamora (*El nacionalismo* 107).
9 Quental may also be following the example of Romantic-era Portuguese historian and writer Alexandre Herculano, who distinguished between the "país real" and the "país legal." See Matos ("Iberismo" 351).
10 See "Do Princípio Federativo e Sua Aplicação à Península Hispânica" (1869), "Os Povos Peninsulares e a Civilização Moderna" (1875), *História da Civilização Ibérica* (1879), "O Iberismo" (in *Portugal Contemporâneo*, 1881),

"Espanha e Portugal" (1882, 1888), "Iberismo" (1889), "Alianças" (1890), and the posthumous *Cartas Peninsulares*.

11 See Maria de Lourdes Pereira (10).

12 See Pires (67, 248). Maria da Conceição Pereira (145–6) and Rocamora (*El nacionalismo* 108) agree with Pires. Lopes, Marques, and Reis offer "gradualist" interpretations of Quental's Iberianism. See also Martínez-Gil (*El naixement* 41).

13 Freeland (110) dates "A Catástrofe" to 1879 or the early 1880s. It was not published until after Eça's death.

14 In this letter, written in the wake of the Britain's humiliating 1890 "Ultimatum" to Portugal, Quental speculates: "[N]ão sei se a união ibérica se realizará: mas, a realizar-se, far-se-á pela força das coisas e não pela intervenção livre e razoável das vontades, que as não há cá para tanto" (I do not know if the Iberian Union will be achieved, but, if it is achieved, this will be due to events rather than free, reasoned intention, which here is wholly non-existent) (*Obra Completa. Cartas* 1: 1013).

15 See also Quental (*Obra Completa. Cartas* 2: 834; *As Tendências Gerais* 58).

16 However, Quental's engagement with *decadência* predates this text; he made several references to it in *Portugal Perante a Revolução*, for exemple.

17 José Ortega y Gasset's *España invertebrada* (1921), which identified Spain's apparent "decline" with the progressive decomposition of its national elements, and with regional separatism, features prominently in this discussion. As Matos notes, Quental did not pioneer the notion of peninsular decline, "porque los primeros liberales ya habían defendido la idea" (because the first liberals had defended the idea earlier) ("Cómo convivir" 257).

18 I am unaware if Quental read Cánovas's book, though both identify the Inquisition, absolute monarchy, and empire as the causes of decline. However, where Quental addresses himself to the "povos peninsulares," Cánovas refers to Spain specifically. See also Boyd (69). See Jutglar on the vast bibliography on "la crisis y la decadencia de la España del siglo XVII" (*La España* 131).

19 See also Harrington (*Public Intellectuals* 17).

20 See Martins (*Civilização Ibérica* 311; *Iberian Civilization* 264).

21 See Pires (64–5); Reis (12).

22 Recall the popularity in Portugal of the expression "de Espanha, nem bom vento, nem bom casamento" (from Spain, come neither favorable winds, nor good marriages). and other *espanholadas*.

23 See liberal politician and Romantic writer Almeida Garrett, who opposed union with Spain but argued in a footnote to his biographical poem *Camões* (1825): "Espanhóis somos, e de Espanhóis nos devemos prezar todos os que habitamos esta península" (We are Spaniards, and all of us who live on this peninsula should feel proud to be Spaniards) (2: 432).

24 As Rocamora notes, idealization of the Middle Ages was typical of Romanticism, and in this sense, the young Quental and Martins were good Romantics. See Rocamora (*El nacionalismo* 108, 183–4).
25 Quental's reference to the Iberians lifting themselves up may recall the *Sursum corda* (Lift up your hearts), from the Catholic Eucharistic prayer.
26 See also Quental (*Prosas* 1: 152).
27 As Kamen notes, an analogous phenomenon occurred in nineteenth-century Spanish intellectual life, though here, "the Spanish were visualized as a great people who had developed fully in the Middle Ages, but after the year 1516 were ruined by despotic foreign rulers [beginning with the Bourbons] from whom they were not rescued until the nineteenth century" (3).
28 See Maria de Lourdes Pereira (12).
29 Quental's argument recalls Unamuno's 1895 statement in "La tradición eterna," which would later be published in *En torno al casticismo* (1902), that while scientific principles are universally applicable, they manifest themselves in particular cultural contexts – hence, "la ciencia no se da nunca pura" (science never comes to us in its pure form) (*OC* 1: 788).
30 See Catroga (*Antero* 126) for the "importância (relativa) do elemento rácico" ([relative] importance of the racial element) in Quental.

3. "A Ribbon of Silver"

1 See Popescu (9); Donnan and Wilson (13); Diener and Hagan (3).
2 Couto Mixto (Portuguese: *Couto Misto*) was a small territory located on the Portuguese–Galician border, comprising three hamlets. The houses of Braganza and Monterrei both held jurisdiction, but until 1864 it was technically not a part of Portugal or Spain.
3 See Hooper (2).
4 See Cuesta ("Portugal-Galicia" 9).
5 The stories in question are "De otros tiempos" (1915), which takes place on the Portuguese–Galician frontier, and "La aventura" (1899), and "Cenizas" (1902), in which characters cross the border to Portugal before journeying to the New World.
6 Pereira-Muro notes for late nineteenth-century Galician regionalists, "[a]unque se llaman a sí mismos 'regionalistas,' en todos existe una confusa noción y un uso aleatorio de los términos 'patria,' 'nación' y 'región'" (though they call themselves "regionalists," they all exhibit a confused idea and make aleatory use of the terms *patria, nación* and *región*) (69).
7 See Valera's series of articles "Historia de la civilización ibérica" (1887) and Cuesta ("Curros" 390, note 6). For Valera and Martins, see Tobar (183, 195).

8 See Martins (quoted in Araújo 79).
9 See Quirk. See also Gabilondo ("Towards" 262), who argues that Pardo Bazán "translated" her texts from an "impossible 'original' Galician position/literature" to Spanish.
10 See Hooper (22). For Pardo Bazán and Galician letters, see Pereira-Muro (109).
11 See Beramendi (450).
12 See Unamuno's "El bizkaitarrismo y el vascuence" (1901) (4: 251–5).
13 See Unamuno (*OC* 4: 156).
14 See Araújo (150–4); Risco; Harrington ("Catalanism"; *Public Intellectuals*).
15 See Dios (363–74) for the nearly three hundred Portuguese-language books in Unamuno's library.
16 See Unamuno (*OC* 4: 1362; 8: 1016).
17 See also Matos ("Portugal," 76) on the "non-existence of nationality at the time [of Portugal's independence]" and on the young country's "non-organic character."
18 See Davies; Beramendi (344).
19 "Who has not read her verses? Who has not … sighed because of her melancholy *saudades*?"
20 Murguía makes the same double reference in the first edition of his *Historia de Galicia* (1865). He eliminated the reference to *dialecto* in the second, 1901 edition in favour of *idioma*. See Beramendi (181).
21 See Brañas (159, 215).
22 I owe this observation on the geographic mobility of *terra* in Galician culture to Sharon Roseman.
23 This discrepancy may reflect the evolving meaning of *patria*. As Hobsbawm observes: "In Spanish *patria* did not become coterminous with Spain until late in the nineteenth century. In the eighteenth it still meant simply the place or town where a person was born" (148).
24 See Beramendi and Seixas (53).
25 See Gabilondo ("Towards" 250); Hooper and Moruxa (7).
26 Pardo Bazán refers to Eça in *La cuestión palpitante* (3: 633). See also a letter, probably dating from 1890, from Clarín to Pardo Bazán in which he mentions the Portuguese novelist (quoted in Bravo-Villasante [136–8]).
27 "The setting afternoon sun lit in gold / the towers of Lisbon, / and the lapping water of the Tagus, / shone like fire"; "I thought I saw from Lusitanian ships, / the sacred waves aflame, / and the numen of glory, / illuminated on the horizon."
28 See Maragall's 1906 article "El ideal ibérico" (*OC* 2: 725).
29 See Brañas (24–5); Maragall (*OC* 2: 628–31); Unamuno (*OC* 10: 86).

30 Surgical metaphors are common in discussions on intra-Iberian relations, and regarding Portugal's historical separation from the rest of the peninsula. Quental, in *Portugal Perante a Revolução de Espanha* (1868), writes of "Portugal, membro amputado desnecessariamente, ainda que sem violência, do grande corpo da Península Ibérica" (Portugal, a limb amputated unnecessarily, though without violence, from the great body of the Iberian Peninsula) (118). See also Resina ("Introduction" 2); Seixas ("Iberia" 83).
31 See Martins (*Civilização Ibérica* 268).
32 For similar descriptions, see Unamuno (*OC* 1: 307; 6: 509).
33 Unamuno's reference to "Pan y Cristo" in this poem recalls Teixeira de Pascoaes's *Jesus e Pan* (1903).

4. Miguel de Unamuno

1 On *intrahistoria,* see Unamuno (*OC* 1: 797). On Castilian protagonism in Spain, see Unamuno (1: 802).
2 See Dios (quoted in Unamuno, *Escritos* 16); Mora (67).
3 See Harrington (*Public Intellectuals* 216–17).
4 See Unamuno (*OC* 4: 526–9, 1081–4).
5 Unamuno's pessimistic characterization of Portugal was seemingly confirmed when republican agitators assassinated King D. Carlos I and heir apparent Luís Filipe in 1908, paving the way for Portugal to become a republic in 1910. Unamuno wrote on the regicide in several articles, collected in *Por tierras de Portugal y de España* (1911).
6 Morejón's *Unamuno y Portugal* remains the most comprehensive book on this topic. The *Epistolário Português de Unamuno* and the *Escritos de Unamuno sobre Portugal,* both edited by Ángel Marcos de Dios, are also essential.
7 Unamuno initially considered publishing these pieces in a book dedicated entirely to Portugal. See Unamuno (*OC* 1: 245).
8 For Unamuno's view that Spanish writers should read Portuguese texts in the original, see Unamuno (*OC* 1: 188). Unamuno viewed Castilian and Portuguese as similar, even "irmãs gêmeas" (twin sisters) (*Escritos* 226).
9 See *Epistolário Português de Unamuno,* appendix II, for his Portuguese collection (Dios 363–74).
10 It is difficult to ascertain whether Unamuno truly disliked Camões, or if this judgment was analogous to his contrarian declaration that, while he revered *Don Quijote,* he did not care about Cervantes.
11 Unamuno was a great reader of Quental and Martins, and a friend of Guerra Junqueiro. See Unamuno (*OC* 1: 191; 4: 1329, 1349).

12 See Unamuno (*OC* 4: 1081, 1357).
13 See Martins's call in his article "Alianças" (1890) for Portugal to "return" to Spain by forming a strong alliance with its peninsular neighbour. See Martins (*Dispersos* 219).
14 See Harrington ("Catalanism" 270).
15 Unamuno acknowledged that Habsburg mistakes undermined Portugal's incorporation into Spain between 1580 and 1640. See Unamuno (*OC* 4: 524, 557).
16 Unamuno termed Quental "la más trágica figura de nuestra literatura ibérica" (the most tragic figure of our Iberian literature), Martins "el único historiador artista de [la Península]" ([the Peninsula's] only artistic historian] and the "único historiador verdaderamente genial que ha producido la península Ibérica en el pasado siglo" (the only truly talented historian that the Iberian Peninsula produced during the past century), and Junqueiro "el gran poeta portugués, o mejor, ibérico" (*the* great Portuguese, or rather, Iberian poet). See Unamuno (*OC* 1: 191; 4: 1329, 1349).
17 The title of Unamuno's article is misleading. Rather than critique the dialectical method, Unamuno critiques Spain's intellectual climate during the first years of the twentieth century.
18 For interpretations of Unamuno that link him to Kierkegaard or that downplay Hegel's influence, see Arroyo ("Hacia"; "Unamuno"); Batchelor; Evans; Marías; Mora; París; Vauthier. See Fiddian for a partial corrective.
19 This term may be translated as "super-Castilian" or "over-Castilian" and recalls Nietzsche's *Übermensch*.
20 See Epps (115–16) for a fair-minded assessment of Unamuno's shifting views.
21 See also Unamuno (*Escritos* 187–8, 246, 249).
22 For tripartite Iberianism, see Harrington ("Hidden").
23 Regarding the Spain/Europe relationship, see Unamuno (*OC* 1: 866; 3: 725).
24 See Newcomb, "A Poetry."
25 This is taken from the subtitle of Unamuno's undated "Paisaje teresiano: El campo es una metáfora," published in *Andanzas y visiones españolas* (1922). See Unamuno (*OC* 1: 494–7).
26 See also Unamuno's declaration to Maragall, from a 6 June 1900 letter: "La poesía castellana no me resulta; la encuentro seca y fría" (Castilian poetry does not speak to me; I find it dry and cold) (Unamuno and Maragall 10).
27 Unamuno seemed to view Catalan, like Portuguese, as playing a compensatory role vis-à-vis Castilian. See Unamuno (*OC* 4: 544–5; 9: 322).

28 This picture of the Minho is typical of Unamuno's descriptions of northern Portugal, and of the Portuguese people and language. See also Unamuno (*OC* 1: 427–8).
29 Unamuno employs the Galician spelling of *meigice*, though he describes it as a Portuguese word. The Portuguese spelling is *meiguice*.
30 I have consulted with *cervantistas* and none has corroborated this statement. Nonetheless, Unamuno's probable misattribution has gained currency in academic and pseudo-academic discourse on Luso–Hispanic relations. Spanish poet Antonio de Trueba attributed the formulation to the historian and political economist Sismondi. See Trueba (229, note 1). Trueba is a possible source for Unamuno's misattribution.
31 For other references to "castellano sin huesos," see Unamuno (*Escritos* 226; *OC* 4: 1358).
32 Unamuno referred to the "dos Repúblicas del extremo occidental de Europa" (two Republics at Europe's Western edge) in "Nueva vuelta a Portugal" (1935). See Unamuno (*OC* 4: 1361).
33 *Paisanaje*, a portmanteau of *paisano* and *paisaje*, refers in Unamuno, who viewed the natural and human landscapes as intertwined, to the "human landscape." He used the term as early as 1895, in the essay "Sobre el marasmo actual de España," later collected in *En torno al casticismo*.

5. Joan Maragall

1 See: Cambó (quoted in Maragall, *OC* 2: 1070); Marfany ("Joan Maragall" 209).
2 The *Sardana* is a folk dance that serves as a symbol of Catalan identity. The *Senyera* refers to the Catalan flag, comprised of four red stripes against a gold background. The pattern appears in flags and coats of arms throughout the "Països Catalans."
3 Angel Smith characterizes nineteenth-century Catalanism in terms of advocacy for "Catalan political autonomy," defence of "an autonomous Catalan cultural sphere," and a desire that "the Catalan language … be used in the areas of politics and high culture." Smith notes a similar ideological eclecticism for *modernisme*, the aesthetic movement with which Maragall identified. See Angel Smith (173–4).
4 Maragall reviewed and respected Azorín's work. See Maragall (*OC* 2: 150; 606–8).
5 See Marfany ("Joan Maragall" 218); McRoberts (27); Epps (97–8).
6 Here I borrow from the title of José Álvarez Junco's *Mater Dolorosa: La idea de España en el siglo XIX* (2001).

7 On emotions in *fin-de-siècle* Spanish essay writing, see Krauel (*Imperial*).
8 For another reference to Maragall's anguish regarding Spain, see Maragall (*OC* 2: 653).
9 See Anderson (quoted in Saler, 186); Martínez-Gil (*El naixement* 206).
10 For another "diagnostic" of a "sick" Spain, see Maragall (*OC* 2: 723).
11 See also Maragall's controversial article "La patria nueva" (1902): "Aquí hay algo vivo gobernado por algo muerto" (Here we have something living governed by something dead). Here he refers to "la gran momia política" (the great political mummy) and "la vasta necrópolis nacional" (the vast national necropolis) (*OC* 2: 653).
12 See Chabás (120); King (237).
13 Maragall's relationship to *modernisme*, an aesthetic movement that emerged in Catalonia during the 1890s, was similarly changeable, and in consequence is difficult to characterize. See Marfany ("Modernisme" 36).
14 "Tripartite Iberianism" is Harrington's term, and describes "the rich vein of decentralizing thought [in early twentieth-century Catalonia] which presumes the existence of three distinct but mutually dependent culture-nations within the Iberian Peninsula: Catalonia, Castile, and Portugal" ("Belief" 226, note 3).
15 See Martínez-Gil (*El naixement* 225) for Prat's influence, and Harrington ("The Hidden" 143–5) for Ribera i Rovira's influence.
16 See Esquirol (203); Martínez-Gil (*El naixement* 212); Harrington ("Agents" 106, note 21; *Public Intellectuals* 27). For Maragall as a Catalanist, though not a militant, see Marfany ("Joan Maragall" 208). See Krauel on "Maragall's peculiar relationship to social insurgency" ("Emotions" 193). See Etherington for a succinct analysis of the embrace by the Barcelona industrial bourgeoisie, to which Maragall belonged, of Catalanism.
17 See Marfany ("Joan Maragall" 220); Terry (3–4).
18 Unamuno described Jacint Verdaguer and Maragall as "los dos mejores poetas españoles vivos" (the two best living Spanish poets) in a 28 July 1898 letter to Pedro Mugica, and wrote in "Sobre la literatura catalana" (1906) that Maragall was "el poeta más intimo, más noble, más llano que canta en España, [y] canta en catalán" (the most intimate, noblest, plainest poet of Spain, [and] one who writes in Catalan) (quoted in Bastons 32–3).
19 Here Maragall recalls Almirall, who contrasts the Castilian and Catalan characters as follows: "Lo carácter catalá es lo revers de la medalla del genuhí castellá. En los bons temps, aquest era lo tipo de generalisador, y nosaltres eram eminentment analisadors. Ells se exaltaven per una abtracció idealista: nosaltres buscavam sempre ventatjas positivas" (The Catalan character is the reverse side of the medal of the genuine Castilian character.

In the good times, the Castilians were generalizers, while we were eminently analytical. They exalted in idealistic abstraction: we always looked for positive gains) (*Lo catalanisme* 54).

20 See Maragall (*OC* 2: 150–1).

21 Valentí Almirall referred to this in an 1880 article as the problem of "sintetitza[ndo] en Castella la nació espanyola" (synthesizing in Castile the whole of the Spanish nation) (*OC* 2: 327).

22 For a similar anecdote, see Unamuno (*Escritos* 190).

23 Note the resemblance between Maragall's "gran patria ibérica" and the title of Prat's 1916 manifesto *Per Catalunya i per l'Espanya gran* (For Catalonia and the Great Spain).

24 "Or de llei" is classified as a poem from Maragall's first years in the 1961 Editorial Selecta edition of his *Obres Completes*. See Maragall (*OC* 1: 193, note). Martínez-Gil notes that the poem anticipates Maragall's later interest in "l'ideal de federació ibèrica" (192).

25 See Martínez-Gil ("A Visão" 60, note 3).

26 See Ribera i Rovira (67).

27 See Martínez-Gil (*El naixement* 112); Harrington ("The Hidden" 143–5).

28 Resina takes the word "modalities," as in *Iberian Modalities: A Relational Approach* (2013), from this letter. See Resina ("Introduction" 14–15). For another reference to "modalities" in Maragall, see "El ideal ibérico" (Maragall, *OC:* 726).

29 See Harrington ("Catalanism" 266); Epps (119–20); Llopis (178–9).

30 See "Or de llei" for another mention by Maragall of the "sweetness" of Portuguese in comparison to Castilian (*OC* 1: 194).

31 For Luso-Catalan affinity, see Rocamora (*El nacionalismo* 105).

32 For Catalan federalism, see Jutglar (*Pi y Margall*) and Angel Smith (172).

33 See Jutglar (*Pi y Margall* 1: 284) for "unidad en la variedad." Maragall's critique of pact-based federalism as cold and abstract was shared by Catalanism more broadly. See Harrington (*Public Intellectuals* 33); Jutglar (*Pi y Margall* 2: 696–7).

34 Joaquim Cases-Carbó echoed the argument for Catalonia to lead Spain to unity with Portugal in his article "El problema peninsular" (1924). See Cases-Carbó (9).

35 "Portugal had the strength to seize this right, this freedom, during its time"; "The Catalan problem that now confronts us is identical to the Portuguese problem, merely delayed by a few centuries. The Portuguese resolved it, and we would like to resolve it."

36 See Martínez-Gil (*El naixement* 220–1, note 3).

37 See Marfany ("Joan Maragall" 241). For Prat's anti-liberalism, see Angel Smith (204).

38 The *Epistolario entre Miguel de Unamuno y Juan Maragall y escritos complementarios* (1951) registers thirty-seven letters exchanged between the two writers.
39 See Harrington ("The Hidden" 159).
40 See Maragall (*OC* 1: 740).
41 See Epps for discussion of the Europe/Africa opposition in Maragall and Unamuno's correspondence.
42 Here too Maragall recalls Almirall, who declared: "L'ús de la nostra llengua es la manifestació mes eloqüent de la nostra personalitat y un argument incontestable en pro de la justicia de la nostra causa. Mentres visqui la llengua catalana, tot acte d'unificació, portat á efecte en cualsevol terreno, será un acte de veritable tirania" (The use of our language is the most eloquent manifestation of our personality and an incontestable argument for the justice of our cause. As long as the Catalan language exists, all actions toward unification, occurring anywhere, will be acts of true tyranny) (*Lo catalanisme* 90).

6. The Iberianist Legacy

1 Martins seems to view both historical pessimism and Iberianism as typically Portuguese. See Martins (*Portugal Contemporâneo* 3: 249).
2 See Torga's diary entry for 11 November 1942 (2: 75).
3 See Maravall (17). See also Rocamora (*El nacionalismo* 116).
4 For instance, Madariaga was cited by Mexican philosopher Samuel Ramos in *El perfil del hombre y la cultura en México* (1934). See Ramos (37–40, 62).
5 Madariaga seems to have understood the term "Iberianism" as more or less synonymous with peninsular traditionalism or, for Unamuno, *casticismo*. See Madariaga (*Memorias* 130).
6 See also Madariaga's article "Los vascos y el sentido común": "Yo llevo apellido vasco, y si algo soy, soy gallego" (My last name is Basque, but if I'm anything, I'm Galician) (quoted in Madariaga, *Memorias* 347).
7 See Madariaga (*Memorias* 266).
8 For Madariaga on Unamuno, see Madariaga (*Genius* 45, 87–110; *Memorias* 32; *Memorias (1921–1936)* 223).
9 See Madariaga (*Anarchy* 18) for his disappointment with the post–First World War order in Europe.
10 See Pi y Margall (*Las nacionalidades* 79–81).
11 See Kahan's *Aristocratic Liberalism*. For Madariaga's politics, see Madariaga (*Anarchy*; *Democracy*; "A Letter").
12 For Madariaga and Ortega, see Fox (117, 123); Keown (23–4).

13 See Madariaga (*Memorias* 109; *Democracy* 112–14); Preston (161).
14 See also Madariaga (*Memorias (1921–1936)* 228).
15 See Madariaga (*Anarchy* 200; *Democracy*); Pi y Margall (*Las nacionalidades* 294).
16 See Martins (*Civilização Ibérica* 33; *Iberian Civilization* 13).
17 See also Madariaga (*España* 238–9).
18 See also Madariaga (*España* 243).
19 See Unamuno (*OC* 1: 803); Ortega (*España* 47–8).
20 See also Madariaga (*Memorias* 57, 211).
21 See Madariaga (*Memorias* 47, 89, 121, 175–6, 224).
22 See Madariaga (*Memorias* 53) for a more explicit criticism of the "adhesión condicional a España que profesan muchos catalanes y vascos" (many Catalans and Basques' conditional adhesion to Spain).
23 See Madariaga's article "La nacionalidad española" (17 April 1923) (quoted in *Memorias* 213–15).
24 On the name of post-1640 Spain, see Martínez-Gil (*El naixement* 12); Cases-Carbó (7).
25 See Pi y Margall (*Las nacionalidades* 225–6) for the 1580–1640 period in Portugal. Pi blames "el principio unitario" (the unitary principle), noting: "Bajo el principio federativo, ó no se habria separado ó, si lo hubiese hecho, habria vuelto espontáneamente al seno de la antigua patria" (Under the federative principle, [Portugal] either would not have separated [from Spain], or if it had, it would have spontaneously returned to the fold) (255).
26 See Madariaga (*Memorias* 115).
27 See also article 225 of the 1976 Portuguese Constitution, concerning autonomy for the Azores and Madeira.

Conclusion: Iberianism's Lessons

1 See Gabilondo ("Spanish" 27); Faber (8).
2 See the Centro de Estudos Ibéricos (Guarda, Portugal), founded 2001, and the Instituto de Estudos Ibéricos (Universidade do Porto), founded 2002. Stanford University's Department of Spanish and Portuguese renamed itself the Department of Iberian and Latin American Cultures, effective 1 September 2009. The University of Toronto began publishing its Toronto Iberic series in 2010.
3 On comparativism, see Viestenz (18); Gabilondo ("Spanish" 46).
4 See also Loureiro (65, 68–74).
5 Note that the RAE acknowledges the pluralism of Hispanic languages and literatures (*lenguas, literaturas)*, but implies that Hispanic culture (*cultura*) is singular.

6 See Armistead and Silverman (650).
7 See also Del Valle (79).
8 See Clover (113) on the impossibility of "saving the humanities."
9 See, for instance, Irwin on "postnationalist American studies."
10 See Resina (*Del hispanismo* 137).
11 A peninsularist colleague informed me that when she studied Vicente as a graduate student in Spanish, she did not read his Portuguese plays. As a graduate student in Portuguese, I did not read his Castilian plays. Though this approach respects a certain disciplinary logic, it nonetheless creates an artificial distinction that is unnecessary given the close linguistic proximity of Spanish and Portuguese. Further, as Harrington notes, it is antihistorical, given that when writers like Alfonso X, Vicente, or Juan Boscán wrote across Iberian languages, they did not "[view] themselves as writing in a foreign language" (*Public Intellectuals* 13).

Works Cited

Abreu, Luís Machado de. "Pendências Iberistas no Oitocentismo Português." *Revista da Universidade de Aveiro – Letras*, no. 13 (1996): 53–68.

Almirall, Valentí. *Lo Catalanisme: Motius que'l llegitiman fonaments cientifichs y solucions practicas*. Barcelona: Llibreria de Verdaguer; Llibreria de Lopez, 1886.

– *Obra Completa*. Ed. Josep M. Figueres. 2 vols. Barcelona: Institut d'Estudis Catalans, 2009–13.

Anderson, Benedict. *Imagined Communities: Reflections on the Origin and Spread of Nationalism*. Rev. ed. London: Verso, 2002.

Araújo, José David Santos. *Portugal e Galiza: Encantos e encontros*. Santiago de Compostela: Vento do Sul, 2004.

Armistead, Samuel G., and Joseph H. Silverman. "The Traditional Balladry of the Sephardic Jews: A Collaborative Research Project." *La Rassegna Meniale di Israel*, 3rd ser., vol. 49, no. 9/12 (September–December 1983): 641–67.

Arroyo, Ciriaco Morón. "Hacia el sistema de Unamuno." *Cuadernos de la Cátedra Miguel de Unamuno*, 32 (1997): 169–87.

– "Unamuno y Hegel." In *Miguel de Unamuno*, ed. Antonio Sánchez-Barbudo. Madrid: Ediciones Taurus, 1974. 151–79.

Bastons, Carles. "Traducción de Maragall i Unamuno: Els lligams d'una amistat." In *Joan Maragall y Miguel de Unamuno, una amistad paradigmtica. Cartas, artículos, dedicatorias, poemas*, ed. Carles Bastons. Lleida: Editorial Milenio, 2006. 27–47.

Batchelor, R.E. *Unamuno Novelist: A European Perspective*. Oxford: Dolphin, 1972.

Beramendi, Justo. *De provincia a nación: Historia do galeguismo politico*. Vigo: Edicións Xerais de Galicia, 2007.

Beramendi, Justo, and Xosé M. Núñez Seixas. *O nacionalismo galego*. 2nd ed. Vigo: Edicións A Nosa Terra, 1996.

Berkowitz, Peter. "Nietzsche's Ethics of History." *Review of Politics* 56, no. 1 (Winter 1994): 5–27.

Bhabha, Homi K. *The Location of Culture*. Routledge: London and New York, 1994.

The Bible. Authorized King James Version with Apocrypha. Oxford: Oxford University Press, 2008.

Bou, Enric. "On Rivers and Maps: Iberian Approaches to Comparatism." In *New Spain, New Literatures*, ed. Luis Martín-Estudillo and Nicholas Spadaccini. Nashville: Vanderbilt University Press, 2010. 3–26.

Boyd, Carolyn P. *Historia Patria: Politics, History, and National Identity in Spain, 1875–1975.* Princeton: Princeton University Press, 1997.

Brañas, Alfredo. *El regionalismo: Estudio sociológico, histórico y literario.* Barcelona: J. Molinas, 1889.

Bravo-Villasante, Carmen. *Vida y obra de Emilia Pardo Bazán.* Madrid: Revista de Occidente, 1962.

Brobjer, Thomas H. "Nietzsche's View of the Value of Historical Studies and Methods." *Journal of the History of Ideas* 65, no. 2 (April 2004): 301–22.

Bryson, Michael. "Dismemberment and Community: Sacrifice and the Communal Body in the Hebrew Scriptures." *Religion & Literature* 35, no. 1 (Spring 2003): 1–21.

Camões, Luís de. *Os Lusíadas.* São Paulo: Editôra Cultrix, 1966.

Camões, Luiz de. *The Lusiads.* Trans. Leonard Bacon. New York: The Hispanic Society of America, 1950.

Cánovas del Castillo, Antonio. *Historia de la decadencia de España desde el advenimiento de Felipe III al trono hasta la muerte de Carlos III.* Madrid: J. Ruiz, 1910.

Carreiro, José Bruno. *Antero de Quental: Subsídios para a sua Biografia.* 2 vols. Ponta Delgada: Instituto Cultural de Ponta Delgada; Braga: Pax, 1981.

Cases-Carbó, Joaquim. *El problema peninsular 1924–1932.* Barcelona: Llibreria Catalònia, 1933.

Castro, Rosalía de. *Obra galega completa.* 5th ed. Madrid: Akal, 1982.

Catroga, Fernando. *Antero de Quental: História, Socialismo, Política.* Lisbon: Editorial Notícias, 2001.

– "Nacionalismo e Ecumenismo: A Questão Ibérica na Segunda Metade do Século XIX." *Cultura – História e Filosofia* 4 (1985): 419–63.

– "Política, História e Revolução em Antero de Quental." *Revista de História das Ideias* (Faculdade de Letras da Universidade de Coimbra) 13 (1991): 7–55.

Cela, Camilo José. *A vueltas con España.* Madrid: Seminarios y Ediciones; Ediciones Castilla, 1973.

Chabás, Juan. *Juan Maragall. Poeta y ciudadano.* Madrid: Espasa-Calpe, 1935.

Clarín (Leopoldo Alas). *La Regenta.* 2 vols. Madrid: F. Fé, 1900.

Clover, Joshua. "Value | Theory | Crisis." *PMLA* 127, no. 1 (January 2012): 107–14.

Constitución española. Cortes Generales "BOE" no. 31, 29 December 1978. http://www.boe.es/buscar/pdf/1978/BOE-A-1978-31229-consolidado.pdf

Constituição da República Portuguesa. VII Revisão Constitucional (2005). http://www.parlamento.pt/Legislacao/Paginas/ConstituicaoRepublicaPortuguesa.aspx#art225

Costa, Joaquín. *Reconstitución y europeización de España y otros escritos.* Ed. Sebastián Martín-Retornillo y Baquer. Madrid: Instituto de Estúdios de Administración Local, 1981.

Cuesta, Pilar Vázquez. "Antero de Quental Iberista?" *Congresso Anteriano Internacional – Actas.* Universidade dos Açores, 14–18 October 1991. Ponta Delgada: Universidade dos Açores, 1993. 161–82.

– "Curros, os escritores portugueses e o Ultimatum." *Grial* 12, no. 36 (October–December 1974): 385–425.

– "Portugal-Galicia, Galicia-Portugal: Un diálogo asimétrico." *Colóquio/Letras* 137–8 (1995): 5–21.

Curros Enríquez, Manuel. *La lira Lusitana, La señorita de aldea, De mi álbum, Artículos y poesías en gallego y castellano.* Madrid: Suc. de Hernando, 1912.

– *Obra poética completa.* Madrid: Editora Nacional, 1977.

Davies, Catherine. "Rosalía de Castro's Later Poetry and Anti-Regionalism in Spain." *Modern Language Review* 79, no. 3 (July 1984): 609–19.

De la Campa, Román. "Hispanism and Its Lines of Flight." In *Ideologies of Hispanism,* ed. Mabel Moraña. Nashville: Vanderbilt University Press, 2005. 300–10.

Del Valle, José. "Menéndez Pidal, National Regeneration and the Linguistic Utopia." In *The Battle over Spanish between 1800 and 2000: Language Ideologies and Hispanic Intellectuals,* ed. José del Valle and Luis Gabriel-Stheeman. London and New York: Routledge, 2002. 78–105.

Del Valle, José, and Luis Gabriel-Stheeman. "Nationalism, *Hispanismo,* and Monoglossic Culture." In *The Battle over Spanish between 1800 and 2000: Language Ideologies and Hispanic Intellectuals.* London and New York: Routledge, 2002. 1–13.

Diener, Alexander C., and Joshua Hagen, eds. *Borderlines and Borderlands: Political Oddities at the Edge of the Nation-State.* Lanham, MD: Rowman & Littlefield, 2010.

Dios, Ángel Marcos de, ed. *Epistolário português de Unamuno.* Paris: Fundação Calouste Gulbenkian; Centro Cultural Português, 1978.

Donnan, Hastings, and Thomas M. Wilson. *Borders: Frontiers of Identity, Nation and State.* Oxford and New York: Berg, 1999.

Eça de Queirós, José Maria de. *Os Maias: Episódios da Vida Romântica.* Lisbon: Editora Ulisseia, 2000.

– "Um Génio que Era um Santo." In *Anthero de Quental in memoriam,* ed. Ana Maria Almeida Martins. Lisbon: Editorial Presença; Casa dos Açores, 1993. 481–522.

– *Obras de Eça de Queiroz.* Vol. 3. Porto: Lello & Irmão, [1912?].

Entralgo, Pedro Laín. "Mi Maragall." In Joan Maragall, *Obres completes*, vol. 2. Barcelona: Editorial Selecta, 1961. 13–31.

Epps, Brad. "Between Europe and America: Modernity, Race, and Nationality in the Correspondence of Miguel de Unamuno and Joan Maragall." *Anales de la Literatura Española Contemporánea* 30 nos. 1–2 (2005): 97–132.

Epps, Brad, and Luis Fernández Cifuentes. "Spain beyond Spain: Modernity, Literary History, and National Identity." In *Spain beyond Spain: Modernity, Literary History, and National Identity*, ed. Brad Epps and Luis Fernández Cifuentes. Lewisburg: Bucknell University Press, 2005. 11–45.

Esquirol. Jesús Revelles. "L'iberisme de Joan Maragall. Un projecte germinador." In *Joan Maragall, paraula i pensament*, ed. Josep-Maria Terricabras. Girona: Càtedra Ferrater Mora; Documenta Universitaria, 2011. 203–15.

Etherington, John. "Nationalism, Nation and Territory: Jacint Verdaguer and the Catalan *Renaixença*." *Ethnic and Racial Studies* 33, no. 10 (November 2010): 1814–32.

Evans, Jan E. *Unamuno and Kierkegaard: Paths to Selfhood in Fiction*. Lanham, MD: Lexington, 2005.

Faber, Sebastiaan. "Economies of Prestige: The Place of Iberian Studies in the American University." *Hispanic Research Journal* 9, no. 1 (2008): 7–32.

Fiddian, R.W. "Unamuno-Bergson: A Reconsideration." *Modern Language Review* 69, no. 4 (October 1974): 787–95.

Figueiredo, Fidelino de. *História d'um "Vencido da Vida."* Lisbon: Parceria Antonio Maria Pereira, 1930.

– "Prefácio" to J.P. de Oliveira Martins, *História da Civilização Ibérica*. 10th ed. Lisbon: Guimarães & Cia. Editores, 1972. 9–20.

Fox, E. Inman. "El 'hombre nuevo': La tutela del pueblo y el liberalismo español." *Revista Canadiense de Estudios Hispánicos* 21, no. 1 (Fall 1996): 117–30.

Freeland, Alan. "Imagined Endings: National Catastrophe in the Fiction of Eça de Queirós." *Portuguese Studies* 15 (1999): 105–18.

Gabilondo, Joseba. "Spanish Nationalist Excess: A Decolonial and Postnational Critique of Iberian Studies." *Prosopopeya*, no. 8 (2013–14): 23–60.

– "Towards a Postnational History of Galician Literature: On Pardo Bazán's Transnational and Translational Position." *Bulletin of Hispanic Studies* 86, no. 2 (2009): 249–69.

Galdós, Benito Pérez. *El doctor Centeno*. 2 vols. Madrid: Impr. y litograta de la La Guianada, 1886.

– *Halma*. Madrid: Sucesores de Hernando, 1913.

Ganivet, Ángel. *Idearium español. El porvenir de España.* Ed. E. Inman Fox. Madrid: Espasa Calpe, 1999.

Garrett, Almeida. *Obras.* 2 vols. Porto: Lello & Irmão, 1966.

Gaziel (Agustí Calvet Pascual). "La pàtria segons Maragall." In *Joan Maragall. Conferències en commemoració del centenari de la seva naixença (1860) i del cinquantenari de la seva mort (1911).* Barcelona: Institut d'Estudis Catalans, 1963. 137–67.

Harrington, Thomas S. "Agents of an Intersystem: Contributions of the Cuba-based Diaspora to the Construction of the Nation in Galicia and Catalonia." *Catalan Review* 15, no. 2 (2001): 95–114.

– "Belief, Institutional Practices, and Intra-Iberian Relations." In *Spain beyond Spain: Modernity, Literary History, and National Identity*, ed. Brad Epps and Luis Fernández Cifuentes. Lewisburg: Bucknell University Press, 2005. 205–30.

– "Catalanism in the Portuguese Mirror: Skirmishes between 'Unitarians' and 'Pluralists' for Control of the Movement (1900–1925)." *Revista de Estudios Hispánicos* 35 (2001): 257–80.

– "The Hidden History of Tripartite Iberianism." *A Comparative History of Literatures in the Iberian Peninsula.* Vol. 1. Ed. Fernando Cabo Aseguinolaza et al. Amsterdam and Philadelphia: John Benjamins Publishing Co., 2010. 138–62.

– *Public Intellectuals and Nation Building in the Iberian Peninsula, 1900–1925: The Alchemy of Identity.* Lewisburg: Bucknell University Press, 2015.

Herder, J.G. *On Social and Political Culture.* Trans. F.M. Barnard. Cambridge: Cambridge University Press, 1969.

"Hispanismo." In *Diccionario de la lengua española.* Real Academia Española. Amended 22nd edition. http://lema.rae.es/drae/cgi-bin/aviso_dle.cgi?url=&val=hispanismo

Hobsbawm, E.J. *The Age of Empire 1875–1914.* London: Weidenfeld and Nicolson, 1987.

Holton, R.J. "The Idea of Crisis in Modern Society." *British Journal of Sociology* 38, no. 4 (December 1987): 502–20.

Hooper, Kirsty. *Writing Galicia into the World: New Cartographies, New Poetics.* Liverpool: Liverpool University Press, 2011.

Hooper, Kirsty, and Manuel Puga Moruxa, eds. *Contemporary Galician Cultural Studies: Between the Local and the Global.* New York: Modern Language Association of America, 2011.

Hughes, Robert. *Barcelona.* New York: Alfred A. Knopf, 1992.

Irwin, Robert McKee. "*Ramona* and Postnationalist American Studies: On 'Our America' and the Mexican Borderlands." *American Quarterly* 55, no. 4 (December 2003): 539–67.

Isasi, Santiago Pérez, and Ângela Fernandes. "Looking at Iberia in/from Europe." In *Looking at Iberia: A Comparative European Perspective*, ed. Santiago Pérez Isasi and Ângela Fernandes. Bern: Peter Lang, 2013. 1–8.

Junco, José Álvarez. *Mater Dolorosa: La idea de España en el siglo XIX*. Madrid: Taurus, 2001.

Jutglar, Antoni. *La España que no pudo ser*. Barcelona: Anthropos, 1983.

– *Pi y Margall y el federalismo español*. 2 vols. Madrid: Taurus, 1975–6.

Kahan, Alan S. *Aristocratic Liberalism: The Social and Political Thought of Jacob Burckhardt, John Stuart Mill, and Alexis de Tocqueville*. Oxford: Oxford University Press, 1992.

Kamen, Henry. *The Disinherited: Exile and the Making of Spanish Culture, 1492–1975*. New York: HarperCollins, 2007.

– *Imagining Spain: Historical Myth & National Identity*. New Haven and London: Yale University Press, 2008.

Keown, Dominic. "Dine with the Opposition? ¡No, gracias! Hispanism versus Iberian Studies in Great Britain and Ireland." In *Iberian Modalities: A Relational Approach to the Study of Culture in the Iberian Peninsula*, ed. Joan Ramon Resina. Liverpool: Liverpool University Press, 2013. 23–36.

King, Stewart. "From Literature to Letters: Rethinking Catalan Literary History." In *New Spain, New Literatures*, ed. Luis Martín-Estudillo and Nicholas Spadaccini. Nashville: Vanderbilt University Press, 2010. 233–44.

Kojève, Alexander. *Introduction to the Reading of Hegel: Lectures on the* Phenomenology of Spirit. Ed. Raymond Queneau and Allan Bloom, trans. James H. Nichols. Ithaca: Cornell University Press, 1980.

Koselleck, Reinhart. "Crisis." Trans. Michaela W. Richter. *Journal of the History of Ideas*. 67, no. 2 (April 2006): 357–400.

Krauel, Javier. "Emotions and Nationalism: The Case of Joan Maragall's Compassionate Love of Country." *Hispanic Research Journal* 15, no. 3 (June 2014): 191–208.

– *Imperial Emotions: Cultural Responses to Myths of Empire in* Fin-de-Siècle *Spain*. Liverpool: Liverpool University Press, 2013.

Laqueur, Walter. "Fin-de-sìecle: Once More with Feeling." *Journal of Contemporary History* 31, no. 1 (January 1996): 5–47.

Leone, Carlos. *Dez críticas*. Lisbon: Edições Colibri, 1999.

Llopis, Juan M. Ribera. "Centre-Peninsular Considerations on Catalan Literary Regeneration: An Everlasting Circle?" In *Looking at Iberia: A Comparative*

European Perspective, ed. Santiago Pérez Isasi and Ângela Fernandes. Bern: Peter Lang, 2013. 165–80.

Lopes, Óscar. *Antero de Quental – Vida e Legado de uma Utopia*. Lisbon: Caminho, 1993.

López, Ana María Freire. *Emilia Pardo Bazán, Portugal y la literatura portuguesa (con cartas inéditas de la escritora a Teófilo Braga y José Ramalho Ortigão)*. Digital edition. Alicante: Biblioteca Virtual Miguel de Cervantes, 2012. http://bib.cervantesvirtual.com/obra/emilia-pardo-bazan-portugal-y-la-literatura-portuguesa-con-cartas-ineditas-de-la-escritora-a-teofilo-braga-y-jose-ramalho-ortigao

Loureiro, Angel G. "Spanish Nationalism and the Ghost of Empire." *Journal of Spanish Cultural Studies* 4, no. 1 (2003): 65–76.

Lourenço, Eduardo. *O Outro Lado da Lua – A Ibéria segundo Eduardo Lourenço*. Ed. Maria Manuel Baptista. Porto: Campo das Letras; Guarda: Centro de Estudos Ibéricos, 2005.

Madariaga, Salvador de. *Anarchy or Hierarchy*. London: George Allen & Unwin Ltd., 1937.

– *Democracy versus Liberty? The Faith of a Liberal Heretic*. London: Pall Mall Press Limited, 1958.

– *Englishmen, Frenchmen, Spaniards*. 2nd ed. New York: Hill and Wang, 1969.

– *España. Ensayo de Historia contemporánea*. 7th ed. Buenos Aires: Editorial Sudamericana, 1964.

– *The Genius of Spain and Other Essays on Spanish Contemporary Literature*. Freeport, New York: Books for Libraries Press, 1968.

– "A Letter of Remonstrance." *The Antioch Review* 18, no. 2 (Summer 1958): 255–6.

– *Memorias (1921–1936). Amanecer sin mediodía*. 3rd ed. Madrid: Espasa-Calpe, 1974.

– *Memorias de un federalista*. Buenos Aires: Editorial Sudamericana, 1967.

– *Spain: A Modern History*. New York: Frederick A. Praeger, 1958.

Magalhães, Gabriel. "A atitude ibérica da Geração de 70. Variações na unidade." *Península. Revista de Estudos Ibéricos*, no. 4 (2007): 157–75.

Maragall, Joan. *Obres completes*. 2 vols. Barcelona: Editorial Selecta, 1960–1.

Maravall, José Antonio. "Prólogo." In J.P. de Oliveira Martins, *Historia de la civilización ibérica*. Trans. José Albiñana Mompó. Madrid: Seminarios y Ediciones, S.A., 1972. 7–18.

Marfany, Joan-Lluís. "Joan Maragall." In *Història de la literatura catalana*. Ed. Joaquim Molas et al. Vol. 8. Barcelona: Editorial Ariel, 1986. 187–246.

– "Modernisme i noucentisme, amb algunes consideracions sobre el concepte de moviment cultural." *Els Marges* 26 (1982): 31–42.

Marías, Julián. *Miguel de Unamuno*. Madrid: Espasa-Calpe, 1943.

Marinho, Maria José. *Da "Revista do Ocidente" à "Revista Ocidental."* Facsimile copy archived in the National Library, Lisbon. L.42767V.

Marques, Fernando Pereira. "A questão ibérica em Antero de Quental." *Res-Publica* 5/6 (2007): 73–80.

Martínez-Gil, Víctor. *El naixement de l'iberisme catalanista*. Barcelona: Curial, 1997.

– "A Visão Luso-Catalã da Ibéria." In *ACT 25 – Catalunya, Catalunha*, ed. Esther Gimeno Ugalde et al. Centro de Estudos Comparatistas, Universidade de Lisboa. Ribeirão: Edições Húmus; Barcelona: Onada Edicions, 2013. 55–87.

Mas y Sanz, Sinibaldo. *A Iberia*. Trans. Latino Coelho. 2nd ed. Lisbon: Typ. Universal, 1853.

Mascarenhas, Manuela. *A Questão Ibérica: 1850–1870*. Braga: Livraria Cruz, 1980.

Masur, Gerhard. *Prophets of Yesterday: Studies in European Culture 1890–1914*. New York: Macmillan, 1961.

Matos, Sérgio Campos. "¿Cómo convivir con la pérdida? Historiografía, conciencia histórica y política en Portugal dentro del contexto peninsular." In *El pasado en construcción: Revisionismos históricos en la historiografía contemporánea*, ed. C. Forcadell, I. Perió, and M. Yusta. Zaragoza: Institución Fernando el Católico, 2015. 249–74.

– "A Crise do Final de Oitocentos em Portugal: Uma revisão." In *Crises em Portugal nos Séculos XIX e XX*, ed. Sérgio Campos Matos. Lisbon: Centro de História da Universidade de Lisboa, 2002. 99–115.

– *Historiografia e Memoria Nacional no Portugal do Século XIX (1846–1898)*. Lisbon: Edições Colibri, 1998.

– "Iberismo e Identidade Nacional (1851–1910)." *Clio* (Centro de História da Universidade de Lisboa), new ser., 14/15 (2006): 349–400.

– "Nota de Apresentação." In *Crises em Portugal nos Séculos XIX e XX*, ed. Sérgio Campos Matos. Lisbon: Centro de História da Universidade de Lisboa, 2002. 9–10.

– "Portugal: The Nineteenth-Century Debate on the Formation of the Nation." *Portuguese Studies* 13 (1997): 66–74.

Mazzini, Giuseppe. *Selected Writings*. Ed. N. Gangulee. London: Lindsay Drummond, 1945.

McRoberts, Kenneth. *Catalonia: Nation Building without a State*. Don Mills, ON: Oxford University Press, 2001.

Medeiros, António. *Two Sides of One River: Nationalism and Ethnography in Galicia and Portugal*. Trans. Martin Earl. New York: Berghahn Books, 2013.

Medina, João. *Ortega y Gasset no Exílio Português (com um excurso sobre a lusofilia de Miguel de Unamuno).* Lisbon: Centro de História da Universidade de Lisboa, 2004.

Mignolo, Walter. "The Many Faces of Cosmo-polis: Border Thinking and Critical Cosmopolitanism." *Public Culture* 12, no. 3 (Fall 2000): 721–48.

Mora, José Ferreter. *Unamuno: A Philosophy of History.* Trans. Philip Silver. Berkeley and Los Angeles: University of California Press, 1962.

Moraña, Mabel. "Introduction: Mapping Hispanism." In *Ideologies of Hispanism*, ed. Mabel Moraña. Nashville: Vanderbilt University Press, 2005. ix–xxi.

Morejón, Julio García. *Unamuno y Portugal.* 2nd corr. and exp. ed. Madrid: Editorial Gredos, 1971.

Murguía, Manuel. *Galicia.* Barcelona: Establecimiento Tipográfico-editorial de Daniel Cortezo y Cia, 1888.

Navajas, Gonzalo. "La modernidad como crisis. El modelo español del declive." *Anales de la literatura española contemporánea* 23, no. 1/2 (1998): 277–94.

Nebrija, Antonio de. "On Language and Empire: The Prologue to *Grammar of the Castilian Language* (1492)." Trans. Magalí Armillas-Tiseyra. *PMLA* 131, no. 1 (January 2016): 197–208.

Newcomb, Robert Patrick. "A Poetry of Flesh and Bone: Miguel de Unamuno and Miguel Torga." *Portuguese Studies* 30, no. 1 (2014): 21–36.

Nietzsche, Friedrich. "On the Utility and Liability of History for Life." In *Unfashionable Observations.* Vol. 2. Trans. Richard T. Gray. Palo Alto: Stanford University Press, 1998. 85–167.

Nogueira, José Félix Henriques. *Obra Completa, Seguida de Marginália, Esboço Bibliográfico, Apêndice Documental e Notas.* 2 vols. Ed. António Carlos Leal da Silva. Lisbon: Imprensa Nacional–Casa da Moeda, 1980.

Nordau, Max. *Degeneration.* Lincoln and London: University of Nebraska Press, 1993.

Nozick, Martin. *Miguel de Unamuno.* New York: Twayne, 1971.

Oliveira Martins, J.P. de. *Correspondencia.* Ed. Francisco d'Assis Oliveira Martins. Lisbon: Parceria Antonio Maria Pereira, 1926.

– *Dispersos.* Ed. António Sérgio and Faria de Vasconcelos. 2 vols. Lisbon: Biblioteca Nacional, 1923–4.

– "Do princípio federativo e sua aplicação à Península Hispânica." In *Obras completas. Jornal.* Lisbon: Guimarães Editores, 1960. 9–42.

– *História da Civilização Ibérica.* Lisbon: Guimarães & Cia. Editores, 1972.

– *Historia de Portugal.* 2 vols. Lisbon: Parceria Antonio Maria Pereira, 1901.

– *A History of Iberian Civilization*. Trans. Audrey F.G. Bell. New York: Cooper Square Publishers, 1969.
– *Portugal Contemporâneo*. 3 vols. Lisbon: Guimarães, 1953.
– "Os povos peninsulares e a civilização moderna." In *Páginas desconhecidas*, ed. Lopes D'Oliveira. Lisbon: Seara Nova, 1948. 65–97.
Ortega y Gasset, José. *España invertebrada*. 8th ed. Madrid: Revista de Occidente, 1952.
– *Man and Crisis*. Trans. Mildred Adams. New York: W.W. Norton and Company, 1962.
– *Obras completas*. Vol. 5. Madrid: Alianza Editorial; Revista de Occidente, 1983.
Ortega y Gasset, José, and Miguel de Unamuno. *Epistolario completo Ortega–Unamuno*. Ed. Laureano Robles Carcedo and Antonio Ramos Gascón. Madrid: Ediciones El Arquero, 1987.
Ortigão, Ramalho, and Eça de Queiróz. *As Farpas*. Ed. Gilberto Freyre. 2 vols. Rio de Janeiro: Dois Mundos, 1943.
Pardo Bazán, Emilia. *Obras Completas*. 3 vols. Madrid: Aguilar, 1957.
– *Poesías inéditas u olvidadas*. Ed. Maurice Hemingway. Exeter: University of Exeter Press, 1996.
París, Carlos. *Unamuno: Estructura de su mundo intelectual*. Barcelona: Anthropos, 1989.
Pereira, Maria da Conceição. "A Questão Ibérica: Imprensa e Opinião (1850–1870)." Dissertação para Doutoramento em História Moderna e Contemporánea apresentada à Faculdade de Letras da Universidade do Porto. Porto: Universidade do Porto, 1995.
Pereira, Maria de Lourdes. "Em Busca de uma Memória Ibérica." *Res Publica* 5/6 (2007): 7–15.
Pereira-Muro, Carmen. *Género, nación y literatura: Emilia Pardo Bazán en la literatura gallega y española*. West Lafayette, IN: Purdue University Press, 2013.
Pérez, Jorge. "¿De qué hablamos cuando hablamos de estudios ibéricos?" Theorizing Iberian Studies. Modern Language Association Convention, Vancouver, 9 January 2015.
Pi y Margall, Francisco. *Las nacionalidades*. 2nd ed. Madrid: Imprenta y Librería de Eduardo Martinez, 1877.
– *La reacción y la revolución: Estudios políticos y sociales*. Ed. Antoni Jutglar. Barcelona: Anthropos, 1982.
Pidal, Ramón Menéndez. *Los españoles en la historia*. 2nd ed. Madrid: Espasa-Calpe, 1971.
– "La lengua española." *Hispania* 1 (February 1918): 1–14.

Pires, António Machado. *A Ideia de Decadência na Geração de 70*. 2nd ed. Lisbon: Vega, 1992.

Popescu, Gabriel. *Bordering and Order the Twenty-first Century: Understanding Borders*. Lanham: Rowman & Littlefield, 2012.

Prat de la Riba, Enric. *La nacionalitat catalana*. Barcelona: Tip. L'Anuari de la Exportació, 1906.

Preston, Paul. "A Quixote in Politics: Salvador de Madariaga." In *¡Comrades! Portraits from the Spanish Civil War*. London: HarperCollins, 1999. 141–65.

Proudhon, P.-J. *The Principle of Federation*. Trans. Richard Vernon. Toronto: University of Toronto Press, 1979.

Quental, Antero de. *Causas da Decadência dos Povos Peninsulares no Últimos Três Séculos: Discurso pronunciado na noite de 27 de Maio de 1871, na sala do Casino Lisbonense*. Lisbon: Contexto, 2001.

– *Obra Completa. Cartas 1–2*. Ed. Ana Maria Almeida Martins. Ponta Delgada: Universidade dos Açores; Lisbon: Editorial Comunicação, 1989.

– "O Que É a Internacional." *Prosas Sócio-Políticas*. Ed. Joel Serrão. Lisbon: Imprensa Nacional–Casa da Moeda, 1982. 330–52.

– *Poesia Completa*. Ed. Fernando Pinto do Amaral. Lisbon: Publicações Dom Quixote, 2001.

– "Portugal Perante a Revolução de Espanha." In *Obras completas. Política*. 1st ed. Ponta Delgada: Universidade dos Açores, 1994. 105–28.

– *Prosas*. 3 vols. Coimbra: Imprensa da Universidade, 1923–31.

– *As Tendências Gerais da Filosofia na Segunda Metade do Sec. XIX*. Ed. Marcello Fernandos and Nazaré Barros. Lisbon: Lisboa Editora, 2000.

Quirk, Ronald J. "El problema del habla regional en *Los Pazos de Ulloa*." *INTI*, no. 2 (October 1975): 31–43.

Ramos, Samuel. *El perfil del hombre y la cultura en México*. 4th ed. Mexico City: Universidad Nacional Autónoma de México, 1963.

Reis, Carlos. "Portugal ante la revolución de España: De Antero de Quental a Fernando Pessoa." *Semiosfera*, segunda época, no. 2 (March 2014): 10–31.

Renan, Ernest. "What Is a Nation"? In *Nationalism in Europe, 1815 to the Present. A Reader*, ed. Stuart Woolf. London and New York: Routledge, 1996. 48–60.

Resina, Joan Ramon. *Del hispanismo a los estudios ibéricos: Una propuesta federativa para el ámbito cultural*. Madrid: Biblioteca Nueva, 2009.

– "Introduction: Iberian Modalities: The Logic of an Intercultural Field." In *Iberian Modalities: A Relational Approach to the Study of Culture in the Iberian Peninsula*, ed. Joan Ramon Resina. Liverpool: Liverpool University Press, 2013. 1–19.

– "The Scale of the Nation in a Shrinking World." *Diacritics* 33, no. 3/4 (Autumn–Winter 2003): 45–74.

– "Whose Hispanism? Cultural Trauma, Disciplined Memory, and Symbolic Dominance." In *Ideologies of Hispanism*, ed. Mabel Moraña. Nashville: Vanderbilt University Press, 2005. 160–86.

Ribera i Rovira, Ignasi de L. *Iberisme*. Barcelona: Llibreria "L'Avenç," 1907.

Risco, Vicente. "Teixeira de Pascoaes na súa época." *Grial* 9, t. 9, no. 32 (April–June 1971): 227–30.

Rocamora, José Antonio. "Causas do surgimento e do fracasso do nacionalismo ibérico." *Análise Social*, 4th series, vol. 28, no. 122 (1993): 631–52.

– *El nacionalismo ibérico 1792–1936*. Valladolid: Universidad de Valladolid; Salamanca: Gráficas Varona, 1994.

Rosa, João Guimarães. "A Terceira Margem do Rio." In *Primeiras Estórias*, 15th ed.; 4th reprinting. Rio de Janeiro: Editora Nova Fronteira, 2003. 79–85.

Sabaté, Flocal, and Luís Adão da Fonseca, eds. *Catalonia and Portugal: The Iberian Peninsula from the Periphery*. Bern: Peter Lang, 2015.

Saler, Michael, ed. *The Fin-de-Siècle World*. London and New York: Routledge, 2015.

Saramago, José. *A Jangada de Pedra*. 15th printing. São Paulo: Companhia das Letras, 2001.

– *The Stone Raft*. Trans. Giovanni Pontiero. San Diego: Harvest, 1996.

Saraiva, António José. *A Tertúlia Ocidental: Estudos sobre Antero de Quental, Oliveira Martins, Eça de Queiroz e outros*. 2nd ed. Lisbon: Gradiva, 1995.

Seixas, Xosé M. Núñez. "Iberia Reborn: Portugal through the Lens of Catalan and Galician Nationalism (1850-1950). In *Iberian Modalities: A Relational Approach to the Study of Culture in the Iberian Peninsula*, ed. Joan Ramon Resina. Liverpool: Liverpool University Press, 2013. 83–98.

Serra, Pedro, and Ana María García Martín. "Oliveira Martins visto por intelectuais espanhóis nas correspondências de Juan Valera e Marcelino Menéndez y Pelayo." *Revista da Universidade de Coimbra* 38 (1999): 159–73.

Serrão, Joel. "Compreender Oliveira Martins." In *Portugueses Somos*. Lisbon: Livros Horizonte, 1975. 37–56.

Smith, Angel. *The Origins of Catalan Nationalism, 1770–1898*. Houndsmills, Basingstoke, Hampshire: Palgrave Macmillan, 2014.

Smith, Anthony D. *The Ethnic Origins of Nations*. Oxford, UK, and Cambridge, MA: Blackwell, 1986.

Terricabras, Josep-Maria. "Presentació." In *Joan Maragall, paraula i pensament*, ed. Josep-Maria Terricabras. Girona: Càtedra Ferrator Mora; Documenta Universitaria, 2011. 9–12.

Terry, Arthur. "The Poetry of Joan Maragall." Sheffield: The Anglo-Catalan Society, 2001.

Tobar, Leonardo Romero. "Juan Valera's Iberism." In *Looking at Iberia: A Comparative European Perspective*, ed. Santiago Pérez Isasi and Ângela Fernandes. Bern: Peter Lang, 2013. 181–99.

Torga, Miguel. *Díario*. 16 vols. Coimbra: self-published, 1941–93.

Trueba, Antonio de. *El gabán y la chaqueta*. Vol. 1. Madrid: El Cosmos, 1884.

Turgenev, Ivan. *Fathers and Sons*. Trans. Peter Carson. New York: Penguin, 2009.

Unamuno, Miguel de. *Epistolario inédito I (1894–1914)*. Ed. Laureano Robles. Madrid: Espasa Calpe, 1991.

– *Escritos de Unamuno sobre Portugal*. Ed. Ángel Marcos de Dios. Paris: Fundação Calouste Gulbenkian; Centro Cultural Português, 1985.

– *Obras completas*. Ed. Manuel García Blanco. 9 vols. Madrid: Escelicer, 1966–71.

Unamuno, Miguel de, and Juan Maragall. *Epistolario entre Miguel de Unamuno y Juan Maragall y escritos complementarios*. Barcelona: Edimar, 1951.

Valera, Juan. "Historia de la civilización ibérica." In *Obras completas. Historia y política (1869–1887)*. Vol. 38. Madrid: Imprenta Alemana, 1914.

Vauthier, Bénédicte. *Arte de escribir e ironía en la obra narrativa de Miguel de Unamuno*. Salamanca: Ediciones Universidad de Salamanca, 2004.

Verde, Cesário. *The Feeling of a Westerner*. Trans. Richard Zenith. Luso-Asio-Afro-Brazilian Studies & Theory 2. Dartmouth, MA: University of Massachussetts Dartmouth, 2011.

– *O Livro de Cesário Verde seguido de algumas poesias dispersas*. 12th ed. Ed. Cabral do Nascimento. Lisbon: Editorial Minerva, n.d.

Viestenz, William. *By the Grace of God: Francoist Spain and the Sacred Roots of Political Imagination*. Toronto: University of Toronto Press, 2014.

Williams, Raymond. "Nationalist." In *Keywords*. New York: Oxford University Press, 1983. 213–14.

Index

Toronto Iberic

1 Anthony J. Cascardi, *Cervantes, Literature, and the Discourse of Politics*
2 Jessica A. Boon, *The Mystical Science of the Soul: Medieval Cognition in Bernardino de Laredo's Recollection Method*
3 Susan Byrne, *Law and History in Cervantes' Don Quixote*
4 Mary E. Barnard and Frederick A. de Armas (eds), *Objects of Culture in the Literature of Imperial Spain*
5 Nil Santiáñez, *Topographies of Fascism: Habitus, Space, and Writing in Twentieth-Century Spain*
6 Nelson Orringer, *Lorca in Tune with Falla: Literary and Musical Interludes*
7 Ana M. Gómez-Bravo, *Textual Agency: Writing Culture and Social Networks in Fifteenth-Century Spain*
8 Javier Irigoyen-García, *The Spanish Arcadia: Sheep Herding, Pastoral Discourse, and Ethnicity in Early Modern Spain*
9 Stephanie Sieburth, *Survival Songs: Conchita Piquer's* Coplas *and Franco's Regime of Terror*
10 Christine Arkinstall, *Spanish Female Writers and the Freethinking Press, 1879–1926*
11 Margaret Boyle, *Unruly Women: Performance, Penitence, and Punishment in Early Modern Spain*

12 Evelina Gužauskytė, *Christopher Columbus's Naming in the* diarios *of the Four Voyages (1492–1504): A Discourse of Negotiation*
13 Mary E. Barnard, *Garcilaso de la Vega and the Material Culture of Renaissance Europe*
14 William Viestenz, *By the Grace of God: Francoist Spain and the Sacred Roots of Political Imagination*
15 Michael Scham, Lector Ludens*: The Representation of Games and Play in Cervantes*
16 Stephen Rupp, *Heroic Forms: Cervantes and the Literature of War*
17 Enrique Fernandez, *Anxieties of Interiority and Dissection in Early Modern Spain*
18 Susan Byrne, *Ficino in Spain*
19 Patricia M. Keller, *Ghostly Landscapes: Film, Photography, and the Aesthetics of Haunting in Contemporary Spanish Culture*
20 Carolyn A. Nadeau, *Food Matters: Alonso Quijano's Diet and the Discourse of Food in Early Modern Spain*
21 Cristian Berco, *From Body to Community: Venereal Disease and Society in Baroque Spain*
22 Elizabeth R. Wright, *The Epic of Juan Latino: Dilemmas of Race and Religion in Renaissance Spain*
23 Ryan D. Giles, *Inscribed Power: Amulets and Magic in Early Spanish Literature*
24 Jorge Pérez, *Confessional Cinema: Religion, Film, and Modernity in Spain's Development Years (1960–1975)*
25 Juan Ramon Resina, *Josep Pla: Seeing the World in the Form of Articles*
26 Javier Irigoyen-Garcia, *"Moors Dressed as Moors": Clothing, Social Distinction, and Ethnicity in Early Modern Iberia*
27 Jean Dangler, *Edging Toward Iberia*
28 Ryan D. Giles and Steven Wagschal (eds): *Beyond Sight: Engaging the Senses in Iberian Literatures and Cultures, 1200–1750*
29 Silvia Bermúdez, *Rocking the Boat: Migration and Race in Contemporary Spanish Music*
30 Hilaire Kallendorf, *Ambiguous Antidotes: Virtue as Vaccine for Vice in Early Modern Spain*
31 Leslie Harkema, *Spanish Modernism and the Poetics of Youth: From Miguel de Unamuno to* La Joven Literatura
32 Benjamin Fraser, *Cognitive Disability Aesthetics: Visual Culture, Disability Representations, and the (In)Visibility of Cognitive Difference*
33 Robert Patrick Newcomb, *Iberianism and Crisis: Spain and Portugal at the Turn of the Twentieth Century*

www.ingramcontent.com/pod-product-compliance
Lightning Source LLC
LaVergne TN
LVHW090156080826
844660LV00013B/831/J
9781487502966